THE SHATTERED DREAM

THE SHATTERED DREAM

*Herbert Hoover and
the Great Depression*

By GENE SMITH

McGraw-Hill Book Company

New York   St. Louis   San Francisco   Bogotá   Guatemala
Hamburg   Lisbon   Madrid   Mexico   Montreal   Panama
Paris   San Juan   São Paulo   Tokyo   Toronto

Reprinted by arrangement with William Morrow and Company
First McGraw-Hill Paperback Edition 1984

1 2 3 4 5 6 7 8 9 FGRFGR 8 7 6 5 4

0-07-058474-5

Library of Congress Cataloging in Publication Data

Smith, Gene.
  The shattered dream.

  Originally published: New York : Morrow, 1970.
  Bibliography: p.
  1. United States—Politics and government—1929–1933.
2. Hoover, Herbert, 1874–1964. 3. Roosevelt, Franklin D.
(Franklin Delano), 1882–1945. 4. Depressions—1929—
United States. I. Title.
E801.S6 1984   973.91'6   84-10080
ISBN 0-07-058474-5 (pbk.)

To Jayne

Contents

All this reminds me of the small girl who said, "Mother, you know that beautiful jug you said had been handed down to us from generation to generation?" Mother replied, "Yes, Ann, what of it?" And Ann answered solemnly, "This generation dropped it."

—HERBERT CLARK HOOVER

PART I

The Search for El Dorado

Chapter One

HERBERT HOOVER turned fifty-four on August 10, 1928. The birthday party was held in his Moorish-style mansion and the main presentation was a giant birthday card affixed with hundreds of signatures, those of the President and Mrs. Coolidge at the top. Half of California (and all of Palo Alto) seemed to be in the house.

Also present were the luminaries of the Republican Party, county and state chairmen, congressmen and senators. Almost to a man they disliked their host, for he was not of their type, did not respect them, and had never pretended otherwise. But they insisted on being individually presented to him so that they could offer their politicians' florid expressions of support. Being closeted with them in his upstairs study made Hoover "want to yell," wrote the reporter Charles Michelson.

The politicians were there because earlier in the summer the Republican convention in Kansas City had nominated Secretary of Commerce Herbert Hoover for the Presidency of the United States. Officially, the candidate would be made aware of this on August 11, the day after his birthday, when the Notification Committee, led by Senator George Moses of New Hampshire, would tender him the prize in the football stadium of the Leland Stanford University.

August 11 was bright and not too warm, with a golden

California sun and brilliant blue sky. Six microphones sat upon the podium of the speakers' platform, their wires linked into a gigantic radio hookup of forty thousand miles of line connecting one hundred stations manned by nearly two thousand technicians. Half a dozen bands roamed the stadium, and at every entrance were thousands of little American flags on sticks. Everybody coming in was given a flag to wave. Overhead, daylight fireworks blasted off into the cloudless sky. Anchored balloons hovered over the scene, and airplanes swooped and dived. Volunteers recruited from the university student body directed the parking of automobiles in lanes running through the acres of wooded fields surrounding the stadium, but despite their efforts the largest traffic jam in the history of Palo Alto soon developed.

Upward of seventy-five thousand people came. When they were seated, the various bands were rounded up and consolidated into one enormous assemblage of two hundred and forty pieces. John Philip Sousa conducted.

Then the Notification Committee and the Secretary of Commerce came up to the canopied platform hung with gold and blue bunting. The Stanford officers' training unit had wanted to greet the Secretary with an artillery salute, but Hoover forbade it. He issued a statement which pointed out that while a Cabinet official was entitled to a salute when performing official business connected with his department, "I am not in that position on this occasion, so there will be no salute." (To his friends he said, "No damned salute.")

Senator Moses, forced into a promise to limit his notification speech to seven minutes, spoke in his bombastic, phrase-making way. Then Herbert Clark Hoover, Stanford '95, got up: "You bring, Mr. Chairman, formal notice of my nomination by the Republican Party to the Presidency of the United States—I accept." The abruptness startled the professional politicians who would have drawn out and savored the great moment.

Hoover spoke of himself for a moment to the crowd and the great radio audience, the largest in history:

"My country owes me no debt. It gave me, as it gives every boy and girl, a chance. It gave me schooling, independence of action, opportunity for service and honor. In no other land could a boy from a country village, without inheritance or influential friends, look forward with unbounded hope. My whole life has taught me what America means. I am indebted to my country beyond any human power to repay."

He was the American Dream come true, the penniless orphan become multimillionaire, the farm boy named for high office, the raw frontier's son who went into the great world and came back rich and famous.

He said:

"We in America today are nearer to the final triumph over poverty than ever before in the history of any land. The poorhouse is vanishing from among us. We have not yet reached the goal, but, given a chance to go forward with the policies of the last eight years, we shall soon with the help of God be in sight of the day when poverty will be banished from this nation."

His opponent in the election was the governor of the State of New York, Alfred Emanuel Smith. Smith was shrewd, liberal, progressive, a fine administrator. He was accounted the best politician in America. But he was of the sidewalks of the great city and the uneducated thrusting immigrants pushing up against Protestant, traditional America. He would not compromise on his derby and cigar or grating New York pronunciation—"nuttin'" for "nothing" and, of course, his trademark, "rad-io" for "radio." He was aggressively Catholic and believed and said that the ten-year experiment with Prohibition had been a mistake.

To the small towns out on the plains and to the D.A.R. and the W.C.T.U. he was the Devil with cloven hoof and a direct line to Rome. And he was, they said, vulgar. His wife was common. He called her Katy.

Hoover against Smith, thought the reporter Thomas Stokes, was a contest between the high stiff collar, the solid businessman with a wife concerned with uplift movements, and the brown derby reeking of Tammany Hall, a short, overweight, redfaced, dumpy wife, ignorance of everything west of the Hudson: the new people. Out on the prairies, campaigning, Smith stared at the endless miles rolling by, and asked in wonder, "What do the people *do* out here? How do they stand it?" And Hoover's theme song was "Onward Christian Soldiers."

Over and beyond the candidates was Coolidge Prosperity. "Republican efficiency," said the political advertisements in the newspapers, "has filled the workingman's dinner pail—and his gasoline tank besides—made telephone, radio, and sanitary plumbing standard household equipment and placed the whole nation in the silk-stocking class.

"Republican prosperity has reduced hours and increased earning capacity, silenced discontent, put the proverbial 'chicken in every pot' and a car in every backyard, to boot.

"Wages, dividends, progress and prosperity say 'Vote for Hoover.'"

The Republican candidate himself was sober and solemn, speaking in a flat, metallic voice. At first he indicated that he would do no campaigning beyond offering three or four radio addresses. But his advisers told him that he would have to get out and be seen by the voters. The idea made him ill at ease and it was difficult to make him consent. Finally he agreed to do it. "But," he said, "I'll not kiss any babies."

People came to his rallies and at once were bored. But their boredom was a kind of tribute; it was the boredom greeting the professor's lectures at college or the minister's talk on the Meaning of the Book. These were experts and should be looked up to.

In the public estimation, wrote the journalist Charles Michelson, Hoover was "an almost supernatural figure whose wisdom encompassed all branches, whose judgment was never at fault, who knew the answers to all questions and could see in the dark."

"If any difficult situation should arise," said Secretary of State Charles Evans Hughes, Hoover was "the one man who more than anyone else could be depended upon to bring the widest knowledge and the greatest resourcefulness to the devising of means to meeting the emergency."

Hughes and Senator William Borah of Idaho carried most of the load in the campaign. Hoover kept one hand rattling the keys in his left trousers pocket as his right shoulder worked up and down and he read from laboriously prepared texts: "I have endeavored to present to you the policies which have made and will make for the prosperity of our country. They hold the hope of the final abolition of poverty." His eyes never left the page. He never mentioned Al Smith's name.

When it was over and Hoover went back to Palo Alto to vote, ten thousand people met the train. Stanford student musicians followed his auto up Palm Drive to the polling station on the university grounds, blaring "Come, Join the Band." Overhead, an aviator circled, dropping firecrackers that exploded in the air and released the flags of all the countries of the world. In the living room of his house he set up a blackboard and all through the evening he chalked in the figures while his wife chatted with friends in front of the fireplace.

Across the nation Al Smith sat in the 69th Regiment Armory in Manhattan with an unlit cigar drooping from his lips. The returns for him were so catastrophic that Smith's daughter ran to a telephone and called Herbert Bayard Swope, her father's friend and the editor of the *New York World*. She asked Swope if it were possible that states Democratic since before the Civil War were actually going Republican. Surely, she said, there had been some mistake. Swope told her there was no mistake.

It was 12:30 A.M. New York time, 9:30 P.M. in Palo Alto, when the United Press wire brought in Smith's message conceding the election. It was read aloud and a ripple of reserved handclapping went through the big drawing room looking out over the San Juan Mountains. To the reporter Thomas Stokes it was as if the people were infected by the attitude of their host. "His personality permeated the room. He showed no outward excitement."

The President-Elect said, "He should have conceded three hours ago, or, better still, three months ago."

The remark coming from anyone else would have seemed utterly cruel, but it was simply the reaction of a mind trained in dealing with realities.

His margin was 444 electoral votes to 87, 40 states to 8, twenty-one and a half million votes to fifteen million. No such victory had ever been accorded any candidate in the history of the American Union. Virginia, North Carolina, Florida, Texas, Kentucky, Tennessee, and Maryland went for him, and at once it was said that his victory in the South had finally ended the Civil War.

In the morning, when, it seemed, all Palo Alto slept, he and his wife rose and went for a long tramp through the hills in back of the university. Long ago they had walked there alone—campus sweethearts. When they returned to their house the Secret Service men were waiting.

Chapter Two

IN HIS HOME in Palo Alto Hoover set to work almost at once upon his coming Presidency. He drew up plans to coordinate, with his future Cabinet, a study for the reorganization of the ten major federal departments which would eliminate all overlapping of government functions. He asked leading experts to submit programs for dealing with the improvement of agricultural practices and pricing techniques, flood control, manufacturing routines, child welfare, home building, disarmament moves, economic projections, and reduction of unemployment. Soon he had dozens of packed filing cases.

In December he went south on a Navy destroyer, visiting the countries along the east coasts of Central and South America. The leaders of the various nations, enormously complimented by his expression of interest, competed with one another to honor him with parades, fireworks, and speeches of welcome. The officers and enlisted men of the ship found him an enthusiastic fisherman and imperturbable sailor who stood at the rail, field glasses in hand, watching the progress of tropical storms. On New Year's Eve the crew and passengers held a costume party and Mrs. Hoover insisted that her husband wear a paper fireman's hat. When the reporters asked if he had any statement with which to mark the passing of 1928 and the coming of 1929, he simply said, "Happy New Year."

Hoover's inauguration day was Monday, March 4, 1929. By Saturday night Washington was jammed with the greatest crowd of its history—two hundred thousand visitors, equivalent to half the population of the city. Additional automobiles and special trains poured in, filled with people anxious to see the proceedings. It was impossible to walk through the hotel lobbies and the downtown streets were a solid mass of people who would be participating in Monday's inaugural parade: Pawnee braves in regalia, cowboy bands, high school drill teams, American Legion units with robin's-egg-blue breeches and silver-plated drill rifles.

On Sunday, the day before the inauguration, the President and Mrs. Coolidge went to church through lanes of people calling, "Good-bye, Mr. President," and "Thank you, thank you." Expressionless as always, the President took off his high silk hat as he walked by. The crowds at the President-Elect's church were far greater in size and more vocal, calling out good wishes so loudly that he frowned in disapproval.

Monday dawned cold and wet. Calvin Coolidge looked out at the South Lawn of the White House and said to his wife, "Well, Grace, it always rains on moving day." Then in their top hats and morning attire, Coolidge wearing a batwing collar, the President-Elect in his usual high, stiff one, they sat side by side in an open touring car and rode down Pennsylvania Avenue.

The brilliantly groomed Percherons of the White Horse Battery led with their heavy guns; then came a battery pulled by black horses and then another pulled by chestnuts. The machine-gun battalions had teams of shining mules, and just in front of the car carrying the President and the President-Elect, the Third United States Cavalry moved at a slow, clattering trot. Above, the dirigible *Los Angeles*, silver and thin, maneuvered through the clouds along with double-winged Army bombers.

They came to the great massed crowd at the Capitol. The lawns stretching out to the Library of Congress were dark with people in rain gear. It was the first inauguration brought to the entire nation by radio and to the outlying Pacific possessions by short wave, the first ever recorded by talking motion pictures. Hoover came up to the podium with his speech in his hand. The spectacular crowds under vari-hued umbrellas reflecting every color of the rainbow pressed up against the heavy cables strung by the police.

"I have no fears for the future of our country. It is bright with hope," he finished, and they cheered.

Calvin Coolidge said, "Mr. President." Coolidge smiled as no one had ever seen him smile before; the *New York World* headlined on the front page the next day that the ex-President's warmth and sudden human display was "thrilling." Then he went off to a private car attached to the Montreal Limited which would take him home to New England.

President Hoover went to his touring car. The top had been put up to protect him from the rain, but he ordered it let down. The people along the Avenue might want to see their new President.

That day the market drove on up, the *New York Herald-Tribune* reporting that "messages from virtually every city in the country, from Maine to California and from Washington State to Florida, have directed brokers in New York to buy stocks, indicating a conviction that the Hoover Administration is to inaugurate a period of unparalleled prosperity. Confidence in this prosperity, belief that times with Mr. Hoover at the helm will be even better than they are now has been manifest ever since election. . . . There has been an almost unprecedented display of conviction on the part of the investing public that with Hoover at the throttle the signal is full steam ahead."

"Oh you Herbie!" shouted a boy, and Hoover lifted his silk top hat.

A telephone appeared on the desk of the President of the United States. There had never been one there before. (Other Presidents thought it undignified to speak from their desks on the telephone; on the rare occasions when they used the instrument they did so from a special adjoining room.) An elaborate buzzer system was set up to summon the five secretaries to the President. (All other Presidents had made do with a single secretary.)

The uniforms of the White House police were smartened up, and the reporters' lounge enlarged. In the family living quarters all the furniture was endlessly shifted around. Mrs. Hoover, spending lavishly of her husband's private fortune, redid practically every room, installing new fixtures, purchasing period pieces, making one room into a tropical paradise complete with exotic birds in cages. Along the Rapidan River in Virginia, three hours from Washington, construction was begun on a Presidential retreat built with more than a quarter of a million dollars of the President's own money.

Efficiency and an end to waste characterized the conduct of the Executive Offices. Memoranda from the five private secretaries were to be signed in typewriter and then initialed by hand. Whenever possible thoughts would be committed to paper, thereby replacing protracted personal talks and saving time. In a short while memoranda were pouring forth to the various commissions the President set up to deal with all the problems considered in the immediate post-election days and neatly itemized in the packed filing cases. He outlined additional fields of inquiry to be explored by hundreds of experts: prohibition, child care, the probable sociological, racial and economic trends of the United States for the next half century.

The new President was notable for not blindly following Presidential traditions. That the President must never be directly quoted by reporters had been an unbreakable, if unwritten, law. Hoover thrust the rule aside and instituted three different types of news conferences: one in which he could be quoted, one in which his thoughts could be attributed to a "White House source" or a "high Administration official," and one in which he would simply offer background information for the reporters' better understanding of given situations. The reporters liked him, respected him, freely said that he was the man best prepared for the Presidency in their time.

The country thought of him as a thinking machine, perhaps icy in his ways. He closed the White House stables and retired the White House yacht; the country marveled at his dedication to his job. And the stock market began climbing to new heights each day in the golden summer of 1929. General Electric went from 268 to 391; AT & T from 209 to 303; everything went up. He put a bill through Congress to aid the farmers by establishing price supports for commodities and called a special session to consider tariff revision. And the market went up still more, that wonderful market for whose stocks Indian maharajahs sold their jewels and Hungarian magnates their land. In the three months of summer, the average rose by 25 percent.

The White House permanent staff never ceased to marvel at the new President's capacity for work. Theodore Roosevelt went for cross-country runs and boxed with an instructor; Taft went golfing; Wilson spent his afternoons motoring through Maryland and Virginia; Harding drank and played cards; and Coolidge slept away his days with his feet up on the desk. None of this was for Hoover. He did not go to the theater or to sporting events; he did not go for walks or rides; he did not gossip. He worked. Washington had never seen a President who worked as hard.

The congressmen, particularly the members of the Senate, did not warm to him. They resented having to go through the screen of Presidential secretaries asking the senator to state in writing why the President should receive him. For the most part they were big, bluff, hearty men fond of a joke or a good story. Majority Leader James Watson of Indiana was typical, complaining that never in his life had he heard the President laugh, never heard him tell a funny story, never heard of him telling *anybody* a funny story. (Watson himself could tell yarns by the hour to the newspaper boys or to his colleagues.) The Republican senators resented having to defer to a President who as recently as 1920 had not been sure of which party he preferred. They disliked sitting in his office waiting for him to speak first—he never did—and then receiving the cold itemization of his wishes, the curt dismissal. Harding had been at home in the Senate which he left to go to the Presidency, and Harding's poker games had continued up on the White House second-floor living quarters along with the drinking and wenching. Coolidge in his chill way knew how to cozy along the senators' pet projects, for he had been in their business all his mature life.

But Hoover was "no politician." His handling of the tariff revision bill showed that, for despite his better instincts he permitted himself to be pushed into raising tariff barriers to heights which severely hampered trade with foreign nations. Stung by criticisms attending the passage of the Smoot-Hawley tariff bill, the President refused to reconsider his choice of Judge John Parker to fill a vacant seat on the United States Supreme Court. Congress had pushed him around on the tariff question, he told his friends, but he would not listen to Senatorial questions about Parker's suitability. In the end, the Senate refused to confirm Parker's nomination.

And on September 3, 1929, the market reached, according to all the indices, the highest point in history. It hovered there for a moment, like a rising flood. It crashed over the dam on Thursday, October 24. The loss of values in the day's trading amounted to almost as great a sum as America had spent to fight the World War. Enormous crowds gathered in front of the New York Stock Exchange building and outside the offices of every brokerage office in the country. At Broad and Wall streets the people simply stood and looked at the Stock Exchange. The sound of the floor men yelling sell orders inside could be plainly heard for a block in each direction; it was like the roar of a maddened beast. The governors of the Exchange ordered the Visitors' Gallery hurriedly cleared so that outsiders would not see the scene on the floor as the traders rushed to the trading stations, ties askew and with ruffled hair, trying to unload stocks for whatever they would bring. Ten- and twenty-point drops were common—thirty points, fifty points. There was no bottom.

Outside the branch offices all over the country people stood jammed elbow to elbow peering at the translux flashing the unbelievable prices. Men gulped, shook their heads, softly said, "No." Others grinned, and the writer Edwin Lefèvre, looking at them, thought to himself that they were trying to minimize the damage in their own minds, or preparing to explain at home when evening came.

Hideous rumors spread in all the great cities. The brokers inside had weapons and were physically slaughtering one another. The investors who had lost their money were going to burn the Exchange. (When this rumor reached the New York City Commissioner of Police, strong contingents of mounted officers

were sent to Wall Street.) In downtown New York, not far from
the Exchange, someone peered up at a skyscraper and saw a man
on a ledge. In a moment the rumor spread that it was a broker
who was going to jump. At once there was a crowd of thousands
looking up at a puzzled window cleaner. The same thing, or
something like it, happened in almost every city.

In Washington, the Federal Reserve Board met, and Secretary of the Treasury Andrew William Mellon, in an unusual
move, attended. Then he hurried to confer with the President,
who already had been on the phone to New York with the leading bankers and the head of Morgan's. When the market finally
closed for the day, the tape was hours late. The telegraph operators handling out-of-town business worked over their keys until
morning, and the brokers trying to straighten out the immense
volume of paper work did not sleep at all. Midnight soup was
served to the office girls working in the brilliantly lit-up offices.

The next morning, Friday, the President issued a statement:
"The fundamental business of the country, that is, the production and distribution of commodities, is on a sound and prosperous basis." The advisory services said, "Stocks have hit bottom.
. . . Immense amount of good by shaking down prices. . . .
Technical conditions. . . ." But millions upon millions of shares
were dumped for whatever they could bring. Nothing that any
trader did was right. Suddenly for an hour or a day the market
would shoot up, drawing in billions of dollars; then it would
plummet again.

The market's crash did not frighten the President. All his
life he had been a man who arranged and shaped and directed
events. So he leaped forward into territory where no President
had ever ventured before. "The cure for such storms is action,"
he said. Within days after the crash he held nine major conferences at the White House. Individually he talked with business leaders, labor representatives, construction men, the members
of the Federal Reserve Board, the U.S. Chamber of Commerce,
men from the national farm organizations, men from the public utilities. They came from all over the country to Washington, and limousines waited at Union Station to take them to

the White House, where the President steadily said that his main interest was in preventing unemployment stemming from the crash, that the first casualty must be profits, not wages. He got the employers to promise they would not cut down the pay checks of their men, and the unions to promise they would not press for raises. It was the perfect compromise with no intimidation, no favoritism, no handouts. All would give a little. All would work for the common good. And there would be no sacrifice of dignity.

He called for, and got, a reduction in taxes. The top rate for corporations was reduced from 12 percent to 11 percent, with corresponding decreases for the average American taxpayer who earned $5,500 a year and paid less than $200 a year. In a series of telegrams to the governor of each state and the mayor of each major city, he asked for the construction of local public works.

In March of 1930, just one year after his inauguration and five months after the crash, he said that unemployment in the United States would vanish within "sixty days." For a brief moment it seemed he was correct, and all the indices went up. Then they slipped back. In May he said, "We have now passed the worst and with continued unity of effort we shall rapidly recover." Later in May he said business would be normal by fall. But it was not.

His public pronouncements ceased for a while, but his work increased. He studied the reports of car loadings and commodity prices, pork futures and automobile sales, real estate foreclosures and department store volume. He worked far into the night, awoke at three or four, and immediately switched on the light to read some more. Then he went back to sleep for an hour or so; he arose at seven. He took no precipitate steps, saying the most dangerous thing in the world was a man with emotion but no ideas. But what they called the panic and then the crisis and at last the Depression deepened, men shuffling through the rain—somehow it always seemed to be raining—into the schoolhouses where the charitable agencies handed out stew and coffee. The factories fell silent and the birds built their nests in the high roofs. The banks foreclosed on the farms; and in the cities the sidewalk curbings crumbled and there was no money to repair them, no money to open the blocks and blocks of closed stores in the emptied streets.

A great silence settled over America.

Hoover worked on. He never smiled. But then, that had always been his way. That, and success.

Chapter Three

HOOVER WAS BORN in 1874 in West Branch, Iowa, the middle frontier, the West. Across the grassy prairies the Indian trails were widening into straight earth-packed tracks, and three years earlier the railroad had arrived.

West Branch's population was less than three hundred, and the streets were dusty in summer and muddy with Iowa's dark soil in the spring and fall. In winter the two forks of the little Wapsinonoc River froze solid and children went flying down Cook's Hill on homemade sleds and then thawed out their hands and feet in icy water. When the ice broke there was fishing for sunfish or catfish with a butcher-string line and ten-for-a-penny hooks. The children used willow poles and half an angleworm, which they spat on for luck.

There were woods near the town with rabbits to be trapped in cracker boxes; and out on the undulating prairies the Indian boys showed how a pigeon could be brought down by a dozen boys firing bows and arrows in unison.

Children in Iowa in those years did chores: hoeing the garden, planting corn, milking the cow, sawing wood for the stove. Christmas was popcorn balls cemented with sorghum molasses. They wore homespun clothes dyed with butternuts, and no shoes in the summer. (Jesse Clark Hoover's younger son, Bertie, stepped on a hot iron chip from his father's blacksmith shop and seared his foot permanently.) In West Branch people made their own rugs and soap; women canned fruit and vegetables. All around were the woods and prairies and great stretching cornfields which would make Springdale Township's name known as one of the richest corn areas of the entire world. Through the front yard would come the stock being herded toward the railroad loading platforms.

Every four years there were torchlight parades in honor of the Republican Presidential candidates. There was a Grand Army of the Republic post for the young veterans of the Union Army cherishing their sabers and the heavy Colts and carbines that had licked Johnny Reb. Sidewalks consisting of wooden planks went along the two main streets—ideal for courting couples out for a walk, people said—and there was a hotel offering a room for a dollar a night and free cartage of luggage from the station a block away. There was no saloon and, until the railroad brought drifters into town, no jail. (The drifters ceased to drop off the freights into West Branch when a lockup was fitted out and the rock-breaking routine for prisoners became known up and down the line.)

The Hoover house was fourteen feet wide, twenty feet long, divided into two rooms. The smaller room was the bedroom, with the three children—there was an older brother; there would be a younger sister—sleeping together in a trundle bed that rolled out from under their parents' bed. There were holes in the wooden walls and floors where the timber had been lashed together as it floated down the Mississippi to the landings at Davenport. Hoover's paternal great-grandparents had come out by covered wagon from Miami County, Ohio, traveling through the Indian country, molding bullets to take down the prairie chickens and deer, settling into shacks out on the open plains while they built their house. His mother's father came down from Canada.

Hoover's people were Quakers. His mother, Huldah, dressed in dark colors and wore a bonnet of the Prairie Schooner type. His father, Jesse, wore a broadbrim hat and a collarless coat of blue or brown. He was the village blacksmith, with his forge behind the house.

West Branch was somber. There were no brick houses, for

the Quakers thought brick and porches and cupolas and Victorian gewgaws were showy and perhaps even sinful. Only whitewash and robin's-egg-blue paint was acceptable on the inside walls. For hours, absolute silence was maintained at the First Day and Fourth Day meetings until a sister or a brother was moved by the Spirit to speak. Outside the Meeting House the ox-teams of the families from the outlying settlements stood at the hitching post; on Sundays their owners came to dinner in the town homes without invitation but always with a welcome. Huldah Minthorn Hoover was known as an eloquent and impassioned speaker at Meeting—the Spirit had even moved her to break into solemn song at her father's funeral—and her house was always crowded on the Sabbath. Three or four of the countryfolk always came for dinner and sometimes there were as many as a dozen guests. Hospitality was the first rule after reverence for the Divine.

In the Quaker homes there were no books save the Bible, the encyclopedia, and those novels wherein it was shown how the hero overcame the Demon Rum. (When Tad and Bertie Hoover came into possession of a copy of an innocent boys' magazine, *The Youth's Companion*, they hid it away behind their father's blacksmith shop.) Huldah Hoover went by buggy down the straight, rolling trails in nearby towns—Downey, West Liberty, Centreville—to speak the Word, to preach Peace and Temperance; she had the call. "Thee little 'you,' thee," the Quaker children said to each other as the ultimate insult; and Tad and Bertie and little May were taught to scrape up the crumbs around their places at table—waste is a sin.

Nothing but the absolute truth was acceptable in any circumstance. Once Uncle Allan Hoover demanded to know why his son and his nephew Bertie were giggling and carrying on in such a demonstrative and un-Quakerish fashion. He wished he had not asked when they told him, in front of his hired man, that the hired man's consumption of apples, thirteen in one sitting, had struck them as funny.

Out to the west was El Dorado, and over the mountains were more mountains with more gold. But the Quakers sought only the Inner Light in every man which told him the Right and the Truth: "One, with God, is a majority." Conscience and thrift, plain living, that was the way, and helping others with the barn-raising and corn-husking, feeding the husband who waited while the midwife was with his woman, taking care of the woman's children when she was sick.

Jesse Hoover died at thirty-four of the fever. The Elders thought his wife's stone for him was too large and ornate and they asked her to put a smaller one in its place. Three years later she was dead herself, at thirty-five: typhoid. They put her with her husband and their pioneer parents in the village grave-yard located on a slight rise on the prairie. Bertie, her second son, eight, took it in stoic silence. Then the children were farmed out to relatives; the inheritance, a few hundred dollars, was put in the hands of an unpaid outsider—a local grand old man—so that it could not be said that a cousin or uncle was managing it for anyone's benefit but the three small orphans.

Uncle Allan Hoover took Bertie to his farm. The estate paid six dollars a month for the boy's board, but during the summers he worked and so the charge was reduced to four dollars. At nine years of age he was partially self-supporting, picking thistles, cleaning the barn, and helping the workers at threshing time. School was a mile-and-a-half walk through the prairie winds in the fall, the brutal snows in winter and the dragging mud in the spring. He was quiet, serious, extremely shy, inarticulate. He thought a long time before speaking, learned to sit still through the interminable Meetings, did not show emotion: a Quaker.

At ten years of age he left West Branch for the Oregon home of his mother's brother, Uncle Henry Minthorn, whose only son had recently died. The emigrant train taking new settlers west had cars fitted up with bare bunks and a kitchen stove; his relatives in West Branch gave him a roll of bedding, fried chicken, ham, bread, meat pies. For seven days the slow, rocking cars headed across the mountains, out into the West of 1884, and then up into Portland, where the uncle waited at the depot. He was a country doctor, dour, Quakerish, serving a clientele in the Willamette Valley. Bertie was put to work caring for the doctor's team, splitting the wood, driving the horses on calls made in after-school hours. Between long silences his uncle talked on occasion of how, back in Iowa as a boy, he helped smuggle slaves out of the South via the Underground Railway before running away from his pacifist home to join a Union regiment at Davenport.

Bertie was fifteen years old when his uncle moved the 40 miles from Portland to Salem to take over a Quaker land-settlement agency selling sections up along the wet forest trails. Bertie was the office boy. Together with a boy who worked in the insurance office next door he reconditioned sewing machines and tried to peddle them to housewives. He bought a bicycle whose expense consumed several months of his less than five-dollars-a-week salary, the bicycle being a new safety type with cushion tires. He enrolled in a business college and worked on his math and Latin. He began to read novels, and *David Copperfield* lived on forever in his orphan-boy's mind as the most important book he had ever read.

He was extremely diligent, very earnest, mechanically minded, and, in a vague way, ambitious. He considered becoming a bookkeeper, then discarded the idea. (In his boyhood, back in Iowa, he had wanted to run the locomotives.) When adults were kind to him he was always moved: a teacher helping with higher mathematics, a woman who planned a reading program.

One day an eastern engineer drifted into his uncle's land-settlement office, made Bertie's acquaintance and talked with him about engineering. The office boy took what the man said to heart and for a year mulled it over in his mind, sending away for catalogues on engineering courses, hanging around the town's little foundry and sawmill and repair shops. At a mining prospect in the Cascades he talked with a mining engineer. The man's carefully scientific calculation that the mine was no good spoke to something in him, in his nature and imagination. Perhaps it was the precision, the chance to weigh facts one against the other. He decided to become a mining engineer and never for a moment regretted the decision. Engineers build, create, construct. They cannot bury their mistakes. Only performance counts. "The engineer simply cannot deny that he did it," he said later, looking back.

It was 1891. He was sixteen. The newly formed and free Leland Stanford, Jr., University in Palo Alto, California, was holding entrance examinations for potential applicants. A Quaker, Joseph Swain, had been appointed to conduct the examinations in Portland. Uncle Henry and the rest of the family wanted Bertie to go to a Quaker college in Indiana, but he fought the idea after learning the place had no engineering courses. He told them that, after all, a Quaker was in charge of the Portland examinations, and they let him go there for the tests. He did very well in mathematics, badly in the other subjects. Joseph Swain was understanding and kind when he reviewed the test results with Bertie. He suggested that the boy go down to California for the summer and take special tutoring with a woman near the college. Then perhaps he might be able to pass the examinations in the fall. Hoover had a total of $160 in savings from his office job, some money made weeding onions in the bottomlands north of Newberg, two suits and his bicycle. Two hundred dollars was coming to him from his father's estate. His uncle gave him $50, his aunt gave him food, and he went South. That summer he ground away with the woman tutor and in the end he was conditionally admitted to Stanford, the conditions arising from deficiencies in several subjects, primarily English and composition.

The week before the college formally opened its doors for the first class, he moved into Encina Hall—one of the school's first two boys. The formal opening was October 1, 1891. There were four hundred students. Hoover was two months past his seventeenth birthday.

He got a job in a school office for five dollars a week and another job typing in the Department of Geology and Mining—he had learned to operate a machine during his office-boy days. He picked up laundry—he called his route the "Red Star Service"—and delivered newspapers, although he still had difficulty approaching people. He was tall and skinny—"gawky" was what most people immediately thought—very boyish, almost childish-looking. His shyness was such that he would never speak until spoken to, and he would rarely meet the other person's eyes.

His grades were not good—in four years he never got an "A"—but he became in his way an important man on the fledgling campus. He failed to make the baseball team as a shortstop, but the team made him manager in charge of arranging games, collecting gate money and buying equipment and uniforms. The college started a football team and he managed that, too. Throughout, he remained almost completely aloof from his world. He simply never spoke. His fellow students saw him trudging through the Quadrangle with his eyes perpetually on the ground, and although they could respect his achievements, they found it impossible to warm to him.

Fraternity and sorority chapters were started at Stanford and of course Hoover did not become a pledge. He was one of those whom the Greek-letter students called a "barbarian," and as a "barb" he helped organize an anti-fraternity and -sorority ticket to campaign in the student elections. Hoover was elected manager of all student enterprises. He set up a constitution and a bookkeeping system, and with only minor changes they lasted half a century.

The head of the Department of Geology and Mining became interested in him and arranged jobs during the summer vacations. At the end of his freshman year he mapped geologic outcrops on the north side of the Ozarks in Arkansas, and after his sophomore and junior years he worked for the U.S. Geological Survey in California and Nevada, down on the desert floor and up in the High Sierra. He camped out for weeks on end, and traveled by horseback. All the jobs together, along with the money he had when he entered Stanford, allowed him to graduate in a solvent state—with forty dollars.

He had something else: an "understanding" with a young lady. She was Miss Lou Henry, once of Waterloo, Iowa, but now along with her family of Monterey, California. She was the only child of a physician who had wanted a boy, and who had taught her to ride, hunt and fish. She was far quicker than Bert Hoover, gay, clear-sighted, and realistically skeptical about life. She was Stanford's first girl Geology major and he met her when his professor showed her some specimens and said they were probably pre-Carboniferous.

"What is your opinion, Hoover?" asked the professor.

Her blue eyes and roguish grin paralyzed him. Blushing and tongue-tied, he could not answer the professor's question. She liked parties and for her he learned to dance. It was not easy. Lou Henry was the only woman in his life, ever.

Hoover left Stanford in 1895, just past twenty-one years of age. Miss Henry was finishing her freshman year. He wanted to be near her, and so with forty dollars in his pocket he looked for a job in the California gold-mining fields around Nevada City and Grass Valley, where he had been with the Geological Survey the preceding two summers. There were no jobs. The money dwindled away and he ended by living on credit from an innkeeper until he found work pushing a mining car for the night shift in the lower levels of the Reward Mine. He earned two dollars a day, worked ten hours per shift, seven days a week. In the blasting and drilling of the Reward he learned those things that could not be taught in college, and they promoted him to full-fledged miner.

But after a few weeks the job gave out and he went tramping the gold-field employment offices. Finally he caught on at the Mayflower Mine; after work he spent his time around harsh and unpaved Nevada City's assay office and National Hotel and Wells Fargo Express office talking about mining. He saw Louis Janin, a well-known mining engineer he had met before and asked him for a job. Janin told him he had no mine jobs. The only job vacant in his organization was that of copyist in the office. Hoover said he could run a typewriter and Janin laughed and took him on. After a few days indoors he was sent on a project to northern Colorado, and after that to a mine at Steeple Rock, New Mexico. The miners were Mexicans carrying guns and brawling in the streets and cheap barrooms.

It was the beginning of the Hoover who never wore a white collar, who was dirty, ate wherever he could, went down into the mines, slept on the desert floor, sought gold, zinc, stone, metal, all that made for a twentieth century beyond the dreams of his grim pioneering people. Engineering was an old profession, but it was in its modern guise a new one also, and peculiarly American, for the Europeans were too hidebound really to understand it. Hoover had fallen in love with it, the solid calculation, balance, evaluation, judgment.

After New Mexico and the hot desert and freezing mountains came a call from Australia asking Janin to recommend an expert schooled in American gold-mining practices. It was late 1897; Hoover was twenty-three years old. Janin asked him if he would go, and so he was off to the London office of Bewick, Moreing & Co., the controlling company of the Australian mine. He carried in his bag his first set of dinner clothes because the boss said the English would expect him to have one. He took the rattler back East, stopped at that West Branch in whose little weekly his father had once advertised his blacksmith's implements under the romantic heading of "Ho for Kansas!" Then at Davenport he crossed the Mississippi for the first time, went on to New York and a White Star steamer outward bound for Southampton. In the English country place of the head of Bewick, Moreing & Co., the footman unpacking his things frightened him, but he went down to dinner and, a few days later, to a Western Australia crying out for the thrusting American frontier technology.

His mine was the Coolgardie, three hundred miles from the smallpox-quarantined port of Albany. It was like the California of '49, he thought to himself, with the same wild optimism, prostitution, and champagne gulped down in anticipation of the big strike. He laid out plants, did development work, ordered American equipment sent out, examined the new prospects in the brutal desert where bushes were the principal fuel, and water from the scratched-out wells sold at the rate of ten cents for four gallons. It was prohibitively expensive to grow green things, but he started a garden and fought off the terrible heat and the desert ants to bring through two cabbages at a cost of $250 worth of water apiece. Miners gathered in the evening to watch something grow in that parched and arid place. At midnight the temperature stood at 100 degrees; and across a thousand miles of flat desert there was not a running stream, no roads beyond primitive tracks.

Hoover traveled to the outlying mines by Afghan camel, sleeping on the ground during the cold nights which broke with the swarming flies of daybreak. He lived off bread, cocoa and sardines heated in the can over a fire, the flies and sand mixing with the food and drink. Deep in the interior of Western Australia he looked at the Welsh-owned Sons of Swalia prospect and reported to London by cable that he thought the mine worthwhile. On his say-so Bewick, Moreing & Co. invested half a million dollars in the strike and made him mine manager with a salary of $10,000 a year. In time the Sons of Swalia brought in some fifty-five million dollars worth of gold.

The British asked him to go to China at a salary of twenty thousand. He accepted and cabled Miss Lou Henry to ask for her hand. They had seen each other only two or three times in the nearly four years since he had left Stanford, where she had remained to get her degree. But they had corresponded steadily. She cabled "Yes" and he made for London and then New York and the long rolling train ride across the country to California and his wedding day—the day he arrived, February 10, 1899. They were both twenty-four years old.

The next day they sailed for Peking. This was the China of Western nations vying for concessions and corruption in the court of the Young Emperor Kwang Hsu. The Hoovers settled in a rented house in the International Settlement at Tientsin. The former Lou Henry learned Chinese—she had a gift for languages—while her husband writhed his way through the tortuous Palace intrigue common to all business enterprises in Imperial China. In the interior he traveled on horseback, escorted by a hundred Chinese cavalrymen with advance heralds and rear guards. His Oriental advisers told him that to go with less pomp would mean loss of face. The Chinese provincial inns abounded with bedbugs and spiders; the cook worked over charcoal-fired pots set up in the open courtyards. The ancient mines were milled by the power of endlessly circling ponies or mules; the coolies made six cents a day.

He was twenty-five years old and still so youthful-looking with his round, unlined face and straight mouse-colored hair that all along the China Coast he was known as "Boy" Hoover. He went to Shantung, Manchuria, Shansi and Shensi provinces, and to the Mongol capital of Urga in the Gobi Desert, where he found the ceremonies of hospitality unchanged from the days of Marco Polo. He called upon Living Buddhas in Tibetan lamaseries, local war lords and American missionaries. He spent a

Christmas at Kalgan, a gate in the Great Wall, and showed three hundred Chinese mission children how to use four second-hand footballs sent out by people in the States. He was asked to look at the Sorrow of China, the Yellow River. Despite his explanation that he was not that kind of an engineer, the Chinese insisted. So he went by houseboat with Mrs. Hoover, who was delighted to be in the midst of the teeming waterway life.

The new century came, and with it rumors of an uprising of the Society of the Mailed Fists: the Boxers. The Young Emperor was gone and the Dowager Empress encouraged the Boxers to expel all the foreigners with fire and sword. All through the spring of 1900 the rumors grew more frightening. Hoover left an outlying prospect where his men had outlined a field of anthracite greater than all the world's other existing supplies put together, and returned to Tientsin to be with his wife. They were there on June 10 when the first artillery shells came looping toward the foreigners living in the International Settlement, protected by one thousand troops of various Western nationalities. Outside the gates were twenty-five thousand Boxers screaming for blood and imbued with the belief that supernatural powers would keep them from harm.

Hoover worked with the loyal Christian Chinese to remove from the great warehouses sacks of sugar, peanuts, rice, and grain which could be used for barricades against the shelling and small-arms fire. Mrs. Hoover acted as a volunteer in the hospital, hugging the walls when she rode her bicycle to her work so as to avoid enemy fire. One of her tires was hit by a bullet; a shell blew out the front door of their house.

Across the street from their home an artillery salvo smashed into the compound where the Chinese Director of Railways was taking shelter with his wife and children; the wife and one child died. Hoover rushed over with an aide and carried the other children to Mrs. Hoover, who took charge of them. Eighteen years later, in Washington, the wife of the Chinese Minister, Mrs. Wellington Koo, said, "I have met you before. I am Tong Shao-yi's daughter whom you carried across the street during the siege of Tientsin."

The battle lasted a month. Before the Western troops from Taku arrived people went half mad with fear and walked about asking the men if they intended to shoot their wives when the Boxers broke through. Later Hoover would say that he never heard a sound more beautiful than the bugles of the Welsh Fusiliers and American Marines playing "There'll Be a Hot Time in the Old Town Tonight" when their relief column finally came marching into the Settlement. The column had machine guns and some artillery, but the Boxers outside closed the ring again and held for three more weeks until more Western troops arrived to drive the besiegers away. Most of the wounded and women and children went off under guard down the river. The Hoovers, however, stayed on, Mrs. Hoover refusing to desert her post in the hospital and the seriously wounded who could not be moved.

The Western commander, an American Marine colonel, asked Hoover to guide his men in a sortie against the enemy. Hoover did, and in the open plains outside the Settlement they came under Chinese fire. Several Marines were hit. Hoover was so frightened he could hardly move. He asked a Marine officer for the rifle of one of the wounded men. As soon as it was in his hand he completely lost his fear. But he was a Quaker and pacifist and did not fire the weapon. A few days later additional relief forces arrived and the siege was lifted.

The Dowager Empress and her government who had countenanced the Boxer Rebellion fled into interior China and the Westerners seized the spoils of war: the mines, shops, harbor works, steamers, coal stocks and yards. The Hoovers went across a Red Sea broiling under the August sun, and then back to America, and then out again to the East where Mrs. Hoover set up residence in Japan while her husband went on to Shanghai. From there in the dead of winter he took a steamer for Chinwangtao in North China. When the boat arrived the waters of Chinwangtao were frozen. The ship's captain suggested the passengers go ashore by crossing the ice on foot. Off the shallow beach the ice had turned to mush and, carrying his satchel, Hoover plunged into hip-deep water. He stumbled seven miles inland as the temperature dropped to below zero. Finally he lit a bonfire to halt a Western troop train heading for Tientsin. Unshaven, covered with mud, he sat in a car filled with sleeping privates of the Russian Army and so arrived at Tientsin.

Foreign troops were all over the city. When he bought a cow for dairy use the German contingent immediately stole her and he went wandering the streets with a lantern to find her. Bandits plagued the area; the Boxers had all but dismantled the railroads; every Chinese official demanded a bribe for performing the slightest service—it was a ghastly business for a solemn, methodical engineer solely interested in extracting valuables from the ground. He doggedly battled his way toward creating an ice-free port at Chinwangtao so that he could ship out coal.

He was twenty-seven when, in late 1901, Bewick, Moreing & Co. cabled to ask if he would accept a junior partnership in their worldwide enterprises, with a base in London. He picked up Mrs. Hoover, and via Nagasaki went on to the States, and then to England.

Chapter Four

HOOVER BECAME the richest engineer of his time. He sought gold, lead, zinc, copper, tin. He went to India, New Zealand, the Hawaiian Islands, Egypt, Korea, Russia, France, Ceylon, crossing the Pacific ten times and the Atlantic twenty-five or more. Mrs. Hoover gave him two boys, both born in London: Herbert, Jr., in 1903 and Allan in 1907. The family went everywhere with him, always avoiding hotels in favor of a quickly settled, although always temporary, home. Lou Henry Hoover, quick and smiling, easily adapted to their constant moving. Her geological training at Stanford made her able to appreciate his work and help him with it. When he went into remote places where a woman and children would not find even minimum comfort and safety, she waited with the boys at their base. He always hurried to get back. As his fortune grew there were many servants, but he stayed close to his boys. He like to build things with them, little dams, pools in streams. He was always good with children, able to talk with them, friendly, completely relaxed. With adults he remained as reserved as he had always been. When someone spoke to him he always seemed to be studying the buttons on his vest, or looking at the other person's shoes. Or he doodled page after page of geometric forms. When he did speak, his eyes were always downcast.

In London in the last years before the War, the family had

a flat at Hyde Park Gate and later their Red House at Campden
Hill, ancient, with a garden and fine oak- and walnut-paneled
walls, fireplaces, and leaded-glass bookcases. In the summer they
were at cottages at Swanage, Dorsetshire or Stratford-on-Avon.
Great Britain was wonderful in those days, Hoover remembered
afterward—calm, well ordered, so comfortable for those with
money. But the class-consciousness and the servility of the masses
bothered him. His position and eminence would have permitted
him to make a splash in society or even Court circles, but neither
he nor the former Lou Henry wanted that. Instead, their guests
tended to be old friends from Stanford days, or engineers and
their wives whom they had met on strikes in the East.

After a decade as partner with Bewick, Moreing & Co., he
went into business for himself, with offices in New York, San
Francisco, London, St. Petersburg and Paris. All carried a simple
HERBERT C. HOOVER on the door. He was still under thirty-five
years of age, "The highest-paid man of his age in the world!"
wrote Mrs. Leland Stanford to a friend. In part he went on his
own for the sake of the boys, for it meant he could take on fewer
prospects and spend more time in the United States. He wanted
them to have an American education. With Mrs. Hoover's father
they kept a small home in California where the boys were settled
so that they could attend the Stanford University children's
school and later Palo Alto High School. During the summers the
children came to the Red House in London and the rented
English countryside cottages.

He spread out all over the world—Alaska, Burma, Mexico,
Siberia—specializing in taking over badly run engineering projects and making them pay. He conceived of himself as a doctor
to sick concerns and loved making order out of chaos and bringing efficiency to ventures struck by incompetency or bad luck.
He seemed able to marshal all the relevant facts in every project
in his mind, and never forgot anything. On the long sea voyages
he worked in his cabin with secretaries and aides, and when he
arrived at the mine or mines in question, he knew more about
the problem than the resident engineers. His associates and employees spoke of him among themselves by a nickname which
lasted all his life: The Chief.

At home and abroad he and Mrs. Hoover worked on their translation of the works of the Latin scholar Agricola, who in the sixteenth century had assembled all knowledge of mining, metallurgy and industrial chemistry. For two hundred years afterward the work had been the great textbook of these subjects, even when Latin became a dead language. It had never been translated into English. Agricola's Latin terms for technical matters had always defied researchers, for he was dealing with practices and methods forgotten for centuries. The Hoovers ran experiments in laboratories to test what they thought Agricola was saying, and pored through ancient manuscripts to gain insight into his thinking. After years of work they had their translation printed on paper similar to that used in the sixteenth century. Their studies had ranged back as far as the mining practices of Greece and Rome as described by Agricola. They printed 3000 copies and gave half that number to engineer friends and engineering institutions.

In 1914 Hoover turned forty with a fortune approaching ten million dollars. He began to think about seeking some kind of job in public service at home, and said to his very closest friends that a man who had enough money to give his family a comfortable living had an obligation to do something for his generation. Agricola had quoted the Greek philosopher Antiphanes: "Now, by the gods, why is it necessary for a man to grow rich? Why does he possess much money unless that he may, as much as possible, help his friends, and sow the seeds of a harvest of gratitude, sweetest of the goddesses?"

Perhaps he would give up business matters to devote himself to Stanford University's welfare as teacher or business manager. Already his work as Trustee made the President of the University, David Starr Jordan, write a friend: "It is marvelous how Hoover is handling our board. Almost every reform we have dreamed of has slipped through as if oiled . . . Hoover gave them in ten days more ideas than they had had before in ten years."

In the summer of 1914 the War came, and suddenly the job found him. Almost with the first movements of the opposing forces, London was filled with hordes of American tourists fleeing the Continent. They discovered that the British banks were closed and that shops, hotels and business outfits were refusing to accept travelers' checks, lines of credit, and even American money. The tourists stormed around their Consulate demanding that something be done for them. The Consul was a friend of Hoover's and the Consulate was only a block from Hoover's London office. The Consul called to ask if Hoover would lend a hand in helping his fellow Americans.

Hoover went over and listened in deep silence with downcast eyes. Then he telephoned his offices to order that all the gold and British money on hand be brought over. In his methodical way he divided the crowd of about one thousand into five equidistant lines, set up a row of tables, and started changing dollars into pounds and gold. Some of the frightened tourists said they had no money at all, and he asked them to reaffirm this on their words of honor. When they did, he lent them his own funds. There was no question of collateral or interest. Finally they were all taken care of, and went away searching for meals and hotel rooms. The Consul called up Ambassador Walter Hines Page and reported. Ambassador Page at once said he had a mob of thousands asking for help, and could Hoover come right over to the Embassy?

Hoover learned Ambassador Page expected that upward of one hundred thousand Americans would need some aid. Hoover got the still-closed banks to release several thousand pounds of his own money, which he distributed. But there were no ships to bring the people home, for all the European liners were being taken off the Atlantic run. So the Americans piled up in London. Mrs. Hoover got together a group of resident American women to help their fleeing countrywomen and the children. She organized excursions to the areas around London and the cathedral towns and Shakespeare country. Meanwhile, her husband had branch committees of his informal aid organization set up in the main Continental cities, usually with engineers he knew in charge. Five hundred volunteers in London grouped the Americans into various categories which determined the type of assistance they were given.

Over a period of six weeks Hoover's people helped one hundred and twenty thousand Americans to exist while space aboard homeward-bound ships was sought. More than a million and a half dollars was lent. Defaults amounted to less than three hundred dollars. Ambassador Page wrote President Wilson: "Life is worth more, too, for knowing Hoover. . . . He's a simple, modest, energetic man who began his career in California and will end it in Heaven."

By the time the operation was half completed, Hoover had so organized the relief program that he was able to spend a part of each day in his office trying to pick up the routine of the international affairs that had been disrupted by the War. But his professional career was in fact finished.

On the Continent the German Army swept over most of Belgium and the War settled down into two opposing trench lines winding up from the Swiss border to the Channel. Behind the German lines Belgium and northern France grew hungry. The Brussels branch of Hoover's impromptu committee endeavored in a small way to relieve the situation by sending an American engineer to London with money to buy food. The man purchased the food but the British refused to allow its shipment to Belgium. Hoover's advice was sought; he suggested that if knowledge of the situation were known in the United States, American public opinion might force a change in the British attitude. He talked to the general manager of the Associated Press, who saw to it that stories of Belgian suffering and British intransigence were sent to American newspapers.

More people arrived from behind the lines to tell of the worsening situation. For lack of anything to do, they talked with Hoover. On October 18, two and a half months after the war began, Ambassador Page telephoned Hoover and asked him to come to the Embassy. Hoover was about to board ship to America where Mrs. Hoover had taken the boys for the beginning of the school year. Instead he went to Page and a group of Belgians at the Embassy. Page told him that William Jennings Bryan, the American Secretary of State, had cabled orders to do whatever might be done for the people behind the German lines. The American government, however, could not become involved. When the ambassador finished, the spokesman of the Belgian group said to Hoover that they were talking about the lives and deaths of millions of people. Would Hoover undertake to lead a campaign to feed these people?

He asked for a day to think it over and spent that night pacing the floor of his bedroom while he thought of the terrible troubles that would surely lie ahead in such an undertaking and the great fortune that might be his in working on during a war which would inevitably drive the prices of metals to unprecedented heights. In the morning he breakfasted with the journalist Will Irwin, an old Stanford friend. "Let the fortune go to hell," Hoover said.

During the long years of the War the Commission for Belgian Relief spent a billion dollars of loans and donations to feed the hungry and aid the sick. Germany would do nothing for the people in the rear of the German lines, and the Allies periodically threatened to end the whole business. Hoover's Commission chartered ships, went through the lines, begged, pleaded, bluffed. Belgium and northern France could produce only a third of the necessary food, so the Commission took over the entire crop to insure that there would be no profiteering. Belgian money was worthless; the Commission printed its own. Commission scientists invented a cracker containing every nutrient needed by the children to survive. The lacework industry of Belgium seemed destined to die; the Commission kept it alive by paying for and then storing the lace against sales when the War ended.

Hoover's ships hit mines in the Channel, and German submarines torpedoed them despite the signs BELGIAN RELIEF COMMISSION stretching from stem to stern. He traveled to Germany and demanded assurance from German officers that it would not happen again. Only the Commission passports allowed a man to cross Europe through the shattered villages and battling armies. Nothing like it had ever been done before, and Hoover had constantly to allay the fears of those on the Allied side who said the German Army was living off the Commission's food, and those on the German side who accused him of being a spy. In the United States people of neutral persuasion complained that an obscure ex-engineer was undertaking dealings with foreign governments that were dangerous in that they might involve America in the War.

Hoover served throughout with no pay, but with something like adulation from those who worked with him. "Those of us who lived through the difficult, almost impossible days," wrote one of his aides, "have come to an almost superstitious belief in his capacity to do anything possible to human power." It seemed to his people that The Chief's brilliance was almost superhuman, for his mind worked, as Will Irwin said, "at thoroughbred speed and with incredible endurance." He thought about a problem in silence, digested the facts, and came up with the solution. And it was the right solution. Belgium's hundreds of thousands who otherwise would have died attested to it.

He remained as he had been. Periodically, the King of the Belgians, in the name of the millions, told Hoover he wished to decorate him with the country's highest orders; but Hoover's Quaker diffidence, which made medals, ribbons and pageantry repellent, and his shyness and fear of speaking before crowds forced him to reply that he could accept no decorations and no public honors. When people tried to thank him for what he had done they found their words did not reach him, for he would stand thin-lipped and silent, his gaze in another direction.

In April of 1917 the United States entered the War. On the day that Congress voted the joint resolution President Wilson cabled Hoover asking that he return to organize the country's food resources. He arrived in Washington on May 5 and was welcomed at the White House on the same day. The newspapers called him the "Food Czar," or the "Food Dictator." But he saw himself campaigning under the Food Administration's theme, "Food Will Win the War." He did not believe Americans had to be forced to save food. Rather, one asked intelligently and explained the mechanics. And, as Hoover knew it would happen, twenty million housewives put stickers in their windows saying that a Food Administration volunteer lived there and that the housewife was "Hooverizing" her food, saving fats and preparing the special nonwasteful meals the Food Administration experts recommended. Her son and daughter grew vegetables on empty lots.

The War ended and Hoover went back to a shattered Europe faced with pestilence and famine. Internal markets, trans-

portation and food distribution systems had withered as a con-
sequence of the seventeen revolutions which erupted within weeks
of the Armistice. Everywhere east of the Rhine were white
faces and dull eyes and thin, anemic people passing empty shops.
Funeral processions continually went by and no children played
in the streets. The Europe of pre-War was dead.

All around was the fear, too terrible to be put into words,
that a wake similar to that of the Thirty Years' War was in
prospect, that a third of the people might die, that the vicious
pocket wars would go on and on, that the old tribal hatreds
stirred by the War might find a new and as frightful expression.
Hoover was asked by the leaders of the Allied governments, assembled in Paris for the Peace Conference, to take charge of
provisioning the hundreds of millions. He accepted, saying that
if the well-to-do would share and give, a tragedy might yet become a triumph.

Hoover sent his emissaries across Europe from Belgium to
Azerbaijan. Behind them he constructed telegraph lines and railroads. His wheat-laden ships sailed into empty harbors all over
the former War zones and his mills on the quay baked bread.
The solvent countries, fearful that if he failed Bolshevism would
succeed, poured credits into his coffers to buy food. Germany
gave up the French gold coins paid out as indemnity after the
Franco-Prussian War nearly half a century before. And, finally,
money was raised by simple charity. For eleven months Hoover
did not take a day off, never went into a shop—others bought his
clothes—and ate on the run, his thoughts constantly haunted
by the millions, particularly the pale, stunted children, their
heads shaved as a precaution against lice, stretching out their
tin plates in canteens and schoolhouses for stew and bread that all
Europe called Hoover Lunches. In Finland a new verb came into
the language: "to hoover" meant to be kind, to help.

He had at his disposal the forces of the American Army
and Navy, and the full backing of the President. Hoover's job,
Wilson said, was second only in importance to the task that
faced General Pershing when he landed in France. Hoover's men
forced hostile armies to lay down their arms, acted as mediators
between mutually distrustful factions trading coal for beef and

eggs for potatoes. Corporals under his command ran trains across fortified national boundaries where no other traffic was passed; and it was said that armed guards would salute a piece of paper with his name written on it.

He sent trainloads of surplus Army clothing across the Continent, and millions of pounds of raw cotton. When typhus broke out he mobilized soldiers to go from west to east spraying delousing powder upon millions of people. Revolution came, Red Terror and White Terror, coup and countercoup, riots, looting— he fed the hungry and clothed the naked, warmed the houses and stoked the factory fires. All over the world he came to be known as the Great Humanitarian, and into his offices there poured a million signatures on a hundred thousand pages, the signatures of children and their childish drawings of him as a new angel of mercy.

"Young man," Admiral Sir Rosslyn Wemyss said to him, "I don't see why you Americans want to feed these Germans."

"Old man," Hoover snarled back, "I don't understand why you British want to starve women and children after they are licked."

In the eyes of the economist John Maynard Keynes, Hoover with his withdrawn and self-effacing air seemed like "a weary Titan" or an "exhausted prizefighter." Alone of all the men in Paris for the Peace Conference, Hoover emerged with an enhanced reputation. Had Hoover's reasoning way and Hoover's decency been universal, Keynes wrote, then a lasting peace might have been fashioned.

In August of 1919 he went to Poland at President Wilson's request. There, by the President's instructions, he told the Poles that America would stand by them in the support of democracy. He forced himself to speak for a few minutes at Kosciusko's tomb in Cracow. The pianist-statesman Paderewski translated his few remarks for an hour. Hoover asked a Polish aide what Paderewski was talking about. The man replied, "Oh, he is making a *real* speech."

In Warsaw fifty thousand school children came to the old racetrack to parade in Hoover's honor. He stood in the grandstand gesturing in an embarrassed and constricted way that made a friend think his hand quickly flapping up and then down was like a limp flag rising momentarily from a mast on an almost windless day. The children, five to twelve years of age, in rags, fed only because of Hoover's work, carried paper banners with the American and Polish colors, along with messages saying that they asked God to bless Herbert Hoover. The general commanding the French military mission burst into tears and said, "There has never been a review of honor in all history which I would prefer for myself to that which has been given you today."

Hoover took away, also, the memory of how, when a rabbit ran among the children, they broke ranks by the thousands to give chase, catch the animal and then bear it to him—a gift.

He returned to America thinking that the Old World and the New would never understand each other, and that Europe's violent and destructive hatreds would bar all further progress on the Continent. The Americans were different. Three hundred years of growing away from their European ancestries had evolved them into a stronger, better race. To explain what he meant he wrote a book, *American Individualism*. Though the public did not read it in great numbers they derived from the title the idea that he had invented two phrases ever after associated with his name: The American Way of Life and Rugged Individualism.

Upon arrival in New York he gave one speech whose composition had poisoned his days on the ship. Then he went on to California where he issued a statement saying that for a month he would devote himself to two small, vigorous boys, that he would reply to no telephone calls, read no letters exceeding one page in length, and that he would decline the honor of speaking at the sixty-four public meetings which had requested him to do so. He said he was making these rules in the belief that "the American people will be gratified to find a citizen who wants to keep still." He opened an engineering office and hinted that he was back in the business for which he had been trained. Then he went camping and fishing with his family in the mountains. But in fact this strictly private way of life was over for him.

It was the cry of fifteen million European children that reached him. The American Relief Administration was still feeding them, but the money was running out. Congress voted Hoover a grant of one hundred million dollars to continue the work, and when that ran out he threw himself into collecting money from private sources. He sat in a New York banquet hall at a rough table set with tin dishes; by him was an empty chair with a lighted candle before it. On the other side sat General Pershing. It was the Invisible Guest who sat at the empty plate, Hoover explained to the thousand-dollar-a-plate guests, the Invisible Guest who symbolized the children. The people would eat as the children ate, their food, from their plates. A man rose and told the deeply moved audience that one thousand dollars each was not enough. When Hoover indicated the diners had been told no additional contribution would be solicited, the man asked if it was not the sense of the meeting that this limitation be put aside. Three million dollars was given that night.

The Russian author Maxim Gorki wrote Hoover asking if Communist Russia might not be helped. Hoover replied that he could feel for the sick and starving of the country, "particularly the children," and that if given a free hand he would do what he could. The Soviet diplomat Maxim Litvinov worked out the details which allowed for the liberation of all American prisoners in Russia and the right for members of the American Relief Administration to travel with no impediments. The entire distribution was on an entirely nonpolitical basis. Eighteen million Russians profited. They ate because of Hoover. Without him it would never have been done, for the Americans as a whole were tired of giving to charity and particularly antagonistic to Bolsheviks. Gorki wrote, "You have saved from death three and one-half million children, five and one-half million adults."

Hoover then turned away from Europe, saying that nothing else could be done for the Old World—it would have to make its own destiny. For a moment he hesitated as to his future course, for he was tendered the largest financial offering that ever came to any engineer. Daniel Guggenheim came to him as the owner, along with his brothers, of the largest mining firm in the world. He asked if Hoover would join them as a partner with a guaranteed minimum increment of half a million dollars a year for the rest of his career. For a week Hoover and his wife considered the offer, and in the end the answer was "No." For the newly elected President, Warren Gamaliel Harding, had asked Hoover to join his Cabinet. The conservative politicians surrounding the pliable Harding were against the offer, fearing Hoover as a liberal and a progressive. But for all the weakness that would make his Presidency the most corrupt in history, Harding had a certain impulse to do the right thing. He wanted Hoover.

There was brought to Harding's home in Marion, Ohio, a very slim, quiet, diffident little man from Pennsylvania who sat waiting on the porch for two hours and who, when introduced to Harding, made no impression on him. For Harding had never heard of Andrew William Mellon of Pittsburgh. But the men behind him had, and they wanted this wraithlike figure in the new Administration as Secretary of the Treasury. Harding said, No Hoover, no Mellon, and so Hoover was given the choice of Interior or Commerce. Commerce was considered the lower post, but Hoover saw it for what it might be, and Harding appointed him to it. On the Stanford campus Mrs. Hoover had built a magnificent rambling home; now they left it for a large brick house on Washington's S Street, just four doors up a hill from where the retired and broken Woodrow Wilson was dying.

Herbert Hoover was the most active and brilliant Cabinet member of his time, second in the public's eye only to the soon legendary Mellon. The Secretary of the Treasury held a position close to that which religion gives its prophets. For Mellon was the man whose word was law, who never made a mistake, who in his whispering manner held the secrets of prosperity and the happiness of millions. But where Mellon was austere and retiring, a thin and saintly old man in the eyes of the American people, Hoover was accessible and filled with dynamic energy. Mellon, so it seemed, performed miracles that saw the United States rise to a way of living undreamed of by any nation in the past, and there was something of the alchemist in his manner. No one dared question him, and he offered few explanations as he went silently about his work, cutting taxes, cutting government expenditures, making surpluses grow and factories work three shifts. No one saw into the sanctum of his mystic thinking from which the unbelievable prosperity emerged: the waffle makers suddenly on everyone's tables; the simply astonishing proliferation of cars; the magnificent new public high schools with marble swimming pools, great auditoriums and immense stadia (better-neighborhood schools sometimes had polo teams); the yachts; the electric washing machines; the wonderful new paved roads; the boom developments making the farmers rich as they sold off their lands for constantly rising prices.

Secretary of Commerce Hoover was far more understandable. To the public his achievements had logic and a down-to-earth quality about them. He was called the Great Engineer and one saw the engineer's methodical path in his doings. When there was a slip in employment he called together leaders from production, distribution, banking, construction, labor, and agriculture. With them he would plan long-term reconstruction. And soon the factories put up MEN WANTED signs and the magazines were swamped with new pages of advertising. There were too many firms making too many versions of the same product—four hundred types of bolts—and he arranged for standardized sizes, which resulted in lower prices for consumers and greater productivity. The world cried out for America's goods, and the Secretary of Commerce worked to make credit available to the foreigners so that Hudsons and Packards might cross African trails and European boulevards.

Waste horrified Hoover; his Department showed businessmen how to fight it with better transport facilities, better use of water resources, and the reduction of seasonal variations in industry. He injected himself into labor disputes and acted as arbitrator in commercial litigations. He helped to develop and apply scientific research methods for labor-saving devices and superior processes. He got private charitable foundations to make grants for the study of food problems, and applied himself to aiding architects in designing better homes.

Hoover wrote a booklet, "How To Own Your Own Home," and the Department of Commerce sold millions of copies. He was very much involved in aeronautical matters, calling conferences to work for better planes and airports and for pilots' examinations. His personal regulation of radio broadcasting led to new laws which made the airwaves public property. Commerce-appointed experts made sense out of the welter of the nation's fishing laws, and Congress at his insistence passed legislation safeguarding the fisheries. In 1927, when the Mississippi River overflowed in the most disastrous flood of its history, six state governors asked the Secretary of Commerce to come and help the million and a half people affected by the thousand miles of rampaging waters. He commanded all the forces of the government: the Army Engineers, the Coast Guard, a naval air contingent and the Weather Bureau.

As the flood moved slowly downstream, Hoover established great tent towns, mobilized hundreds of motorboats, laid electric lines and put up temporary hospitals. In the waters' wake he remedied the damage by providing materials for new homes, feed for the livestock, tools and furniture for the people. The Rockefeller Foundation at his behest furnished funds for 100 health units to operate in the flood areas for a year afterward; the teams stamped out the endemic malaria and typhoid of the entire area, including that part of Arkansas where in the summer of his freshman year the young Bert Hoover had worked at mapping geologic outcrops. The whole of the gigantic undertaking was handled without aid from the federal government; it was all financed under his direction by the Red Cross and private charities, with loans being let at moderate terms but with the understanding that the money would be paid back—as it was, to the last cent.

He left the floodlands thinking that nowhere but in the United States could be found the local leadership and organizational ability to get the job done. In Europe or Asia there would never have been enough feeling of genuine fellowship among the people, not enough independent spirit, too much reliance upon government dictates. He had never been prouder of the Americans.

Chapter Five

HOOVER STAYED eight years as head of the Department of Commerce, hating to go to Cabinet meetings during the Harding days because of the vulgarity and dirty jokes that occupied the President and some of his cronies. (His "playmates," Hoover called them.) He avoided all social dinners with Harding because it struck him as inappropriate that there should be gambling and drinking in the White House. But the President respected him. (Harding called all the members of his Cabinet by their first names except Hoover, Mellon, and Secretary of State Charles Evans Hughes. These three were meticulously addressed as Mr. Secretary.)

Hoover was present on the last trip of Harding's life. The Secretary and Mrs. Hoover were in the West when a telegram reached them asking that they join the President's party en route to Alaska. They met Harding at Tacoma and found him on the verge of a nervous collapse. For at long last he had begun to comprehend the wretched stealing of his playmates. To fight off the nightmare he played bridge from directly after breakfast until midnight. Harding and his party went North by ship, the five other bridge players setting up shifts so that one of their number might now and then be free. It went on for days. Afterward, Hoover never again played the game.

A few days out Harding called Hoover to his cabin and told

him there was great scandal in the Administration. Should it be exposed or buried? Hoover told him the matter should be aired. Harding played ever more feverish bridge and then fell sick. Hoover cabled his Stanford classmate, Dr. Ray Lyman Wilbur, to come to examine the President. The examination was inconclusive. Harding rallied, and then, as his wife read to him from a *Saturday Evening Post* article which praised him, he fell back in his San Francisco hotel sickbed and died.

It was Hoover who telephoned Secretary of State Hughes to tell him the Vice President must be sworn into office at once. Calvin Coolidge was visiting his father in Vermont when a car came chugging up the road to tell him the news—his father's home had no telephone. There was no electricity, but Coolidge's father, a rural justice of the peace, lit a lantern and there in the shadowy house swore in his son as President. Then Coolidge went to Washington to stand at attention as Harding's body was borne from the train, the Secretary of Commerce still suffering from the incessant renditions at each stop of Harding's favorite hymn, "My Redeemer Liveth." The new President said at once he would keep all the fallen leader's men in office—only to learn, as time went by, that quite a good number of them deserved instead incarceration in a penitentiary. He warmed to Mellon (as much, indeed, as he could warm to anyone), for Mellon was of the same cut as he, although of course immeasurably richer.

For Mellon was the finest product of the history of American capitalism. He had vast interests in banking, real estate, metals, and oil. The world's third richest man, so it was said. At his news conferences in the Treasury Building, surrounded by aides to protect him, he smoked little black-paper cigarettes and held up the proceedings when a cigarette went out. As he carefully relit it the sixty-dollar-a-week reporters watched goggle-eyed a man worth one billion dollars putting a match to a stub.

Up Pennsylvania Avenue at Number 1600 the President was that way also, methodically clipping off the ends of his cigars and then carefully locking up the drawer in which he kept them. He liked to push a button that summoned the White House guards. Then, hidden behind the long window curtains, he enjoyed watching them run. On his early morning walks he peered into shop windows along fashionable Connecticut Avenue and cautioned the Secret Service men never to allow their wives to go into those stores. Once he had let Mrs. Coolidge do so and it had ended up costing him a lot of money. Mellon had no wife; he had married many years after most of the men of his generation—he was then in his forties—and the marriage had broken up. But like the President he liked to walk along looking into the store windows. Together the two slim and tiny figures cut taxes to a point where even men making fifty thousand dollars a year paid less than one thousand, and each year they miraculously reduced the debt of the late War by billions.

Coolidge hardly worked at all; he napped in the mornings before lunch, dozed a bit after eating, lay down for a few minutes prior to dinner and then, in his formal attire, sat for just a little while before going off to bed. He spent summers outside of Washington, traveling to his fishing camps by drawing-room accommodations (private cars cost money) and horrifying pure fishermen, his Secretary of Commerce among them, by using a fly instead of real bait. He could upbraid a Secret Service man for taking a dime to buy the five-cents-an-issue *Liberty Magazine* and neglecting to return the nickel change. His silence in public (sometimes in private he could become positively garrulous) was famous. There was a classic jest, perhaps not apocryphal, in which a woman bet him she could make him say more than two words and Coolidge replied, "You lose." He was indeed, in William Allen White's brilliant phrase, "the Puritan in Babylon."

America's money, virtually untaxed during the Coolidge years of 1923–1929, went into the magnificent bull market—"Everyone Should Be Rich," the advertisements said—and into the great land boom where lots sold as stocks did, doubling between sunrise and sunset. (Ex-Secretary of State and ex-Presidential candidate William Jennings Bryan became as something of a common shill preaching that Florida's sun and beaches would make today's small investor tomorrow's millionaire.) Plungers on the stock market cheerfully met interest rates of 20 percent to borrow money, so that for one dollar of margin they might have ten dollars worth of stock which, in a month or ninety days, might be worth fifty or a hundred. The world's luxuries poured forth for the plunger's wife: The African miner and Chinese coolie worked overtime for her; and her husband's golf clubhouse was a mansion built in imitation of the residence of a Scottish Laird.

Herbert Hoover had settled into his job as Secretary of Commerce in 1921 with a shy smile slipping down into his high collar; he had taken the oath and then said—it was so like him—"That ends the ceremony. Now we will have to get to work." He was not really and truly in the spirit of the days which saw blue-collar workers going to the job in a car, not really part of a way of life in which a former barroom fighter—Dempsey—made five thousand dollars a minute while one hundred thousand people roared and the new miracle, radio, brought each blow to the remotest plantations of Louisiana and the reaches of Montana.

It all came true in the roaring twenties: mahogany bars, vacuum cleaners, string quartets for luncheon in the big hotels, double laundry tubs. The dirt street with no pavement past the trolley turn-around on the outskirts of town was paved for the big white-wall-tired motor cars. The Limited went roaring by with a long string of Pullmans carrying two thousand live-wire salesmen affirming that their products were strictly first chop. In the ten years after the War the skylines were transformed; everywhere there were skyscraper grids rising and signs saying, "On this site will be erected . . ."

Washington in those years was a slumbering village for the three hot months of the year and an almost forgotten place for the remaining nine. The Puritan in Babylon rarely smiled and never showed emotion. (The daughter of the late Teddy Roosevelt, once the Princess Alice of Number 1600 Pennsylvania Avenue, remarked that he appeared to have been weaned on a pickle.) But he did what the country wanted. For doing it he was called the Prince of Laissez-Faire. At a press conference he was asked if he thought the gigantic amount of money being borrowed for stock purchases on margin was too high; he held the question over for the next session and then, after consultation with Secretary of the Treasury Mellon, opined it was not. A cousin of his who had been a financial editor sat with him a short time later and asked if this had been a wise or prudent thing to do, to which the President replied that speaking as a Vermont countryman it was his opinion that even one dollar borrowed for stock market speculation was too much money, but that it was not the job of a President to say such a thing. The cousin said he might wish that the President would say that in public, but of course Coolidge would not.

As the 1928 elections approached, the country boiled with discussion of whether Coolidge would run again and thus bid for a longer term in office than any of his predecessors. But the President had nothing to say on this, as on many other subjects. At his press conferences the reporters regularly wrote out their questions and then passed them up to him. One day they all conspired to write down the same question: Would he run again? The President read the slips of paper to himself one by one and then said, "We have a question here about the children in Romania . . ." and lectured for a little.

But his mind seemed to have been made up, although he did not discuss the matter even with the very alert and gracious and utterly different Mrs. Coolidge. He had never felt any great obligation to his office or to the Republican Party, or even to the country. He had never really seemed to care about anything but his son, Calvin, Jr. One day Calvin, fourteen years old, developed a blister on his foot while playing tennis on the White House courts. Blood poisoning resulted. While the boy lay in his room and the doctors looked grim, the President went out onto the lawns and caught a rabbit. With his own hands he brought the little trembling creature as a present to his son's bedside, the servants, who felt for the lad, turning away. Calvin, Jr., died in a hospital and a limousine took the President and First Lady back to the White House. The leader of one hundred and twenty million Americans and the great high priest of Coolidge Prosperity had suddenly become a shrunken little man with his head down. "When he died," Coolidge wrote, "the power and the glory of the Presidency went with him."

On his vacation in the Dakota Black Hills in 1927, Coolidge fished, posed for pictures in a cowboy outfit, and spent hours carefully watching his collie Rob Roy, whose dreams he attempted to analyze by observing the dog's motions while he

slept. Then one day in August he handed each reporter a type-
written note: "I do not choose to run for President in nineteen
twenty-eight."

There was never any further explanation and no one ever
knew if he had really hoped for a draft.

The Secretary of Commerce was in California when the
President's statement was released, and within an hour a flood
of visitors and telegrams poured in asking him to announce his
candidacy. Like everyone else, Hoover was confused by the President's choice of words. "Choose" could mean anything. Hoover
did not speak out but waited for a chance to talk to the President.
A month later in Washington he asked Coolidge if he absolutely
was not going to run, and got no direct reply. After the interview
Hoover told the reporters that he thought Coolidge would be
nominated and would win another term.

But Hoover's friends from Stanford and Belgian Relief Commission days took the President at his word. Hoover for President
clubs sprang up everywhere. The time had been awaiting the
man ever since 1920. As far back as then, even the newspaperman Charles Michelson, later the very greatest of Herbert
Hoover's enemies—his destroyer, some said—had regarded
Hoover as being "the best-qualified possibility that had approached the Presidency in modern times." Even the defeated
Democratic nominee for Vice President in 1920, Franklin Roosevelt, had in that year spoken of Hoover as "a wonder" and expressed the fervent hope that Hoover would be President some-
day. "There could not be a better one," Roosevelt had said.

The intensity of the demand that Hoover succeed him irritated Coolidge. He had never cared for the bustling and eager
young Secretary of Commerce who disturbed peaceful Cabinet
meetings with suggestions about things that might be done.
"Senator," Coolidge once said to James Watson of Indiana, "don't
you know that four-fifths of all our troubles in this life would
disappear if we would only sit down and keep still?" When the
Secretary of Commerce would introduce his new ideas at Cabinet
meetings the President always dealt with them in the same way
in his harsh Vermont drawl: "Waal, might be a good thing.
Might not. We'll see about that lateh." The later never came.

The demands that Hoover declare for the Presidency turned Coolidge acidulous. He took to referring to the Secretary of Commerce as "the wonder boy," "the smart boy," and "the miracle worker." At the same time he prepared himself to return to his half of the rented two-family house in Northampton, Massachusetts, which had always put off the aristocrats in his party who said that no President should have a home address renting for forty dollars a month. In February of the Presidential year, 1928, Hoover asked the President if he intended to allow his name to be filed in the Ohio Republican primary. "No," Coolidge said. Regarding Hoover's proposed filing, the President merely said, "Why not?"

Three months later, Hoover had 400 certain delegates out of a possible 1,084. Still unsure of what the President wanted, or might possibly do, Hoover went to Coolidge to say that if the President so desired, he might have the 400 delegates for a renomination drive. Coolidge said, "If you have four hundred delegates, you better keep them."

The convention met in Kansas City. Mellon, too old for nomination at seventy-three, attended with no great enthusiasm, saying privately that Hoover was an engineer who wanted everything to go in a straight line and everyone to come up to the straight line. The Republican Old Guard was uniformly cold to Hoover's candidacy, jealous of his fame, and resentful of his ways. They remembered with bitterness that he had begun his public career under the hated Wilson, had come out strongly for the League of Nations after the war, and had never kowtowed to the paladins of the Party or paid tribute to their long and faithful service.

But it would have been suicide for the Republicans to nominate anyone else. Hoover would give nothing to the professional politicians. They knew, though, that the people wanted him. He got the nomination on the first ballot.

Election Day came, and with it the great victory, the greatest in American history. There followed the brilliant inaugural. Twenty years earlier Chief Justice William Howard Taft had stood in Hoover's place; now Taft read out the oath of office of the Presidency of the United States and the loudspeakers brought Hoover's response to the crowd of two hundred thousand: "I do." And they roared.

Washington's gentle spring came. Then summer and the delicate early fall. And with the turning of the leaves, so soon after that wet but glorious day of inauguration—*I have no fears for the future of our country. It is bright with hope*—the market crashed.

After that, the great silence.

PART II

The Desperate Years

Chapter Six

W HAT FOLLOWED the crash in 1929 was so gradual that at first it was hardly noticeable. The experts said the market would come back; it went lower each week. New car sales slowed, for the newspapers indicated prices might be cut for the 1930 models. And people planning cruises south decided to cancel their trips. Down the block a TO LET sign appeared. A factory went on half time. Weeds began to grow in the crevices of the unfinished buildings. At the banks the depositors jostled for places in line, and the police had to get rough while wondering if they themselves would have a payday that week. When New York's Bank of the United States failed, a million people, a sixth of the city, lost savings. Immigrant women came to demand their money and, finding their bankbooks were worthless, fell to beating with their hands on the locked plate-glass doors. They screamed through the night for their money, but when no one came out to give it to them, they went away and, so it was said, stayed in their homes as the living dead, until the neighbors or a relative called the police. Then it was the insane asylum.

An executive's secretary who once earned forty dollars a week in the good old days still looked splendid in her neat dress, but, as she walked down the street, she was headed not for the office, for there was no job, but rather for a section of town where she was not likely to be recognized. There she would wait for cars to stop at a traffic light. If a lone man was at the wheel she would offer herself to him.

The society pages still concerned themselves with debuts and parties, but the affairs were different now. The fashionable party arranger Elinor Ferguson thought it seemed like a thousand years since the ballrooms were made up with waterfalls and flower beds for a summer evening dance. She saw a girl who once at a *bal masqué* wore the most dazzling costume Miss Ferguson had ever seen off the stage. It was in the days, she reflected, when American Telephone and Telegraph was soaring toward 300, when U.S. Steel was 260. The girl then was dressed to represent a fountain, her entire costume made of glittering rhinestones and brilliants falling in a shower from her headdress. Now at a party the same girl wore a cotton mesh polo shirt and a pair of cretonne coveralls costing, Miss Ferguson estimated, $2.95.

Eighty percent of the mail during the great days was advertising matter; 60 percent of the newspaper space was ads; along the Pennsy tracks between Washington and New York there were five thousand billboards. Now the mailbox was empty and the papers terribly thin and the billboards were blank. There was nobody in the entry of the huge office buildings. Nobody was in the elevators.

In Chicago the teachers, payless for months on end—tax collections had all but come to a halt—hitchhiked to their schools. One teacher, a former Army officer, slept on a bench in the playground.

In Montana the writer Morris Markey saw a rancher buy bullets on credit. It took the rancher two hours to kill his entire herd. It did not pay to feed them. The price of the meat did not pay for shipment to the railroad. "One way to beat the Depression, eh?" the rancher said grimly.

In New York City the reporter Elmer Davis looked up into the winter sky and saw there a sixty-story city empty above the twentieth floor. He thought: These buildings will stand empty for decades and our descendants will compare them to the pyramids and the great structures of the Roman Empire, architectural monuments to an age of faith. They will never be of use to anyone, save the artists of some future Romantic movement who will find inspiration in the ruins of the Empire State Building at Fifth and 34th.

Herbert Hoover had been born one year after a great depression had run its course; he came out of college and began his career in the midst of another great depression. He did not lose his nerve in 1929. For he had expected the Depression. As Secretary of Commerce he protested to President Coolidge about the easy-money policies which encouraged the mad stock market speculation. And he told the Federal Reserve Board it was utter folly to permit the speculators to run wild with their purchases of stock on 90 percent margin—ten cents down to own a dollar's worth of stock.

President Coolidge, bored and irritated, told the Secretary of Commerce that the Administration had no right to meddle in stock market matters. The Federal Reserve Board ignored what Hoover had said. He turned to the Senate Banking and Currency Committee, writing its members in 1925 that the loose-money policies would bring "inevitable collapse which will bring the greatest calamities upon our farmers, our workers, and legitimate business." Secretary of the Treasury Mellon dismissed his anxiety as "alarmist," his interference as "unwarranted."

As with Hoover, the headlines of 1929 did not faze Mellon, who still sat in his office at the Treasury. That was the way things worked, he told the President. "It will purge the rottenness out of the system. High costs of living and high living will come down. People will work harder, live a more moral life. Values will be adjusted and enterprising people will pick up the wrecks from less competent people."

Mellon was a Social Darwinist. He believed in survival of the fittest. His viewpoint was sustained by long precedent. There had been depressions during the presidencies of Van Buren, Buchanan, Grant, Cleveland, Roosevelt and Wilson. Boom and bust were the system. If there were distress, traditional American charity would take care of it. The system must not be tinkered with.

"Leave it alone," Mellon told the President. He had one formula: "Liquidate labor, liquidate stocks, liquidate the farmers, liquidate real estate."

Mellon's father had gone to England during the depression of the seventies, Mellon told the President. Farms had been foreclosed, railroads were in the hands of receivers, banks had failed, and mobs roamed the streets. Then the "liquidation" had taken its course and Mellon's father received word that orders for steel were pouring into the closed furnaces. He rushed home to find the panic over and the system again working at full speed. It would happen again that way, Mellon said.

But Hoover was the thrusting engineer, an innovator, anxious to perform. And so he held his conferences as soon as the market crashed. He exacted promises, arranged compromises. At first, just after the crash, he appeared successful in his endeavors. "Buy Now" movements were organized to combat slipping prices on all kinds of goods; editorials denounced "riotous savers." For the six months following October of 1929, the country seemed to be in good shape, with more goods being produced each week than had been produced in a month before the War. Steel production came back, along with automobile orders, and the President permitted himself optimistic statements.

But by the spring of 1930 the tide was going the wrong way. When a rare MEN WANTED sign went up in front of a factory, police had to be called out to hold back the crowds seeking jobs. Farm prices kept dropping.

The public was worried but hardly in despair. They were waiting for the turnaround. They were also waiting for a trumpet call from the President. The journalist William Allen White thought to himself that a shallower President would have sounded a tocsin, however empty, with which a worried America might identify. "But President Hoover," White wrote, "was studying the situation, trying to know intelligently what it meant; why it was; what it was. He was interested in facts and not in the psychic relation of those facts to the public and its troubles."

His personality had always impressed people in that way; years earlier the artist S. J. Woolf had been fascinated by the

manner in which the then Secretary of Commerce had speculated on whether tall skyscrapers could withstand earthquakes
and great winds or if they would fall. "He expressed a keen
interest in what would happen. . . . What particularly struck me
at the time was the cold engineering question which he puzzled
over; the other results of such a catastrophe apparently did not
concern him at all." It seemed to Woolf that it was not a matter
of lacking feelings, but rather that Hoover kept his feelings in
the background, "almost as if he were ashamed of being human."

So he silently studied the declining stock market and the
reports of failed banks. He expanded the federal employment
service on terms of voluntary cooperation with state and local
agencies, and asked the Congress to close America's shores to
foreigners. He set up the President's Committee for Unemployment Relief, which consisted of three thousand local groups
working to see that no one went hungry. His entire aim was that
the federal government act as supervisor and coordinator; it
would take no other role.

In his heart he wondered if his optimistic statements were
too hopeful. He decided it was his duty to be optimistic. "I am
convinced we have passed the worst and with continued effort
we shall rapidly recover," he said in his sober way.

Nothing seemed to happen. And because he had done so
much and been so prominent in the fight, every defeat became
in the country's eyes his personal defeat. The phrase "prosperity
is just around the corner," was now said with a derisive air, and
always with attribution to the President. Actually he had never
said it, but people thought he had. Americans began to believe
that Hoover did not know or understand the situation.

Coolidge's old secretary, Edward T. Clark, wrote his former
chief that on "every side" people were saying of Hoover, "Who
advises him?" But Hoover wanted only facts. No one advised
him. He knew what caused the Depression. It was the Great
War's upheaval and dislocation of the American economy, followed by too wild an expansion. And he believed he knew what
to do: move immediately when danger threatened, but do nothing
precipitate. There would be no irresponsible experiments performed simply to "do something."

Then, in early 1931, a year and a half after the crash, it appeared that he had won. Industrial production, payrolls, and stock prices began to go up. Construction contracts rose 25 percent. A quarter of the unemployed found work. One hundred and twenty cities ended relief measures. He permitted himself to believe, and say, that the Depression was over.

And in the moment of what seemed his great victory, the hurricane, which had tantalizingly veered away, turned and came back in even more terrible guise. Europe began to collapse and in its sinking it carried the United States with it.

For a long time, ever since the War, Europe had depended upon American money—loans, purchases, the free spending of the tourists. After 1929 all that faded away, and the European economies sagged. Germany and Austria, the Central Powers who had fought the War against the Allies, suffered the most. Both were unstable states, weak and racked by violent private armies of the Left and Right. In 1931 Germany and Austria moved toward a possible merger that would at least join them economically. France, haunted by the memory of her million and a half dead in the War, felt menaced by the proposed amalgamation. Ever since the War Paris had supported client states ringing the former enemies; now France and her puppets mobilized their forces to strike with discriminatory import quotas, currency exchange rates unfavorable to Austria and Germany, rail rate increases, and closed markets.

Austria and Germany could not withstand the French economic onslaught. The Austrian bank system began to cave under as bills held by foreigners were presented for immediate payment. On May 7, 1931, the United States Ambassador to Germany, Frederic M. Sackett, arrived in Washington. Sackett reported to the President that the German Chancellor, Heinrich von Bruning, had told him that Germany was facing economic ruin, with these foreseeable results: the Weimar Republic would be finished; there would be mobs in the streets of every German town; and the people would throw up a Communist or Fascist dictator. A letter for the President arrived from President von Hindenburg: "The need of the German people which has reached a climax compels me to adopt the unusual step of addressing you personally. . . . All possibilities of improving the situation by domestic measures without relief from abroad are exhausted." He begged for help.

The situation was the same in Austria. Central Europe, the former Austro-Hungarian Empire, depended upon Vienna's banks; suddenly all the banks across hundreds of miles of territory were tottering.

Above the old hatreds and fears unassuaged by the blood-letting of 1914–1918 hung the great issue of intergovernmental debts. Germany owed immense sums for reparations. The Allies owed money to "Uncle Shylock," as America was to the European press. Hoover studied the reports showing that Europe's purchase of commodities in the American market was drying up. And he understood that disaster in Europe would mean the flight from America of European gold worth hundreds of millions of dollars. In the spring Hoover had seemed so close to a great victory. Now it was slipping away. "It is a cruel world," he sighed to Presidential Secretary Theodore Joslin.

He rallied himself and for two days was on the telephone with Congressional leaders lining up support for a stunning move: a one-year delay on all intergovernmental payments. He called it the Moratorium. The former enemy need not make its payments to the former Allies; the United States would not expect the Allies to pay the 1931 installments on their American debts.

"This is perhaps the most daring statement I ever thought of issuing," he said to Secretary Joslin. Something in the daring seized the American people's imagination. The Moratorium, generous and self-serving at the same time, captured them and made them his. Abroad, the move was hailed as the greatest act in international relations since the Armistice thirteen years before.

But the Moratorium accomplished nothing. The European banks failed and a dozen governments came to live in fear of anarchy or the new Dark Ages. Wholesale executions of dissidents were reported in Hungary, pogroms in Poland. British troops fired on Indian mobs; coup followed coup in Latin America; and a hideous series of political assassinations plunged

Japan into a possible civil war. Foreign buying in America almost completely stopped and all the indices slid back to where they had been before the recovery began. There followed a fear that perhaps all this was normal. The hope that the Moratorium had aroused was replaced by something unparalleled on the American continent since the pioneers came: hopelessness.

In the summer of 1931 Great Britain, the first country of the world, went off the gold standard. Seventeen nations followed Britain. It was the most shocking event since the outbreak of the War in 1914. Now the remark "safe as the Bank of England" no longer had any meaning. A new wave of revolutions racked South America. Most terrible of all, rumors spread that there had been a suppressed mutiny in the Royal Navy. "It seemed to me," Hoover said, "the bottom was fast dropping out of the economic world." It was a "nightmare."

All around him the flames devoured American banks. They flickered up in every city and every state, wiping away everything. "No sooner is one leak plugged up than it is necessary to dash over and stop another that has broken out," he said to Secretary Joslin. "There is no end to it." America was now the Gibraltar of the world's security, he told the reporters. The country and the world were at their Verdun; their backs were against the wall; their heels were on the edge of the precipice.

He gathered himself and called a conference of leaders in banking, insurance and loan companies. He was afraid to have them come to his office. Their being seen in the White House might provoke new waves of panic. So he met with them at Secretary Mellon's great floor-through apartment hung with millions of dollars worth of Old Masters. He said to the chiefs of American financial life that perhaps this was the last chance to fight the Depression on their own ground and with their own choice of weapons. If they failed, no one could tell what kind of deluge might sweep down and bury them. He said that all that held the country back was foolish alarm—"senseless bankers' panic and public fear." To instill confidence the money men must cease calling in loans. And they must reach out to find people and situations in which to invest money. To do otherwise was to show lack of faith in the country. It would lead to more business failures. It would mean an end to the beginning of new businesses. It would mean a spiraling down of all activity so that shortly no loan could be counted safe, and no bank immune from runs. He asked the men representing the richer banks to set up a fund to help the poorer banks. The Federal Reserve Banks would help. Together they would save America, save the world.

In another room of Mellon's apartment were real estate and insurance men. Hoover asked them to join together to guarantee mortgages and suspend all foreclosures on farms and homes. Then there would be confidence and an end to corrosive fear. And people would go back to buying. And it would be over.

He spoke to them in his low, even way with eyes downcast. They listened and told him that he was asking too much. The government should do it instead.

These rich and eminent leaders saw a man who, according to the authors Roy Peel and Thomas Donnelly, "invariably appeared solemn and sad, an unhappy man, a man without hope. Instead of radiating confidence and good cheer in the presence of the economic crisis, his portraits made one want to sell short, get the money in gold, and bury it."

It was after midnight when the President and the men parted. The next day they went to their banks and offices and immediately began to call in loans so that they might hoard what they had. Hoover had returned to the White House more depressed than ever before in his life.

Behind the cold orphan boy and expressionless face there lived a romanticized vision of America. "I would that I had the words to say what is in my heart," he often said. But he did not have the words. He wrote all his speeches in his own hand with a short, blunt pencil so that the words would not be committed to paper too quickly, for perhaps then they would be specious and too easy. He was no Theodore Roosevelt, no Wilson. He had no eloquence, no fire; there was no flash. "He had no cry of leadership to offer," wrote Gilbert Seldes. "Perhaps he did not believe in cries."

But he did. His cry was that the Americans remember their great heritage, those things the race called, or had once called, moral fiber, self-sufficiency, pride, self-respect. That beautiful America of songs and legends, he would bring her through with her character unsullied.

He went to Valley Forge in late 1931 as the country prepared to celebrate the two hundredth anniversary of the birth of George Washington. He stood near the huts where the Continental Army had wintered:

It was a triumph of character and idealism and high·intelligence over the counsels of despair or prudence and material comfort . . . and we are still fighting the war of independence. We must not be misled by the claim that the source of all wisdom is in the government. . . . Sirens still sing the song of the easy way for the moment of difficulty, but the common sense of the common man, the inherited tradition of an independent and self-reliant race, the historical memory of Americans who glory in Valley Forge even as they glory in Yorktown—all these tell us the truth for which our ancestors fought and suffered, the truth which echoes upward from this soil of blood and tears, that the way to the nation's greatness is the path of self-reliance, independence and steadfastness in times of trial and stress.

God grant that we may prove worthy of Washington and his men.

He propped up the Federal Farm Loan Banks with a billion dollars for loans to building and loan associations helping the farmers fight foreclosure; he moved to expand the Federal Reserve System so that it could offset the shrinkage in private credit; he got Congress to authorize the National Credit Association aimed at helping the banks pull together; he ruthlessly cut government expenditures. But all the indices slipped down.

The crisis was now psychological. He had put into the country's hands the tools to win a great victory. But he could not allay the country's fears—"Fears," wrote Herbert Bayard Swope of the *New York World*, "of a moratorium on bank payments; fears of the stock exchange shutting down; fears of a suspension of governmental debt payments; fears of life insurance companies—all those vast, vague specters that strike at Man's second greatest desire: security."

Perhaps it was the lack of long tradition with its corresponding ability to see things in perspective. The country began looking as though it were licked.

In the spring of 1931 the writer Louis Adamic visited Lawrence, Massachusetts. It had been the leading wool and worsted city in the United States. Now all the mills and factories were closed and silent. Adamic talked with one of the men who had drawn good wages.

"I don't know nothing," the man said. "Only that I have no job, no job—no job." His voice was shrill, half hysterical.

In the streets of Lawrence, Adamic saw men standing still and slowly clapping their hands from time to time. Or they would swing their arms up and down. They made these motions, Adamic thought, just to do something, to have some activity. He watched a man take a piece of string from a rubbish heap. The man's hands worked with the string, tying and untying knots. His face was haggard, hollow.

Then the man looked up and saw Adamic's pitying eyes. He dropped his string. He seemed all confused. His arms swung in reflex motion. He went away in his split overcoat and shoes with heels worn off, past the rows of unpainted and untenanted houses with broken windowpanes. His arms flapped.

In the coal fields of the Appalachian Mountains, the reporter Morris Markey came upon a group of out-of-work miners. "I don't say they can keep the hard times from coming," one of the men said. "But they can make us understand the whys and wherefores, can't they? That's all I ask, and everybody in the mine is asking the same thing. You go back to New York and tell 'em the miners want to understand what's going on." Markey saw the men sitting and staring out at the road. He saw them walking with bent heads. The big-city jobless walked in the same way. One of the miners said, "You don't go singing no 'Star Spangled Banner' when you got hungry women and young 'uns sitting in the cabin." Markey felt within himself a small, cold terror.

In Chicago, St. Louis and Detroit, it was impossible to walk five blocks without seeing a breadline operated by a church, hospital, Salvation Army unit, rescue mission, or fraternal or religious order. Men stood on the line in all kinds of weather and ate their beans, stew and coffee in full view of any passerby. There was hardly a single block of New York City that each day did not see at least one family numbly sitting on a couch on the sidewalk. Upstairs, their apartment door was bolted up with the eviction notice pasted by the lock. People going by put nickels and dimes in a pot sitting on the family's kitchen table.

A visiting Englishman stopped unemployed and shabby men in the streets of New York: " 'Why in God's name don't you do something about it?' They have always answered, 'Oh, what's the use?' They live from day to day with nothing to fall back on but suicide, with no faith in the present, past or future."

Hoover knew what they were thinking. He read the editorials and saw the cartoons showing him in his inevitable high, starched collar with his hands over his ears, saying to the poor and frightened: "Sorry, I can't hear you." His people wanted him to reach out, to do something dramatic. William Allen White said he should appear at relief stations in the Midwest. "This is not a showman's job. I will not step out of character," Hoover answered. He would not run a "Billy Sunday campaign."

The reporters once had found him easy and affable. But now, beset by anxiety and continually overworked, he treated them as enemies. His only journalist friend was his longtime fishing companion, Mark Sullivan of the *New York Herald-Tribune.* The President's long reports outlining his remedial efforts were numbingly dull, but when the newspapermen sought what they called "human interest" he became angry. When the reporters told him the public was more interested in the details of his granddaughter's birthday party than in the full text of the Moratorium proposals, he snapped that he refused to hold such a low opinion of the intelligence of the American people.

As time went on and 1931 went into its last months he discarded completely the wide-ranging plan of different news categories, and the news conferences were all but abandoned. Instead his secretaries handed out mimeographed copies of announcements uniformly beginning: "The President said: '. . .'" There were always dozens of copies, for he seemed to fear that if a reporter did not get one he might copy it from a colleague and get a word wrong and thus somehow injure the delicate fabric of recovery. He boiled down and digested the releases because he did not trust the reporters to summarize. He reduced them in effect to errand boys for his mimeograph machines. Of course they resented it, and noted with bitter humor that the reporter who had coined the 1928 Republican campaign slogan, "A Chicken in Every Pot and Two Cars in Every Garage," was now broke and seeking loans to feed his three children.

The President endlessly insisted that nothing but fear was holding the country back. When the comedy team of Weber and Fields celebrated their fiftieth jubilee together he sent them a telegram saying America needed jokes to wash away the Depression; wouldn't they think of some? He said the same thing to Raymond Clapper, the head of the United Press Washington office. Jokes and funny stories might build morale, he said. Soon afterward Clapper burst into tears before his wife. "Oh God, I've got to fire six men," he sobbed. "I can't do it. They all have families; they are good men. I can't do it."

But of course he had to do it; revenues were way down. Afterward Mrs. Clapper saw bitterness in her husband's soul. She herself feared robbery, riots, bloodshed, the closing of the banks. Her milkman came to the door asking if she could pay him in advance; none of his other customers had money. And his family was hungry.

The President continued to talk about the return of confidence. He invited the writer Christopher Morley to the White House and told him, "What this country needs is a great poem. Something to lift people out of fear and selfishness. Every once in a while someone catches words out of the air and gives a nation an inspiration. We need something to raise our eyes beyond the immediate horizon. A great nation can't go along just watching its feet. I'd like to see something simple enough for a child to spout in school on Fridays. I keep looking for it but I don't see it. Sometimes a great poem can do more than legislation. . . . Let me know if you find any great poems lying around."

By the fall of 1931 Hoover while dining would sit in complete silence, sunk in concentration. He was capable of utter silence even when greeted by his closest associates. He completely ignored the White House servants; his wife's personal maid heard exactly one sentence from him in her life: once he asked her where Mrs. Hoover was. He did not like seeing the servants in the halls; and so they hid when the White House bells announced his presence, footmen holding trays high in the air as they scurried into hall closets already crowded with maids. The halls were always empty for him as he hurried down to dinner in his tuxedo or tail coat, the last President of the United States to dress for dinner every night of his stay at 1600 Pennsylvania Avenue.

The reporters' dispatches portrayed the President as a man beyond caring. And the people, such as a young woman from Utica, New York, sent him letters filled with anger and despair:

I am only a girl of twenty, but I know what it is to see starvation.

People here are dying day by day.

Young boys go wrong because their folks can't feed them. Girls take the wrong way too because they have to eat, so it is your duty to do something and do it mighty quick.

HELP US! HELP US!

Christmas of 1931 arrived. The President and Mrs. Hoover went shopping for gifts for the grandchildren, inexpensive presents appropriate to the times. It was the mechanical type of toy that most interested him, the store people noted—tiny earth-moving equipment and steam shovels.

New Year's Eve came. Even after dusk men with cheaply printed handouts walked New York's streets trying to drum up passengers for the two-thirds empty cruise ships departing for Caribbean ports at midnight. There was a good deal of public drunkenness and numerous deaths attributed to alcoholic beverages made with antifreeze or chafing-dish fuel.

Nineteen thirty-two dawned rainy.

Chapter Seven

ON THE SIXTH DAY of the new year Father James Cox of Pittsburgh arrived in Washington. He led what the papers called a "hunger march." Days earlier he had addressed a crowd of fifty-five thousand people in Pitt Stadium; fifteen thousand of them went with him to Washington.

His was not the first such group. There had been an avowedly Communist one that sang, "We'll hang Herbie Hoover to a sour apple tree." A Quaker assemblage had also been received in the White House. The Quaker leader stepped forward and said, "How art thee, Herbert?" and then in a quiet way said that unless something was done there must be a revolution.

Father Cox told the President substantially the same thing. The President thanked him for coming. Outside the White House, Father Cox said to the reporters: "The United States is not the firm of Herbert Hoover, Limited. I am the Mayor of Shantytown. That is a town in the heart of Pittsburgh, in the shadows of the skyscrapers owned by one of the richest men in America—Andrew W. Mellon. The men in my town want work but can't get it. So they live in huts and hovels. If the Pilgrim Fathers came here today, would they be satisfied? They came here to give us a country. Now it has been taken away. Who owns it now? The Andrew Mellons."

When he had finished he led his hunger army back to his

Shantytown. Some of his men lingered in Washington for a week. A railroad offered them two cars home, free. So they went back to Pittsburgh, never knowing it was Mellon who had paid for the two cars.

The day after Father Cox was received, the Hoovers entertained in honor of Vice President Curtis and his sister-hostess, Mrs. Dolly Gann. Mrs. Gann's husband, Edward, also attended. The society pages reported that pink carnations, baby primula and adiantums were on the table, and that Hulda Lashankska, soprano, and Paul Shirley, viola d'amore, performed.

The President's face as always did not show the slightest trace of emotion, and looking at him one could not guess whether he had read the newspaper reports of what Father Cox had said. He had, of course, for each day his staff summarized the contents of five hundred newspapers. (Coolidge had been different. He sat for hours poring over one or two papers, reading the want ads and personals, figuring if the price of used cars had gone up.)

In the papers of that day Hoover also read that a young United States congressman had stood up on the floor of the House of Representatives to ask a shocked and suddenly hushed assemblage that they impeach a member of the Cabinet for high crimes of malfeasance. The congressman was Wright Patman, a Texan from a hardshell Baptist district where dancing, card-playing and drinking were frowned on. The Cabinet officer was the Secretary of the Treasury.

Mellon was seventy-six years old; in March he would turn seventy-seven. Physically he seemed hardly changed from the day more than a decade earlier when he had called upon President-Elect Warren Harding in Marion, Ohio. From that meeting he had shortly gone to the Treasury, slipping in by a back door on March 5, 1921, to confer with his predecessor for a few hours before taking up his duties. It was not until a month later that he saw the front anteroom of his office, for he passed each minute of his working day at his desk. One of his first acts as Secretary was to dispatch a circular letter to the country's bankers saying, "The Nation cannot afford extravagance. . . . The people generally must become more interested in saving the government's money than in spending it." He continued as he began, cutting expenditures and working to pay off the national debt created by the War. Economy in all government departments and the reduction of taxes were his two great principles. His scratched and skinny signature, "A. W. Mellon," was exactly like him.

Mellon had no social presence. At his first Cabinet meeting he was baffled when the reporters buttonholed the Secretaries to ask questions. No one had ever done it at the directors' meetings he was used to. At his subsequent press conferences he stuttered and spoke so quietly that his listeners had to strain to hear him. His jacket was always buttoned and he always wore a vest with his dark suit. Watching him light his little black paper cigarettes, the reporter Edward G. Lowry noted, "He doesn't smoke lightly, casually, unconsciously, but precisely, carefully, consciously, as a man computing interest on $87.76 for two months and eight days at 4¾ percent per annum."

He was never excited, always cold, diffident, withdrawn. But somehow these characteristics became drama itself. Everything about him interested the public: his magnificent art collection, his gigantic oil holdings, his aluminum monopoly, his banks, his estates, the fashion in which the dowager hostesses of Washington took him up and the subsequent gossip as to whether he would make one of them the second Mrs. Mellon. Almost every night his one-of-a-kind all-aluminum Pierce-Arrow limousine took him to a dinner or a ball.

The reporter Thomas Stokes mused that it was the newspaper stories reporting his slightest utterance that expanded him: "I have often thought that, in time, those frontpage stories became like a drug to him, that figuratively he hugged the newspaper to his breast and conned it avidly." And of course the stories were all of a kind. They described him as a saintly old gentleman showing the nation how to emulate the individual initiative which had made him and his family rich. His father had educated him and his brother to nurture the monumental fortune. Now as Secretary of the Treasury he would reach beyond mere family and include the entire nation in his teachings.

Mellon was the most eminent American of the twenties. It

was heresy to criticize him, if not to wonder what he and that other silent man, Coolidge, said to each other when they were alone. (In Mellon's absence Coolidge would remark to the Secret Service men that somebody should fix a broken pavement stone near the Treasury, for "Ol' Andy Mellon," counting his coupons, might come along and stub his toe.)

It was the most familiar thing to hear Mellon referred to as the Greatest Secretary of the Treasury since Alexander Hamilton. The title became a cliché. In 1924 the delegates to the Republican Convention rose as one man to give him a standing ovation when his furtive figure slipped up to the platform. He was the man behind Prosperity, wrote Harvey O'Connor, "whose extraordinary rise to pecuniary preeminence gave an implicit endorsement to the policies which he advocated." Robert S. Allen wrote that he sat upon a throne of prestige more powerful than that of the White House.

Much of his work was the release of optimistic statements on projected government receipts and expenditures. Invariably they did not prove optimistic enough. Even with tax cut following tax cut the government ended each year of the twenties with a surplus averaging about a billion dollars. (Mellon did not let expenditures rise much above three billion a year; receipts were generally around four billion.)

Washington hardly knew what to do with the windfalls, so Mellon planned and largely administered the rebuilding of the District of Columbia with a fraction of the surpluses. In secret he planned to finance a magnificent art gallery for whose unparalleled collection of art his scores of Old Masters would be the core.

Then came 1929. Mellon continued to guess wrong, as he always had, on the tax revenues. But where once he had not been cheerful enough, now he was far too optimistic. Year after year the government took in less and less. In fiscal 1929 the tax receipts were five billion, in 1930 four billion, in 1931 three billion. Senators in public debates made bitter jokes about him, calling him "the Greatest Secretary of the Treasury since the Last One" or "the Greatest Deficit of the Treasury." He was derided in the papers; children chanted:

"Mellon pulled the whistle
Hoover rang the bell
Wall Street gave the signal
And the country went to hell."

Now Mellon, the wizard shorn of his artistry, became again the hesitant and uncertain little old man. Thomas Stokes used to see him, a lonely and tragic figure, wandering the streets late at night, peering into the store windows. He clung in his public statements to will-o'-the-wisps, signs of recovery which in the past had lifted the country out of slumps. But nothing worked.

The President had never overly cared for him, nor he for the President. Mellon in Hoover's eyes was unceasingly reactionary, a nineteenth-century man. Hoover to Mellon was a progressive and dangerous innovator. And so they drew apart and increasingly the business of the Treasury was carried on by the Undersecretary, Ogden Livingston Mills of New York, appointed to his post in 1927 on Mellon's recommendation. Mills was accounted the third richest man in Washington, Mellon of course being the first, and Senator James Couzens of Michigan, Henry Ford's old partner, the second.

Mills was the grandson of Darius Ogden Mills, who in 1849 went to California and to the Comstock Lode. His mother was one of the few American hostesses permitted to revolve about Edward VII. When Ward McAllister said that there were only 400 persons in the country worthy of being invited to one's home, Mills's mother had pared the figure to 150. After Mills's graduation from Harvard at nineteen he had gone into politics as a ward worker, which amused his family. The Depression hardly crippled him. He did not give up his yacht, his racing stable, his estates on Long Island and at Staatsburg on the Hudson, nor his Newport villa or his mansion on Fifth Avenue, although it was reported that once just before a dinner party he said to his wife, "Dorothy, there are only ten servants in the house; never before in my life have we had fewer than fifteen."

Mills was smart, capable, arrogant. He had served as U.S. Representative from New York City's Silk Stocking district, and as an Army captain during the War. In 1926 he ran for governor against Al Smith. Al rolled over him.

Mills was with the President every day, sometimes twice or three times a day. Over the telephone that his predecessors had thought undignified to have on the Presidential desk, Hoover and Mills spent hours conversing; and Mellon went further and further into the background. It was Mills talking with the Congressional leaders, Mills explaining away Mellon's overestimate of seven hundred million in anticipated tax receipts for fiscal 1931, Mills interrupting press conferences to say, "What the Secretary means is . . ."

It could not go on forever. On February 3, at ten-thirty at night, the President announced that Mellon would be the new Ambassador to the Court of St. James'. He would replace Charles G. Dawes, Coolidge's former Vice President.

The next day Mellon held his last press conference in his simply furnished office at the Treasury. A fire blazed in the grate underneath a portrait of Alexander Hamilton. Wright Patman said in the House of Representatives that sending Mellon to London while Patman's impeachment charges were still hanging fire was like a judge handing in the verdict while the jury was still out. George Norris of Nebraska said in the Senate, "Poor old Andy. Our ambassadors, when you take their social activities away from them, are only stool pigeons. One of these bright page boys . . . could perform the duties equally as well as the greatest Secretary of the Treasury since Alexander Hamilton."

The reporters asked if he would wear knee britches at Court, as had all other ambassadors save Dawes. He replied he had not given any thought to the problem. It had been raining the day he went to see Harding, he remarked, pointing out that it was raining now on his last day of office. He had thought, the day he saw Harding, that he couldn't break away from business, but of course he had always realized that some day he would have to do so. And so when Harding offered him the Treasury, he accepted.

"I really didn't want to come to Washington," he said. "I did not want absolutely to refuse. There was really no substantial reason why I should refuse."

Had he enjoyed his time in Washington? "Oh, yes, I have

been happy here. The work is congenial and the associations pleasant. It is quite interesting."

They asked him if he had wanted to be President when Coolidge bowed out; he said, "It would not have been practicable at my age."

They asked how he felt toward the reporters and he said he had always found them "educational"—their questions kept him up-to-date. He went back to the past, talking of how America would become great again. They said they were sorry to see him go, and he said, "We have to change about in this world. You cannot keep going on in the same channel all the time."

The next day *The New York Times* said, "If Mr. Mellon had suddenly decided in 1927, 1928, or 1929 to give up the portfolio of Secretary of the Treasury, the Stock Exchange would have been jarred to its foundations, it was remarked by persons who recalled the sharp reactions that were once produced by mere rumors that he would resign." Now the news caused not a ripple in the prices. "The idols of yesterday are no longer worshiped as in the halcyon days."

"Now you are leaving, Mr. Secretary, would you mind telling us when the Depression is going to end?"

"No. I'd like to know that myself."

Chapter Eight

THE MAN MELLON replaced as Ambassador to Great Britain, Charles Dawes, secretly moved into the White House. No one on the outside knew he was there. For five days he conferred with the President and the new Secretary of the Treasury, Ogden Mills.

They had chosen him to head the Administration's ultimate answer to the worsening situation, the Reconstruction Finance Corporation. When the President asked Congress to approve the RFC, many people could not understand it, for it was entirely alien to American ways. What the President proposed was that Congress allocate two billion dollars to the RFC so that the RFC might lend the money to private businesses. Even as recently as Coolidge's time the entire annual federal budget was less than three billion; the proposed 1932 expenditures were less than five. There was no precedent for such an undertaking but Congress went along, although some newspapers said this was the beginning of state socialism, and others, more conservative, said it would soon lead to a Soviet America.

Dawes held a fiery press conference to explain the plan. This, he said, was not charity. The loans would be made with the understanding that they would be paid back. The money would help businesses to help themselves. When the reporters had gone, Dawes turned to Presidential Secretary Joslin. "Did I tell 'em, Ted?" he exulted. "Did I tell 'em? Listen! They like the dramatic. I put it over for them. That's what Hoover ought to do. What they want is a kick. They love it. Make him give it to them every time you can, even if he skins you for it."

Joslin knew. He had been a newspaperman before coming to work for the President. Often he told the President to be affable, tell stories, make jokes. Hoover replied, "I have other things to do when a nation is on fire." Almost every day various groups came to be received at the White House, and the President's conduct when he was with them drove Joslin to despair. Other Presidents had shaken hands with each visitor, but to save time Hoover arranged simply to be photographed with the delegation. Sometimes people would glare at him when he came out to them; others would say, "God bless you and protect you."

Joslin wrote, "He took no notice of either. He might as well have been walking in his sleep. His thoughts were far away. Day after day he went through the motions of walking from his office to the place in the South Grounds where the group was standing, posing, exchanging a brief pleasantry, smiling mechanically and returning to the office."

He developed a routine which could be relied on to bring a smile and he repeated it to each group: "Are you seeing everything you want while in Washington? If not, let me know. I am pretty well known around here. Perhaps I can fix it up for you." He could and would do no more.

Dawes was entirely different. His dynamism was the main reason for his post with the RFC. He had always been cheerful, colorful, fearless, a renowned practical joker. After serving as Coolidge's Vice President he had gone to Great Britain as Ambassador. His informal way was absolutely shocking to the English. A reporter who wondered if he would wear knee britches at Court was asked by Dawes if he wanted a diplomatic answer or the answer the question deserved. The reporter told him he should reply in his own fashion. "Then go plumb to hell and mind your own business," Dawes said.

During the War he had been the chief purchasing agent for the American Expeditionary Force. Dawes obtained the position partly by virtue of being a chum of Pershing's since their boarding house days in Nebraska, but more importantly because of his capability. After the War, at a hearing on corruption in the services, he created an everlasting nickname when he lashed out at his interrogators by saying, "Hell and Maria, we weren't trying to save money, we were trying to win a war."

As ambassador in England "Hell and Maria" went in for incredible practical jokes. His most stunning feat occurred when he hired the buffoonlike comedian Leon Errol to act as waiter for a 1931 Embassy party. Errol, seemingly drunk, told the guests that they were using the wrong silverware for the soup. Diners half finished with their food had their plates yanked out of their hands. Staggering, the comedian-turned-waiter flung a cold lobster into the lap of a duchess and then, taking a lighted candle with him, crawled under the table and was lost to view. The guests looked the other way, but Ambassador Dawes, lolling at the head of the table, could not contain his mirth.

When Dawes came home he found even his richest companions frightened. They had all loaned out money to save friends and in Dawes's eyes their faces were uniformly worried. Suddenly he was not quite the same confident, vibrant man he had been before. But he threw himself into running the RFC. Even before he and the other officers were confirmed by the Senate, bankers and insurance company and railroad presidents flooded into Washington to ask for loans. But they were afraid to be seen coming into the RFC offices, for their being there might trigger off fresh panics that would swamp their enterprises. At night Dawes went to see them in their hotel rooms.

The money began to flow out. At the RFC offices they spoke of themselves as being like firemen trying to save burning houses. Not all the banks could be saved, so they concentrated on the big ones which, if they went under, would drag a hundred smaller ones along. Not all the railroads could be saved, so it was best to save the large one whose bonds were held by insurance companies; for if the railroad died the bonds would be defaulted and the insurance companies would crash. And there were income-producing public works projects that could be assisted: toll bridges, tunnels, docks. But no new city halls or new boulevards. For the money lent for such things might never come back directly and that would lead to an unbalanced budget, the flowing out of gold held by frightened foreigners, a lowering in the price of United States bonds, a lack of faith in the ability of the government to meet its obligations, and, finally, injury to the banks which held those bonds.

The RFC poured out money. But that money was handed out on the theory that recovery would come from the top down. Its recipients were men of affairs. They were, snarled opposition newspapers, "panhandling millionaires."

For America's poor there could be no federal loans and no federal charity. The Senate committee considering direct aid to the unemployed heard endless witnesses who begged the government to give money to individuals. Mayor Frank Murphy of Detroit said of his city, "It used to be the wage earner alone who was on the welfare lists. Now it is the skilled artisan and the cultured citizen. There is one graduate of the U.S. Naval Academy receiving welfare aid and there are many graduates of the University of Detroit and the University of Michigan. Two are from the University of Vienna. . . ." There were forty-five clergymen on welfare in Detroit. Doctors worked for forty cents an hour as taxicab drivers, night watchmen and elevator operators. The city charitable funds were almost gone, and private contributions were down to a trickle.

Palm Beach was undergoing the worst season of its history. "The hostess who used to give luncheon parties every other day for 150 guests now invites in ten comrades for a snack once a week," wrote the society columnist Nancy Randolph, "and the host who used to give dinner dances for 500 persons, hire one of the colony's famous supper clubs and import from Manhattan a special 20-piece orchestra, now asks 20 guests to dine, turns on the radio, pulls up the rugs and tells his pals to hop to it. There are no breadlines in Palm Beach, but neither are there any cake or caviar lines. . . ."

A New Mexico doctor advertised in a local weekly: *Final notice. I am getting tired and disgusted at having to charge baby cases. If you have not got the money to pay for them when they come, for God's sake and Humanity's sake stop getting them.*

Across the nation, in Brooklyn, New York, doctors and lawyers constituted the backbone of the pawnbroker business, representatives of the Brooklyn Pawnbrokers Association reported. Young doctors pawned their microscopes first.

In downtown New York City one night a little girl, holding her father's hand, passed by the Municipal Building. January's winds blew. "Why, Daddy," she said, "there are people lying on the newspapers. And children. Why are they doing that?" There was no answer from her father. When she looked up at him she saw he was crying.

Senator Borah rose in the Senate to demand that the government, if it would not give direct relief, at least give money to the Red Cross for distribution to the needy. Borah was the greatest Senatorial orator of his time. "We will either feed these people," he shouted, "or we will stay here and tell the American people why we do not feed them." The Red Cross leaders declared they did not need or want the funds; they would make do with private charitable contributions. President Hoover congratulated them.

People came to the White House begging him to change his mind and endorse direct aid. He would see them and listen and then pose for the picture. It was always the same tableau: the visitors lined up in a semicircle facing the camera, the President in his high collar and double-breasted blue serge suit. Sometimes they would present a petition and he would receive it in silence, indicating nothing of his attitude. When they spoke to him he doodled squares and circles on a piece of paper—the engineer's mind in motion, according to his friends; the coward's thoughts in flight, according to his enemies.

President Hoover could not bear to see the breadlines or the thin children so remindful of Europe in the War. He never went to the relief stations, never turned his head in the car to look at the men selling apples on the street corners. He fought on, a cigar always gripped between his teeth, his high stiff collar never unbuttoned, his jacket never removed. His eyes turned red at the rims as he went day after day with little more than three hours sleep a night. "As long as I sit at this desk they won't get by," he said, as congressmen called for fiat money, for government intervention in the form of inflationary public works projects, for handouts, subsidies, gifts.

He fought direct relief with all the power left to him. There would be no dole. The dole deadened the will to work, the drive to succeed, the ability of the nation to come back. Rome died as a result of it. England was dying because of it.

Charles Dawes, Ogden Mills and Herbert Hoover worked eighteen-hour days and their Reconstruction Finance Corporation made the biggest individual loans in the history of any nation. But the night courts in New York City found convictions for panhandling on the streets had increased 500 percent in the last six months of 1931—and the 1932 figures were expected to be worse. Only half a dozen Broadway shows were playing. Half a hundred theaters were dark, many with the names of the last attractions to play there in 1929 or 1930 still up on the marquee. And each of the few playgoers found himself asked for a coin two or three times on each block.

The *New York Daily News* reporter Grace Robinson saw a blond young man in night court who, "if he'd been shaved, pressed, and had held his head up, would have been a welcome applicant for any job in former days." The judge said, giving the young man a suspended sentence, "You'll find lots of charitable people in New York who'll hand you nickels and quarters. But you must quit this practice. It's like the drug habit. It will get a hold on you. You look like a strong and healthy young man. Don't get in the rut of these old men who come in here over and over and can't shake the habit of mendicancy."

Miss Robinson thought, "What are magistrates to do? Fill the prisons with men who honestly can't get work?"

Another reporter on her paper talked to a man whose wife was dying in their home where the gas had been cut off, where the fuel box held only a few slats of a soap box, where a dispossess notice was pasted on the door.

"I haven't had a steady job in more than two years," the man said. "Sometimes I feel like a murderer. What's wrong with me, that I can't protect my children?"

Comedians on the vaudeville stage cried out, "What? You say business is better? You mean Hoover died?" In the South farmers cut off the fronts of cars for which there was no gas, attached mules and held what they called Hoovercart races. Government officials tried to get the name changed to "depression chariot," but failed. The original name stuck and goat-pulled Hoovercarts, horse-pulled vehicles, and wagons pulled by teams of men competed for two- or three-dollar purses on Southern fairgrounds tracks.

On the outskirts of every town, along New York's rivers and in Detroit's Grand Circus Park, stood squalid shacks where somehow the unemployed existed from day to day: Hooverville. The Hoover Flag: an empty pocket turned out.

The President continued to talk of how morale must be raised. The crooner Rudy Vallee came to the White House and the President said, "Are you still pleasing people with your songs?"

"I hope so," Vallee said.

"Well, if you can sing a song that would make people forget their troubles and the Depression, I'll give you a medal." Instead, Vallee sang:

> They used to tell me I was building a dream
> And so I followed the mob.
> When there was earth to plow or guns to bear
> I was always there right on the job.

> Once I built a railroad, made it run
> Made it race against time.
> Once I built a railroad, now it's done.
> Brother, can you spare a dime?*

On January 23, 1932, Governor Roosevelt of New York released to the press a letter he had written to the Democratic organization of South Dakota. It said he would be pleased to enter that state's primary election for the nomination to the Presidency.

* "Brother, Can You Spare a Dime?" (Gorney-Harburg) © 1932 by Harms, Inc. Used by permission of Warner Bros. Music. All rights reserved.

PART III

The Governor of New York

Chapter Nine

FRANKLIN ROOSEVELT went into politics in 1910 as a state senator from Dutchess County. He was a tall, thin young man of twenty-eight who looked down his nose at people and spoke in a patrician Groton-Harvard way. "Awful arrogant fellow, that Roosevelt," the Tammany boss Tim Sullivan used to say.

Roosevelt's aristocratic manners grated on his fellow legislators in Albany. (His fellow state senator, James J. Walker of New York City's Greenwich Village, thought to himself that the aloof son-and-heir attitude suggested Roosevelt was on a slumming expedition.) But Roosevelt did make one friend, the majority leader of the Assembly, Alfred E. Smith. His pal Frank would go far, Smith told people.

From Albany Roosevelt went to Washington as Assistant Secretary of the Navy under Secretary Josephus Daniels. He and his shy wife, Anna Eleanor Roosevelt, blossomed in wartime Washington. President Wilson grew fond of him, thinking of him as a great, tall, vigorous young man. Secretary of the Interior Franklin K. Lane took him up and had him in for dinner almost every Sunday night.

There was another rising personage who was often at Lane's house on Sunday nights, the food administrator, Herbert Hoover. Roosevelt and Hoover became close friends. Their wives got along very well. Sometimes the women would help Mrs. Lane with the food while the three men sat smoking together.

When the War ended Roosevelt was thirty-six years old. Hoover was forty-four. Hoover had never been involved in any political activity and was not sure if he was a Democrat or a Republican. Roosevelt looked at his friend and saw a potential Democratic Presidential nominee. He launched a campaign to get Hoover nominated by the Democrats in 1920. Then one night at a dinner party Roosevelt sat by the daughter of Senator Henry Cabot Lodge of Massachusetts. She told him that Hoover was a Republican. He asked her how she knew. She replied that Hoover had told her father.

That ended Roosevelt's campaign for Hoover. He himself was nominated by the Democrats for the Vice Presidency in 1920. Hoover sent him a warm letter saying that although they were not of the same "political tribe," he wished "an old friend" and "great public servant" the best. Hoover said he knew that Roosevelt would serve with distinction if elected. But Roosevelt went down with James Cox of Ohio as Harding and Coolidge swamped them.

A year and a half later infantile paralysis appeared to have ended Roosevelt's political career forever. In 1924, on crutches, he dragged himself to the podium of the Democratic National Convention to nominate his old friend Alfred E. Smith, now governor of New York, for the Presidency. It touched and sobered the delegates to see him so changed from the handsome young athlete he had been as Vice Presidential candidate only four years before. His speech for Smith was brilliant, ending with a quote from Wordsworth that stuck to Smith from then on: the Happy Warrior.

But the speech could not put Smith across. For more than one hundred ballots Smith fought William Gibbs McAdoo for the nomination. In New York's murderous summer heat the delegates, many half drunk on bootleg liquor and fatigue, struck each other with their fists in the runways of Madison Square Garden. They ran out of money, wired home for more, walked about red-eyed and unshaven while bands blared out "The Sidewalks of

New York." With it all came the hissing of the Southern delegates at those who wanted to condemn the Ku Klux Klan by
name; the sound mixed with the noise of Tammany Hall's hood-
lums poisonously abusing McAdoo. The radio reported a convention for the first time in history and night after night the country
went to bed with the hideous proceedings drummed into its ears,
each of the limitless roll calls beginning with the same drugging
words: "Alabama . . . votes . . . twenty-four . . . votes . . . for
. . . Oscar W. Underwood." In the end, each hating the other,
Smith and McAdoo had to capitulate while a compromise candidate, John W. Davis, got the nomination and, shortly, a bad beating from Calvin Coolidge.

Four years later, in 1928, at Houston, Franklin Roosevelt
once more addressed the delegates: "We offer one who has the
will to win, who not only deserves success but commands it.
Victory is his habit—the Happy Warrior, Alfred Smith." This
time they gave Smith the nomination and sent him out to fight
Herbert Hoover.

Smith was optimistic about his chances. But his own state
of New York worried him. He pressed Roosevelt to run for governor—with Roosevelt on the ticket the upstate Protestants might
go Democratic. Roosevelt told him it was out of the question—he
had to spend substantial portions of each year soaking his legs in
the recuperative waters at Warm Springs, Georgia. Smith appealed to Mrs. Roosevelt. "Governor, you know it is impossible,"
she told him.

But he kept pressing. As the summer of 1928 turned into
fall, Roosevelt, fighting to walk again, refused to take Smith's
calls to Georgia. One day Smith cornered Mrs. Roosevelt in Syra-
cuse and she agreed to place a call to her husband; when he
came on the line she simply handed over the phone to Smith. He
obtained Roosevelt's reluctant assent to run.

Smith went down to hideous defeat. That he might lose had
certainly occurred to him, but not that Protestant America would
whisper that he slept with nuns, was of an inferior race, the
Irish, that he was a drunk, that his advisers were the tools of
international Jewry, that he represented the big-city rabble, the

bootlegger, footpad, hoodlum, the filth of Europe come to steal and corrupt what the Anglo-Saxon had built. In his hour of defeat he saw a face of America no one ever knew before.

On election night Roosevelt went to bed thinking he had gone down with Smith. His mother, Sara Delano Roosevelt, sat up alone with a woman reporter. Also studying the returns with a professional eye was the head of the Bronx Democratic organization, "Boss" Ed Flynn. In the early hours of the morning, Flynn telephoned Roosevelt to say it was his opinion that, despite Smith's disaster, Roosevelt had been elected governor of New York. Roosevelt told Flynn he was crazy to wake people up with such a statement. But Flynn was right.

In the first moments of his horror, Smith hardly noticed his protégé's victory. But when Roosevelt was sworn into the office Smith had held for four terms, the Happy Warrior seemed to think he could rule from an Albany hotel room. Tentatively at first, and then more firmly, the new governor resisted the boldly offered suggestions. After a few weeks Smith asked a favor for his old political associate Robert Moses. Governor Roosevelt made it clear that he would do no favors for Moses, for once Moses had refused a favor to Louis Howe. After that things were different between Roosevelt and Smith. The Happy Warrior gave up his rooms in Albany and went to New York City to take a job as head of the Empire State Building.

In Franklin Roosevelt's life Howe was no less important than Mrs. Roosevelt. Howe was five feet tall, weighed one hundred pounds, had a craggy, acne-scarred face and great bulging eyes. He wore incredible clothes, oversized shirt collars, tiny hats. He had a terrible temper which he often lost. When he did so he literally danced with rage, cursed, threw things on the floor and screamed. Howe had been sick all his life and many times appeared about to choke to death. He could only sleep sitting up. Cigarette ashes from his Sweet Caporals covered his clothing and most people found him entirely revolting. A majority of those who knew him thought him the most cynical individual they had ever encountered. He had one faith. That was Roosevelt.

When Roosevelt was a state senator in Albany, Howe, then

a newspaperman, decided that here was a President of the United States. As early as 1912, when Roosevelt was thirty, Howe addressed him as "Dear and Revered Future President." Howe went to Washington with Roosevelt when he was Assistant Secretary of the Navy, superintended his campaign for the Vice Presidency in 1920, and, most important of all, refused to abandon his vision when illness struck Roosevelt in 1921.

Saying that no one must know that Franklin could not walk, Howe lied to reporters and bullied the dazed Mrs. Roosevelt into presenting a cheerful face to her husband. He made her deliver speeches, which she hated, so that her husband's name might be kept before the public. Howe massaged the lifeless legs for hours at a time, read political analyses to the patient, cursed him when he got discouraged. He moved into the Roosevelt town house in New York City, displacing the family's daughter from her room; he ordered Roosevelt to be gay and outgoing when visitors came to call.

There was something wild about his insistence that Franklin would do it yet; Roosevelt's mother thought Howe a combination of madman and devil. Eleanor Roosevelt watched Howe arrange for her husband to be screened off from view when he was lifted into a private railway car and heard him order Roosevelt to wave to the photographers when he was propped up and sitting in a seemingly normal way. In her eyes Howe became not the awful little man that Roosevelt's mother called him, but the dear little man.

Roosevelt became the best-traveled governor in the history of his state. He was incapable of understanding a problem unless he saw it with his own eyes. To this end he had himself driven all over New York, to mental institutions where he tested the soup, to milk-processing plants where he watched the farmers unloading, and, after the crash, to closed factories where he could talk face to face with the distraught owner and the frightened workers.

In 1930, two years after he became governor, he won the most brilliant victory in the history of the state, gaining reelection with a plurality of nearly a million votes. A month later he asked "Boss" Ed Flynn to come to the Governor's Mansion in

Albany. In the library after dinner he said, "Eddie, my reason for asking you to stay overnight is that I believe I can be nominated for the Presidency in 1932."

Louis Howe was the only other person present. They asked Flynn to go about the country gathering friends into a working organization. But Flynn was not a good mixer despite his eminent position as leader of one of the nation's most important Democratic suzerainties. Instead, they selected James Farley, Secretary of the Democratic State Committee. Farley was jovial, commanding, friendly. He had an astonishing memory. He could meet a man at a rail stop and, two years later, remember to ask, "How's that boy of yours in college?" He was also an Exalted Ruler of the Elks. So, ostensibly to visit Elk lodges, he set off on endless travels, shaking hands, remembering names, writing letters to men he had met. He always signed his name in green ink. He always remembered to praise the governor of the State of New York.

So a bandwagon formed for Roosevelt. Roosevelt was handsome, with a magnificent grin and wonderful laugh. The habit of looking down his nose which had irritated people in his youth had been changed into the heads-up attitude of the cripple who smiles at his fate. But there were those who found nothing behind that smile and that gallant floating laugh, the cigarette held jauntily in a long holder. Walter Lippmann in the first month of the new year wrote:

Mr. Roosevelt is, as a matter of fact, an excessively cautious politician. He has been Governor for three years, and I doubt whether anyone can point to a single act of his which involved any political risk. . . . Franklin D. Roosevelt is no crusader. He is no tribune of the people. He is no enemy of entrenched privilege. He is a pleasant man who, without any important qualifications for the office, would very much like to be President. . . . It is in spite of his attractiveness, in spite of his unquestioned personal integrity, in spite of his generous sympathies, that the judgment has formed itself among large numbers of discerning people that here is a man who has made a good governor, who might make a good cabinet officer, but who simply does not measure up to the tremendous demands of the office of President.

The criticism of the most respected columnist in the country
hurt Roosevelt's chances. But even without Lippmann's article
he had many shortcomings. He was a cripple who could give
only the impression of a walk, and that only with very substantial
aid from another person. He had no program to relieve the Depression, only a confident way of saying he would make things
better and a cheery thumbs-up way of talking to people down on
their luck. He was at once for an end to the wild and unprecedented spending of the Hoover Administration and for giving
additional public money to the poor. The contradiction did not
appear to worry him.

He appeared, above all, too soft, too anxious to please and
to be all things to all men. It seemed strange that nothing angered
him, that Louis Howe could safely scream in front of other
people, "Can't you ever get anything through that thick Dutch
head?" The Tammany politicians contemptuously dismissed him
as a mama's boy, which he was. (His widowed mother controlled
all his money, dictated the furnishings of his homes, and decreed
the manner in which his children should be raised.) Serious
students of international affairs expressed doubts about a man
who had fervently espoused Wilson's League of Nations in 1920
and who now came out against American entrance into the
League.

And there was Al Smith, the most dangerous threat Roosevelt faced. Al had never been quite right since the bitter exchange of 1928. Shortly after the stock market crash a very
close friend of his took his own life. It was then that Al learned
that members of his family, aided by his dead friend, had heavily
speculated in the market. They now owed large sums on those
speculations. Al conceived it his duty to make up the money,
and threw himself into promoting the Empire State Building. It
opened in 1931, with Al's grandchildren cutting the entrance
tape. When "Boss" Ed Flynn asked Smith what his political plans
were, Smith took out a piece of paper with large sums written
on it. "Ed, these are all debts that I must clear up. Financially
I am in an extremely bad position." He indicated his future lay
not with politics, but with the Empire State Building. Despite all
he did to publicize it, there were hardly any tenants who could

afford to move in. So he sat in the enormous, almost empty structure, and saw the smiling and aristocratic Franklin Roosevelt bidding to be the party's nominee for President.

In important ways Smith was like Herbert Hoover. Both were poor boys grown eminent. Both believed it was the atmosphere and tradition of America that had permitted this growth. Both had grown away from the world of their boyhoods, Smith more than Hoover. For Smith was more and more entranced by rich men and the appurtenances of wealth. (These values had never particularly attracted Hoover.) As head of the Empire State Building Smith worked in an elegant office and lived at a fashionable address—"from First Avenue to Fifth Avenue," they said of him. He had gone "swell."

Smith had no particular program for beating the Depression. He stood aghast at an unbalanced budget and a government going deeper into debt. But he wanted the Presidency because it would chase away the nightmare face America had shown him in 1928. If he could not have it, then he would at least destroy Roosevelt, the interloper born with the silver spoon in his mouth. Smith announced he would enter several New England primary battles.

Al had been the sharpest political mind of his time. Now it seemed that he could not gauge the hatred and fear that millions felt for him. He afflicted, too, the conscience of those who had turned from the Democrats in 1928 because of him. Professor Felix Frankfurter of Harvard Law School wrote Smith's advisers that the next President would be Smith if the choice were his. But why didn't Smith's people make it clear that this was impossible? Smith's longtime assistant Belle Moscowitz wrote back, "I put the *et tu quo* on you. I don't think you begin to know Roosevelt."

Privately Al Smith and the nomination worried Roosevelt. Publicly he ignored the schism, smiling as always. For years expert forgers operating under Louis Howe had been signing Roosevelt's name on cheery letters sent to thousands of Democratic dignitaries in every state. Now the pace was stepped up. As he traveled Jim Farley constantly sent back lists of new names along with a note on individual tastes or pet projects. Shortly a man Farley named would receive a note ostensibly signed by Roosevelt. It would contain a reference to whatever interested the man plus a bid for support in the coming nomination fight.

Roosevelt and his advisers felt there was no doubt about the outcome of the election. The journalist Jay Franklin wrote, "Some of the Democrats say they need no other issue, no platform, not even a candidate—just the name Herbert Hoover—to sweep the country." In New York the *Daily News* each day printed comments of participants in its straw poll:

"I voted for Hoover in 1928, but why bring that up?" "I've voted Republican all my life but if I had a thousand votes this year they would all go to a Democrat."

It was maddening to Al Smith. For it had been the people nearest to him who had done the most to bring about the hatred of the President. Shortly after the disaster of 1928 Smith's friends had banded together to destroy his conqueror. (No logic, only anger, could explain their action, for Smith had said he was finished with politics.) Led by John J. Raskob, the important Catholic layman and multimillionaire, Smith's people had hired Charles Michelson of the *New York World*. With a salary of $25,000 a year and a lavishly financed staff, Michelson was given the task of examining and airing the sins of Herbert Hoover. No Democratic senator or congressman need ever lack for a clever speech deriding the President. Michelson and his assistants would do the research and writing, and the statesman only had to read it aloud.

Michelson's bureau did its work so well that one of its most-repeated jokes was widely believed to be absolute fact. The story had Mellon and Hoover walking down the street. Hoover took out a nickel and excused himself to Mellon, saying he wanted to step into a telephone booth and call his friend. "Here's a dime," Mellon said. "Why not call both of them?"

Ironically aided by the defamatory campaign mounted by Al Smith's friends, Roosevelt went speechmaking, his way paved for him by the increasing unpopularity of the President and the increasing grimness of the Depression. Wherever he went his staff made elaborate attempts to conceal the real degree of his physical infirmity. Rather than have him slowly hobble down an aisle they carried him up a back fire escape and then into the wings of the platform, so that when he was introduced he would only have to go a few feet to the podium. His six-foot-four-inch son James supported him while blocking from view the lifeless legs locked in heavy metal braces. Roosevelt cried out that the way to recovery was not the "percolator" theory of the President, which held that money poured into the top would sift down to the bottom. Rather, he said, the matter was like yeast: "prosperity will rise upward, through the ranks." He did not specify how he would help the people below, but said of them, "They seem to be beyond the concern of a national Administration which can think in terms only of the top of the social and economic structure."

Roosevelt charged the RFC with worrying only about the big banks, the corporations and the railroads. And he found words that reached out when he spoke of the unemployed man, and the failed small businessman. He called them, all of them in their millions, the Forgotten Man.

Al Smith heard the speech and to him it spoke of class division and an attack on the American Dream. A week later at the Democrats' Jefferson Day rally in Washington he said, "I will take off my coat and fight to the end against any demagogue who persists in any demagogic appeal to the masses of the working people of this country to destroy themselves by setting class against class and rich against poor."

Al from the slums mentioned no names but of course was declaiming against the rich man's son with his New York East Sixties townhouse and his Krum Elbow estate at Hyde Park on the Hudson. And Governor Roosevelt, a twinkle in his eye, responded with a tongue-in-cheek reference to the harum-scarum governor of Oklahoma, asking the reporters, "Wasn't that a terrible attack Al made on Alfalfa Bill Murray?"

Chapter Ten

THERE WAS NO PROOF that the Depression-born revolution-
ary fervor that had toppled seven Latin American governments
would not find its most dramatic display in the United States. In
early March, 1932, in Detroit, the Revolution actually seemed to
have arrived. A gathering of five thousand jobless men marched
upon the River Rouge plant of the Ford Motor Company in Dear-
born. They said they wanted work. The police were waiting at
the Dearborn-Detroit line. They ordered the marchers to disperse.
The men kept coming; tear gas and fire hoses did not stop them.
Suddenly they were a terrible mob, screaming and cursing, and
the police were running for their lives. At the Ford plant the
gates were locked and Ford's private police force was waiting.

Henry Ford had always known in his strange and neurotic
mind that the moment would come when he could use his private
guards. Over the years this force had been trained by brutal
overseers and given free rein in his factories.

Ford had been a farm boy who repaired watches with a nail
sharpened on a grindstone; from that he had advanced to fixing
the threshing machines of neighbors. As an automobile pioneer
he had helped create the new industry, and with his partner
James Couzens in 1914 he had electrified the world by paying
the men a basic wage of five dollars a day. For his spreading
of money and machines he was compared to Lincoln and to

Christ. But in his interior self he remained suspicious of the new world he had helped to make, of kidnapers, Jews, his enemies; everyone who was not of the quiet and bucolic past he romanticized and revered.

Now the Revolution was before his very gates. The running police joined his men and when the mob broke upon the plant, Ford's guards opened up with heavy machine guns. Four marchers died, scores were injured. The others fled, shouting they would return and burn the plant to the ground. They buried their four men a few days later, marching by the thousands with red armbands and signs saying "Ford Gave Bullets for Bread." More frightening still, they demanded the immediate establishment of Soviet America.

"The cylinder-head is cracked," an auto official of Dynamic Detroit told the writer Edmund Wilson. "And when the cylinder-head is cracked, you have to get a new car."

Herbert Hoover did the most elegant entertaining and set the most elaborate table of any President of the United States. Guests were invited on a scale the White House had never seen before. There was a large company for lunch every day, a tea at 4:30, a dinner of at least eighteen to twenty-six covers each night. The food, paid for out of the President's pocket, would not have seemed out of place in the palace of a Chinese mandarin.

The servants could not fathom Hoover. He never looked at them, never spoke. Ordered to keep out of his way, they hardly saw him save for serving him food. At such times a rigid formality was exacted from them. The butlers in their tuxedos with stiff shirts and black ties in the morning and white ties and tails in the evening must always stand at attention when not serving; there must be no talking in the pantry; the silver must never clank against the china when the table was being cleared.

Lou Henry Hoover, the onetime outdoor girl of the California hills, became in the White House the most severe of employers. The servants lived in fear of her glare when the slightest thing went wrong. The butlers and footmen all had to be the exact same height, and she worked out intricate methods by which to give orders. Her hand touching her hair meant dinner should be announced; her hand touching her glasses meant the table should be cleared. She wished to be something like the flawless horseback rider whose instructions to his mount are never discernible. After each ball or reception she sat with the housekeeper and her three secretaries analyzing for hours how the next one might be made better. For dinner seven courses were always served: an entrée, soup, fish, a meat course, salad, dessert and fruit. Meals were served at precisely the same moment of each day, the servants standing like statues in perfect silence, unsmiling and forbidden to display the slightest interest in the table conversation, their expressionless faces not reflecting the wonder with which they viewed the elaborate out-of-season food that, as the Depression deepened, grew ever more elegant.

"There was never a good-morning or even a nod of the head," the head usher, Irving Hoover, wrote of the President. "Never a Merry Christmas or a Happy New Year. All days were alike to him. Sunday was no exception, for he worked just as hard on that day if not harder than on any of the others." In the East Room at Christmas gifts were each year given out: a five-dollar bill for lower servants, and larger amounts for those with greater rank. The President appeared, bowed and left. There was no handshaking.

The servants wondered if he was aware that the faces around him were more strained because they feared that the cuts in their salaries would be made even deeper. But he did not notice them or even the reactions of his guests when, before they had finished eating, he would rise and hurry into the empty halls to go to work. He left behind Mrs. Hoover, straining to be gracious.

It was hard for him when she read the papers and cried. In other circumstances he would have wanted to talk to her about his problems, for he had always respected her opinions. But there was no time. They were alone together only in the moments after breakfast when she trotted along beside him as he went to the office. He ate with incredible speed, wolfing his food down so swiftly as to make the writer Christopher Morley think this was the President's method of dieting.

Sometimes when he was late for lunch Herbert Junior's little girl, Peggy-Ann, would be sent to get him. Armed with Grandmother's orders, the child would run into his office and cry out, "Come on, you lazy man!"

President Hoover's face would break into a smile and he would take her hand in his.

Often both at table in the State Dining Room and at his fishing camp along the Rapidan he sat entirely silent with his eyes down. Mrs. Hoover was gracious and gay, but the President could go through a meal without muttering more than "Good evening" and "Good night." His voice was always low.* "His awful habit," Mrs. Hoover called the hardly audible mumbling. Yet he seemed anxious to have guests. He dined alone with Mrs. Hoover but once each year: February 10, their anniversary.

At the Rapidan River the guests had their own bungalows and invitations to go riding on the bridle paths carefully marked for that purpose, or for walks on the trails. The facilities and food were magnificent. For the women there were flowers and for the gentlemen great long cigars especially made for the President in Havana and smoked by him at the rate of twenty a day. But withal there was a somber quality to it all. "There were never any jokes," wrote Secretary of State Stimson; and Cabinet meetings were like sitting in a "bath of ink."

Shortly after the stock market crash he thought of curtailing the lavish entertaining because of the country's condition. But after thinking it over he changed his mind. To do so would indicate panic on the highest level of the government, lack of confidence in the future. A part of fighting the war of a thousand fronts was to keep up the style of life in the Americans' Executive Mansion. His picture of the American leader was of a man who did not flinch from the country's terrible problems, but rather advanced to meet them. Unfrightened and unbridled ele-

---

* Foreign ambassadors presenting their credentials were told by State Department officials not to think the President's lack of enthusiasm had any diplomatic significance.

gance in the White House and along the Rapidan became a weapon.

President Hoover was always at his desk before eight-thirty in the morning. Secretary of the Treasury Mills met him there. Night after night after dinner they were together in a White House study. The United States government was spending two and a half million dollars a day more than it took in. If that continued, America, like any other bankrupt, would be unable to pay its bills. If bankruptcy came, it would bring what had happened to Germany: hideous inflation, wheelbarrows of dollars to pay for a loaf of bread, meals doubling in price as the diner ate, the end of the middle classes, Bolshevism.

Together Hoover and Mills formulated the most brutal peacetime revenue bill the country had ever seen. The bill called for a rise in estate taxes from 23 percent to 45 percent, an increase in personal income taxes from 23 percent to 45 percent, a rise in corporation taxes, a sales tax, a drastic modification of capital gains advantages. With the unheard of taxes must come ruthless reductions in government expenditures: a cut in the pension paid to General Pershing, a one-week vacation without pay each month for the majority of government employees, decreases in the salary of each member of the Cabinet, $12,000 instead of $15,000, and of the President, $60,000 instead of $75,000. (When a Congressional group asked the President just how much of a cut he wanted to give himself, he said he would reduce his salary by $74,999.00. They indicated this would be illegal, that a $15,000 reduction would be the maximum permissible.)

The revenue bill was sent up to Congress. "The President said: 'Drastic economy requires sacrifice. . . . Rigid economy is a real road to relief to home owners, farmers, workers, and every element of our population.'" For half a year the Congress delayed and wrangled; in the end they gave the President only part of what he asked. Democratic since the 1930 post-crash elections, they balked at anything he asked. He asked Congress for twenty-five million dollars for the relief of animals in Southern drought regions; they tried to authorize the expenditure of sixty million dollars so that humans as well as livestock might be fed. Fearing that this might open the door to other endless requests, he refused to allow the measure. "Prosperity cannot be restored by raids on the public treasury," he declared. There must be no "playing politics with human misery."

The congressmen went almost mad with frustration at the fact that the warehouses were bursting with enough food to feed the population of half the world even as half of America went to bed hungry. It was the first depression in the history of any country where there was enough food to feed everyone. *But who would pay for that food? The city-dwellers could not. The near-bankrupt government could not. And who would pay for its shipment to the cities? The foreclosed farmers?*

Pictures of their impending defeats clouded the eyes of every senator and congressman: bleak declining years in one of Washington's third-rate hotels or "reduced circumstances" at home. Senator Walsh of Massachusetts charged Hoover with failure to remove the "specter of starvation and misery and idleness and unrest." Representative La Guardia cursed the President's proposed sales tax, crying out that it would grind "the face of the poor" and take "milk from babies and bread from mothers." La Guardia was from a poor-immigrant district of New York City and his words about the Reconstruction Finance Corporation were spoken to his shawl-covered Italian mothers and candystore proprietor Jews. The RFC was "the home of financial incurables," and the billions it spent should better be given to the jobless. "It is a wonder the American people have shown the patience they have shown!"

When the President asked Congress to appropriate $120,000 for the Committee on Unemployment Relief's clerical costs Congress spitefully refused. Hoover dug into his own pocket to do it. No one knew of the contribution. Also secret were the loans of the RFC, but it was known that millions of dollars a day were pouring out even as the President refused federal money for direct relief. "What Mr. Hoover wants," said Breckinridge Long, "is bigger and better opportunities for rich men to inherit the earth. It is the plight of the banks and the railroads and the great corporations that stirs his heart most deeply."

Presidential secretary Joslin thought to himself that the White House had become a hell on earth. The President was down to three hours of sleep a night, working from before dawn to long after sundown. Joslin wrote, "He worked those about him until they could hardly drag one foot after the other. He brought in fresh talent from the outside and soon had it fagged out and groggy."

For every argument advanced against him he marshaled half a dozen answers. "He planned and schemed," said Joslin, "worked out formulae, perfecting some, discarding others." He would write a sentence of a letter or address or a message to Congress even when there was just a moment between the departure of one group and the arrival of another. When he summoned interested parties for a conference nothing was left to chance. All the facts must be itemized: the loss of gold reserves figured down to the last dollar of the last day; the drop in steel production to the last unit; the laying-up of ships to the final amount of tonnage. There must be a statement drafted and rewritten with the utmost care and it must be ready for the interested parties to sign.

Joslin thought to himself that the man was steel, not flesh, that his mind was like an unfaltering machine. To his secretary Hoover was the greatest expert in the world on ruined nations. It was unbelievable, Joslin thought, that he would fail.

His incredible eighteen-hour work days made his people think he would break down. But only the trembling hands and insomnia showed the physical toll. He never missed a single day through illness.

The same did not apply to the aides forced to keep up his pace. Their wives came to him to beg for surcease. One woman came secretly to see the President in the Green Room. She told him that for weeks her husband had been unable to sleep for more than a few hours each night. For the previous two nights, she said, he had not slept at all. She pleaded with the President to let her husband resign. But the President could not let him go.

So he was given a few days' leave, and his responsibilities were then lessened for a while.

"My men are dropping around me," the President said to Joslin. "Fighting this Depression is becoming more and more like waging a war."

He realized that he must have physical exercise to keep up his strength, so in his careful way he found the ideal manner to get the most exertion for the least expenditure of time. Each morning he held a medicine-ball game in the company of a varying group which included Mills, Justice Stone, Secretaries Wilbur, Chapin, and Hurley, Assistant Secretary of the Navy Jahncke, White House Physician Boone, Attorney General Mitchell, the secretarial aides Richey, Newton, and Strother, the columnist Mark Sullivan, and any male guests who had spent the night in the White House—of whom each year there were more than one thousand.

The President made no move to dominate the game or have the ball thrown to him more often than to the others. After the game a light breakfast of grapefruit, toast and coffee was served under a magnolia tree said to have been planted by Andrew Jackson in memory of his wife Rachel. In cold weather the men sat swathed in blankets. There was some masculine banter along with the more serious discussions. The President took little part in either, sitting silently until he would go to change before meeting Mrs. Hoover for a more substantial breakfast at exactly eight.

The medicine-ball games were his only entertainment apart from fishing at the camp along the Rapidan. Generally the President fished alone, standing in hipboots in the water. But his hands shook more and more so that he fumbled with the tackle as he put bait on his hooks. Then he caught those hooks in his trousers, hat, and coat.

As the Depression deepened, his Friday afternoon departures for Virginia were increasingly delayed. The cars would be drawn up in the driveway and the reporters alerted, the baggage loaded. But time would pass until, inevitably three or four hours late, he would come out of his office with a dazed look in his eyes to stare uncomprehendingly at the Secret Service men giving him his hat and holding open the door.

"Oh, yes, are we ready to go?" he would say, and settle back in the limousine with his statistical summaries and reports.

As the weather grew warmer there were riots in Great Britain and hunger marches on London. In Germany the former Crown Prince appeared in uniform for the first time since the War. His doing so set off a flock of rumors that the Hohenzollern monarchy was coming back in alliance with Hitler's Nazis. In North China the Japanese sent divisions of elite troops against the Chinese, bombarding and closing a ring around the International Settlement at Shanghai. American troops were alerted and troop ships sailed from Pacific ports. When the Yellow River Patrol was strengthened it seemed as if Hoover the pacifist was bidding for a war with Japan, a war the country could not possibly afford.

Everything, it seemed, was coming apart. When the reporters asked John Maynard Keynes if there had ever been anything like it, he replied that there had, and that it had lasted four hundred years: the Dark Ages.

Chapter Eleven

Eᴀʀʟʏ ɪɴ Aᴘʀɪʟ the annual Governor's Conference was held in Richmond, Virginia, and the President, uninvited and not really wanted, let it be known that he wished to address the men. They had no choice but to accede to his request, and he went down by special train to say that there must be drastic economies. The speech irritated some of the governors. Ritchie of Maryland, a likely prospect for the Democratic Presidential nomination, tartly remarked that his state at least was not in need of the President's advice. Everything possible was already being done.

Roosevelt of New York said, "Very good speech, Mr. President."

The President replied, "Glad to see you again." It had been years since they last met.

The next day Hoover gave a dinner at the White House for the governors and their wives. The guests assembled in the East Room, on their feet as protocol dictated. The time for the President's appearance came and went; they remained standing. Governor Roosevelt laughed and joked with the others as usual, but as time went on his discomfort became acute and his wife knew the pain from his crippled legs must be torture for him. President and Mrs. Hoover came into the East Room half an hour late and Eleanor Roosevelt thought she knew why: it had been done to torment her husband.

Outside there were reporters asking what had gone on at the dinner, but Roosevelt said, "One may not talk when leaving the White House. I've been there before."

June came and it was convention time. Both parties would be meeting in Chicago, the Republicans first, on the fourteenth. For many months it had seemed to Mills that the 1932 Republican platform must at least question the wisdom of the law which since 1921 had made it illegal to buy a drink of liquor or a glass of wine or beer. He begged the President to have the platform call for a referendum on the Prohibition Amendment. The President seemed unable to make up his mind. He could not forget that in 1928 he had called Prohibition "a great social and economic experiment, noble in motive." So while the delegates headed for Chicago, Mills stayed behind in Washington pressing his views on the President. Mills himself was one of the wettest wets in the capital; the President, who had always had magnificent wine cellars before Prohibition, was a dry.

In the end, Mills came to Chicago as one of the last delegates to arrive. He brought with him a platform, largely written by the President, in which the Prohibition issue was referred to in something like double-talk. The newspapers immediately characterized it as a straddle.

Most of the Republican delegates convening in the Chicago Stadium were Federal employees, collectors of customs, marshals, postmasters, receivers in bankruptcy. They took their seats in a hall that was about one-third empty. For all the elaborate decorations of bunting and flags, there was not a single picture of the President in the hall or at the Congress Hotel, which was slipping into bankruptcy even as it served as Republican Headquarters. In fact, noted *Time*, "throughout the length and breadth of the city there was not to be found a single Republican badge, button, sign or slogan urging the selection of anyone for office." Herbert Clark Hoover, wrote the columnist Heywood Broun, was indeed the Forgotten Man.

The Republican keynote speaker was Senator Lester J. Dickinson of Iowa. It had been said of him that he was a hellraiser for agriculture and his nickname for years had been "Hell-raising Dick." Senator Dickinson spoke for a long time until he mentioned the President's name. At the first mention of the leader—Dickinson "howled out" the "horrid" sound, wrote H. L. Mencken—there was listless applause for less than sixty seconds. As the splatter of handclapping died away a band came to the rescue, bursting into "America." The entire demonstration for the President, including the music, took less than two minutes. "The convention," wrote a *New York Times* reporter, "which had hitherto been as apathetic as a lecture audience, had now been lifted to the emotional heights of a faculty tea."

Dickinson went on. But a hubbub of desultory conversation arose all over the hall. Senator Simeon Fess, the chairman of the National Committee, stepped up to the two big white microphone discs: "We are receiving many complaints that the speaker cannot be heard. It is not because the senator is not speaking loud enough. It is because there is too much noise." A number of the delegates responded to Fess's plea by walking out into the lobbies. At the end of the speech, when Dickinson predicted the re-election of the President, there was mild applause lasting perhaps half a minute. *The New York Times* editorial the next day said the speech contained "unconscious humor."

The main issue was whether the party platform would question Prohibition; beyond that there was no suspense or life to the proceedings. Mills's revelation that the President desired a plank that straddled the issue only added to the apathy. The rest of the platform's planks ignored the economic situation of the country. "Ten million American workers and their dependents are threatened with starvation," said the *New Republic*, but the delegates still lived in a "cloistered vision of a happy, vanished, past."

There was no one who could or would replace Hoover as the candidate. Only one man, a "lonely eccentric," said *Time*, opposed the inevitable renomination. He was former Senator Joseph I. France of Maryland, who had appointed himself a candidate. Through the rote speeches praising the President as the captain at the helm, on the bridge, in the pilot house, ex-Senator France stood with a smile on his face chewing gum.

One L. B. Sandblast of the Oregon delegation agreed to nominate him. But when France moved toward the podium to speak, Congressman Bertrand H. Snell physically haited him. The two men struggled in full view of the delegates for a moment before the sergeants-at-arms rushed up. There was a short battle on the stage as flashbulbs popped and a quick rumor spread that a madman was loose. France was roughly dragged away to an anteroom. He said he had intended to nominate Coolidge, with the certain knowledge that the name would have swept the delegates and that they would have nominated the ex-President by acclamation. In fact, the newspapers hinted, something like that was feared and that was perhaps why all the Republican orators avoided mention of Coolidge's name.

Joseph Scott of Los Angeles made the nomination speech for the President, ending, "that glorious Californian, Herbert Hoover." Toy balloons dropped from nets at the top of the hall and the band played "Over There." Then a record of Hoover speaking came over the public address system, but it was of poor quality and could hardly be understood. The band switched to "Onward Christian Soldiers." There were no further demonstrations.

The delegates renominated the 1928 ticket of Hoover and Charles Curtis. As they did so the President listened on a radio placed on the luncheon table in the White House. "Well," he said, "it was not wholly unexpected. Guess I will go back to the office now." None of the aides lunching with him offered congratulations. He rose and rapidly walked from the room. Mrs. Hoover dropped her knitting, jumped up and ran after him.

The message of acceptance had already been written by the President. It was telegraphed to the convention.

"I am deeply grateful. . . . I shall labor as I have labored to meet the effects of the world wide storm which has devastated us with trials and sufferings unequaled. . . . Beyond platforms and measures lies that sacred realm of ideals, of hopes, of aspirations, those things of the spirit which make the greatness and the soul of the Nation. These are our objectives and with unceasing effort, with courage and faith in Almighty God, they will be attained."

Chapter Twelve

THE DEMOCRATS came to Chicago two weeks later, June 27. In the garbage dumps of the city the hungry were seeking what they could find. The smell was sickening, as were the great swarms of summer flies falling upon the heaps of refuse as soon as the garbage trucks pulled away. The people dug in with their hands. They devoured whatever was left on old slices of watermelon and cantaloupe until the rinds were thin as paper. They washed and cooked discarded onions, turnips, potatoes, cabbages, carrots. Sometimes they cut away the rotted parts of the meat, but often they scalded it and then sprinkled it with soda to kill the taste and odor. They made fish-head soup, chicken-claw soup.

At a private incinerator at La Salle and 35th the women complained that men jumped on the trucks before they were unloaded and that it was unfair. Codes were established so that no one should have an undue advantage. At Cicero Avenue and 31st there was a Hooverville two years old. There were three hundred people, drawn there originally and staying there now because of the regular dumping of food. There was a widow who took off her glasses when she ate so that she would not see the maggots.

It was not only the very poor who were suffering in Chicago that June. Samuel Insull was finding it hard going. His life had been an American saga: the penniless boy working as aide to Thomas A. Edison, the entrepreneur out on his own becoming the biggest businessman west of the Alleghenies, the presiding genius of an electrical utility empire which supplied electricity to sections of thirty American states and half a dozen Canadian provinces. His position in the Middle West had been unassailable. He was revered for his immense wealth and the sheer bigness of his enterprises. He was the magnate and patron of the arts entertaining Queen Marie of Romania and bidding his employees to buy his stock, for it could only rise. All the Middle West believed in Insull. Then the Depression came and the empire began to slide downhill.

Insull forsook his charities, his magnificent model farm, the Chicago Opera Company which he had bankrolled for years. Each day he drove in an ancient limousine to his offices where he labored to fight off the hideous rot overtaking his scores of corporations. But it was no good; the holding companies with their reduced income began to lean against each other and then the whole edifice came toppling down. He was out, and took ship abroad saying that he had come to the Golden Land without a cent and that he would leave the same way.

"I've gone from the bottom to the top," he declared, "and now to the bottom again. I only hope I will be able to keep a roof over my head and care for my wife." There followed lurid stories that he was living in a Paris attic renting for pennies a day and that his wife cooked for him on a hot plate.

John D. Rockefeller's eccentric daughter Edith moved to a hotel suite paid for out of an allowance tendered by her brother John D., Jr.; her place on Lake Michigan was too expensive to keep up. Chicago society, with its great Lake Shore mansions, that society supported by Samuel Insull and Edith Rockefeller McCormick, rocked and sank.

Charles G. Dawes returned to Chicago that June. In the middle of the month he resigned from the Reconstruction Finance Corporation, telling the President he wished to reenter the banking business. Ex-Senator Atlee Pomerene of Ohio, who had lost his post in 1916 to Warren Harding, was appointed Dawes's successor. Pomerene told the reporters that when the President called him in to offer the job he had exactly ninety-eight cents in his pocket and that en route to the rendezvous a dozen men had tried to panhandle him.

The Washington reporters asked Dawes how he felt about leaving the public service; he answered he liked it darned well. Then he went to Chicago. The reporters' instincts were aroused by something in his manner and they crowded about him in Union Station.

"If you folks are in such a hurry to get what I've got to say," he told them, "send a man down to the train when it gets into Chicago tomorrow morning. It will be given in Chicago, where it is of major interest, and not here."

In Chicago he silently handed out a typed statement. It said America had reached the turning point. Continued business improvement might be expected. There was nothing more. He shocked the men, for he was uneasy and nervous, nothing like the jolly "Hell 'n' Maria" of the past.

On the day Dawes quit the RFC, twenty-five banks in the Chicago suburbs closed their doors. Gigantic runs began on the Loop banks. It was the crisis of one of those banks which put the worried look on Dawes's face. The bank, the Central Republic, had been created by the merger of a bank Dawes had founded years earlier. Although he had had no contact with it for a long time, he still thought of it as his. Fresh from the train he walked into a meeting of the Central Republic's directors and demanded that he be made chairman of the board. Elected, it was his instinct to pay off the depositors as best he could and then close the doors and go out of business. He would not allow the bank's money to disappear into the wallets of those who believed it was doomed, while the people who believed in Charley Dawes waited faithfully until nothing was left for them. Dawes watched the deposits decrease day by day, from two hundred and forty million to two hundred million to one hundred and twenty million. He decided that the bank must close. For the first time since his return home he slept soundly.

That was Saturday, June 25. On that day the Democrats were pouring into Chicago for their convention. Among them was the Texas banker and RFC official Jesse Jones. Jones checked in at his hotel and then went for a stroll through the Loop. There he saw the tail end of the week's terrible runs. Thousands of people, horrible rumors attending them, swarmed about every bank. Jones watched Melvin A. Traylor, chief executive officer of the First National of Chicago, get up on the pedestal of a marble pillar in his savings department and shout to the wild people that they must not take their money out and thus cripple the bank.

Traylor's bank held, but the next day, Sunday, he came to Jones's hotel room and asked that Jones come with him to a meeting. They went to the boardroom of the Central Republic. Over thirty men, the elite of financial Chicago, were there. To them Charles Dawes quietly said that the Central Republic would not open its doors on Monday morning. It was the first intimation Jones had that the bank of his former chief in the RFC was in any kind of trouble.

Traylor, of Chicago's First National, had already telephoned the President at his camp along the Rapidan. Traylor asked RFC support for the Central Republic. "If we do not get such support by Monday," he told the President, "every Chicago bank—ours among them, of course—will have to close its doors." If the Chicago banks folded, it would mean the Middle West was finished, and that would mean the end of the nation.

When Dawes finished speaking to the financial men in the Central Republic's boardroom, Traylor turned to Jones and asked if he would telephone the President. Jones replied he would have to look at the records. He took off his coat, sent out for sandwiches, worked sixteen hours straight. Then Jones called the President and told him it was far too dangerous for the country to allow the Central Republic to collapse. The President said he would talk to Mills and some other men and call back. After a while the President phoned and told Jones, "Make as good a trade as you can for participation of other banks in the loan, but save the bank."

Jones said to the elite of Chicago assembled in the Central Republic boardroom that together—they as private citizens and he as representative of the government—they would save the Central Republic and all of Chicago's banks. The amount needed for a Central Republic loan was almost one hundred million dollars; to raise it Jones began calling bankers from all over the Middle West. It was a fortunate happenstance that many were in Chicago for the Democratic convention. Mrs. Woodrow Wilson was the guest of Jones and his wife at the convention, so he knew she would be receiving at a suburban country club party that afternoon. He got on the telephone and intercepted the arriving guests to ask that they come to him at the Central Republic's boardroom.

At two in the morning on Monday, Jones had gotten the bankers' bid up to three million dollars. That was the top, they said. That was all they would risk in loans to the Central Republic. Jones pointed out he was talking to them about nearly one hundred million, and if three was all they would offer then they might as well go to bed and let events take their course. They raised their ante to five million as against the government contribution of ninety million. Traylor was their spokesman and there was something in his voice and attitude that told Jones that five was as high as they would go. Jones said the RFC would put up the remaining ninety million. And so they went to bed and five hours later the Central Republic along with the other banks opened for business. Its stock on Friday had been quoted at forty-seven dollars; when word of the desperate last-minute rescue got around the stock soon plunged to a value of just one dollar. But banking in Chicago went on.

Governor Roosevelt was the front-runner as the convention got under way. But he did not have much strength. Ed Flynn and Jim Farley were everywhere praising the governor of their state, but it did not seem to take. He always had been "an utterly impossible man for President of the United States," remarked Supreme Court Justice Harlan Fiske Stone. "Far too feeble and wishy-washy a fellow to make a really effective fight," said H. L. Mencken. Their weakest candidate, thought President Hoover.

Flynn and Farley realized that the two-thirds rule of Democratic conventions might defeat Roosevelt, for their tallies seemed to show that he could never command that figure. They tried to change the two-thirds rule to a simple majority. There was a terrible outcry. Louis Howe came to Chicago and said that this was madness and shortly Governor Roosevelt, who earlier had agreed that this was the best way to insure his nomination, issued a statement that he and his forces had no intention of changing the rule. So they were stuck with it.

Roosevelt did not go to Chicago, but Al did. He had beaten Roosevelt in the Massachusetts primary by three to one and had made an excellent showing in Pennsylvania. Glory opened before him. When Al arrived at the La Salle Street Station in Chicago the reporters asked him what he hoped the convention would do. "Write an honest, concise, clear platform and nominate me."

If not him, who was his second choice?

"I'm for myself alone."

Ed Flynn came to him in his hotel room and Smith said, "Ed, you are not representing the people of Bronx County in your support of Roosevelt. You know the people of Bronx County want you to support me." Flynn and Smith were alone in the room, everyone else having left. Flynn reminded Smith that Smith had indicated to him not long ago that his financial obligations would preclude his running. Now Flynn could not switch from Roosevelt to Smith. It was a very emotional and painful experience for the normally cold and businesslike Ed Flynn. But there was nothing else he could do: he had given his word to Roosevelt. At the end Smith and Flynn shook hands but they were no longer the friends they had been.

All day long the phonographs in the headquarters of the candidates blared out theme songs: "Maryland My Maryland" for Governor Ritchie; "The Sidewalks of New York" for Smith; "The Eyes of Texas Are Upon You" for Speaker of the House of Representatives Garner; and "Carry Me Back to Old Virginny" for Harry Byrd. Among themselves the Roosevelt people went about chanting "Roosevelt for President" to the tune of *Of Thee I Sing*'s "Wintergreen for President," but the governor's official song was "Anchors Aweigh," in remembrance of his Navy Department days. To Louise Stiles, Louis Howe's secretary, the tune did not sound true. Just before Judge John E. Mack of Poughkeepsie, New York, took the podium to put Roosevelt's name into nomination, she plucked up her courage and burst into Howe's hotel room, where he lay on a bed.

"Mein Gawd!" screamed Howe. (He specialized in improbable expressions.) "What's the matter with you? Is the hotel on fire?"

Excitedly she told him that "Anchors Aweigh" was best known as a theme song for a cigarette ad. The right song for Roosevelt, she said, would be "Happy Days Are Here Again."

Howe clutched his head in his hands. "You too!" (Ed Flynn had told him "Anchors Aweigh" was like a funeral march.) "They're driving me nuts out at that hall. 'What'll we play? What'll we play?' That organ player calls me every five minutes. I don't give a damn what they play."

She talked up "Happy Days" and began to sing it, running up and down the room and snapping her fingers in time. Howe moaned, picked up the phone and ordered that when the nomination speech was over the band should play "Happy Days Are Here Again."

At the Chicago Stadium John E. Mack began his nomination speech. As he spoke, Al Smith, dressed in evening clothes, came in and stood listening. At the mention of the name Franklin Delano Roosevelt, Smith rasped, "I can go back to the hotel and listen to that on the rad-io," and turned on his heel. There was an ugly snarl on his lips as he went away. At the end of the speech a huge picture of the candidate was unfurled from the third tier of the balconies. In his room at the Congress Hotel, Louis Howe, his ear to a radio, was seized with one of his frequent asthmatic attacks. He lay on the couch with his knees drawn up to his chest and between spasms of coughing gasped over and over, "Tell them to repeat 'Happy Days Are Here Again.' "

The seconding speeches droned through the hot night and it was not until well past four in the morning when the first ballot was taken. Governor Roosevelt received 661 out of 1100 odd votes. His strength was less than had been supposed. It did not look as if he could get a two-thirds majority. The delegates balloted again and Roosevelt gained some new votes as states deserted their favorite sons. The delegates had been up all night and it was light outside, but they decided to try another ballot. The situation was desperate for Roosevelt. If his position did not improve on this or the next ballot, his strength would surely erode. Already the name of Wilson's Secretary of War, Newton Baker, was on everyone's lips as a compromise candidate. Perhaps no more than a fifth of Roosevelt's delegates were actually voting for him. The rest were out to deny Smith the prize, or under orders to keep it from Newton Baker.

Jim Farley as field commander was fighting off what looked like defeat, offering the Vice Presidency to Byrd or Ritchie if they would hand over their votes. They refused. Roosevelt's people got to Huey Long of Louisiana and told him the Arkansas delegation looked like it was slipping away from Roosevelt; could the "Kingfish" do anything? Arkansas was at the head of the alphabet, and its defection might well set up a mass runaway. Huey Long himself had no respect at all for Roosevelt. He had made this clear earlier to Ed Flynn when, late at night, he had banged on the door of Flynn's hotel room and in his trumpetlike voice blared out that it was Huey Long. When Flynn opened the door Long barged in, half drunk, and surrounded as always with a mass of armed bodyguards. Long told Flynn he had visited each of the candidates, Baker, Byrd, Ritchie, and Smith. They had all disappointed him. Therefore, he announced to Flynn, he would not call on Roosevelt because if Roosevelt disappointed him he would have no one to support. Not seeing Roosevelt, he logically said, he could be his backer. Now in the moment of crisis Long came to the rescue, barging into the Arkansas delegation and telling the men of his neighboring state that if they jumped off the Roosevelt bandwagon he would cross their border and ruin them. He also visited the Mississippi delegation and shook his fist under the nose of Senator Pat Harrison, saying that if he did not hold fast for Roosevelt, "I'll go into Mississippi and break you." There was no question in Flynn's mind that without Huey Long Roosevelt might have lost the nomination then and there.

The third ballot was taken and Roosevelt's lines held but did not materially improve. The sun was long up and the heat of the day was beginning. The delegates were in rumpled clothing and sweating. They adjourned and staggered off to their hotels. The nomination hung in the balance.

Farley went to Louis Howe's room. Howe had been awake all night, lying on the floor under an open window in an attempt to get a breath of air, a radio by his head. His shirt was open and his tie off. He was covered with ashes from his Sweet Caporal cigarettes. Howe had not been out of his clothes for a week. Delegation after delegation had come to his hotel room to listen to Roosevelt speaking over an amplified telephone from Albany, giving his greetings to "my friends from South Dakota" or "my friends from Indiana." Lying on the floor Howe seemed barely able to breathe; the sound of his gasping filled the room. The men who came with Farley were shocked at his appearance. They went outside to wait. Farley lowered himself to the floor and lay next to Howe, who whispered to him. The two figures, the great, hearty Jim Farley and the tiny, fragile Louis Howe lay side by side for a while, and then Farley went out.

Joseph Guffey of Pennsylvania said, "This is the end for Louis, isn't it, Jim? He can't possibly last through the day, can he?"

Farley said, "Of course he'll last. Anything else is nonsense. You know he's not going to die until he sees Roosevelt nominated."

Roosevelt's people scattered to reach all who could get their man across. Howe's secretary, Miss Stiles, was sent to deliver a letter to Mayor Anton Cermak of Chicago, a strong Ritchie supporter, who was staying on a different floor in the Congress Hotel. The reporters were everywhere. To avoid them she raced up and down back stairs and in and out of powder rooms.

Howe himself sent for Harry Byrd of Virginia and bluntly asked what Byrd wanted for his votes. Byrd said he wanted to be United States senator from Virginia.

"Is that your price?" Howe asked.

Byrd repeated that it was. But there already were two Democratic senators from Virginia.

"Very well," Howe said. "We'll put either Glass or Swanson in Franklin's Cabinet."

Virginia was now safe for Roosevelt.

Several of Roosevelt's people placed calls to San Simeon, the California estate of William Randolph Hearst. Hearst did not like Roosevelt except when, as Arthur Krock said, he ruminated upon the fact that Al Smith disliked them both. A stronger emotion came to the publisher when the Roosevelt people told him that if the convention went into a deadlock Newton Baker would be the compromise candidate. To Hearst Baker meant the League of Nations and the World Court, all the internationalism he hated and feared. Hearst got working on the California and Texas delegations. He completely controlled California; Garner of Texas as a Presidential candidate was practically Hearst's singlehanded creation and his influence there was unlimited.

But Texas and California still held to Garner. Calls flew back and forth between Chicago and San Simeon. California's leader was Wilson's son-in-law and sometime Secretary of the Treasury, William Gibbs McAdoo. His murderous struggle with Smith in 1924 had badly split the party. After that epic battle Smith and McAdoo never met again. But when the convention got under way Bernard Baruch had telephoned Smith to ask if he would meet with McAdoo in Baruch's rooms at the Blackstone, the object being to combine to defeat Roosevelt's bid for the nomination.

"Bernie," Al said, "I don't like him, I don't trust him, and I won't be comfortable while I'm with him, but in this fight I would sleep with a Chinaman to win, and I'll come."

He came to Baruch's rooms. McAdoo was already there. McAdoo said, "How are you?"

Al said, "Out of sight."

They shook hands.

"Well," said McAdoo, 1924 never far from his mind, as it was never far from Smith's. "Well, we both got licked."

"Yes," said Smith. "We both got licked."

They agreed they would work together against Roosevelt and parted.

Then the convention got under way and seemed to be approaching a deadlock. Rumors spread that Texas and California would switch from Garner to Roosevelt, with Garner getting the Vice Presidency. Smith heard the rumors and suspected that

McAdoo had thrown his support to Roosevelt and Garner. Smith called Baruch.

"Bernie," he said, "your long-legged friend has run out on us, just as I thought he would."

Baruch said, "Why, Al, you must be mistaken."

"No, I ain't mistaken."

Baruch sent a man to talk to McAdoo. But the man came back saying the California delegation was in caucus and McAdoo could not see him.

Smith placed a call to the Washington hotel where Mr. and Mrs. Garner had lived for all the years of Garner's many terms as representative and Speaker of the House. Smith got Mrs. Garner, the Speaker's longtime secretary, who each day cooked his lunch on a hot plate in the office.

"Mrs. Garner, this is Alfred E. Smith, and I would like to talk to the Speaker."

She told him to call back in twenty minutes. He waited half an hour and then called again. He got a clerk in the hotel who said he would get Garner. After a while the clerk came back on the line and said he could not find the Speaker. Then the clerk said, "Look here, Governor, I'm a friend of yours and I'm going to tell you the truth. He's up on the roof eating dinner, but he don't want to talk to you."

Hearst had ordered the switch out of his fear of Baker.

In Chicago Farley went to Howe and said, "It's in the bag."

Howe said, "Jim, that is fine." Nothing showed in his face as he heard the most thrilling words he had heard in the twenty years since he set out to make a President of Franklin Roosevelt.

Louise Stiles thought to herself that was exactly the way of her boss—the strange little man.

That night the fourth ballot began. When California's turn came McAdoo asked leave to address the convention. He went up to the podium and a hideous roar of boos enveloped him. They knew what he was going to say. Mayor Cermak, with the memory of the letter Louise Stiles carried to him in mind, leaped up and demanded the galleries be in order.

Before his switch from Ritchie to Roosevelt, Cermak had filled the hall to its rafters with unemployed men who for a sandwich and a cup of coffee had contracted to boo Roosevelt's name every time they heard it. That incessant hooting had sawed on the Roosevelt people's nerves, but there was nothing they could do about it.

Now Cermak was one of the Roosevelt people, but he had forgotten to order the men to keep quiet. He waved his arms at them, but the waves of booing only grew louder. The hired jeering was joined by those who hated what had been done to Smith, hated the East, hated the Protestants, hated the Depression. Even those who hated Smith booed.

As the booing increased in volume it was obvious to those who watched that William McAdoo was enjoying the sound. Once before he had heard that sound. It was in 1924. He had waited eight years to pay back Al Smith and Al Smith's people. A sly smile gradually uncovered McAdoo's teeth. His eight-year wait was over. And he would be getting the party's nomination for senator. "California," he called, when at last he could be heard, "California came here to nominate a President of the United States. It did not come here to deadlock this convention. California casts forty-four votes for Franklin D. Roosevelt." After that the delegations came tumbling down.

In Lincoln's study in the White House the President listened to the radio and thought that once the people saw the paucity of Roosevelt's ideas and the weaknesses of his personality and thinking, it would be not impossible for the Republicans to win the election. (At the medicine-ball session the next morning his fellow players would agree, saying that apart from everything else, it was hard to believe that the American people would actually elect a hopeless cripple as their leader.)

As soon as the news was in, Louis Howe called Albany, where the governor sat chain-smoking cigarettes in his study. Roosevelt asked Howe to request the delegates to stay in session; he would fly to them, arriving between two and three o'clock the next afternoon. The governor's wife, in a pale-green chiffon hostess gown, went into the kitchen and began cooking scrambled eggs for her husband.

A girl reporter asked Mrs. Roosevelt, "Aren't you *thrilled* at the idea of living in the White House?" The governor's wife stared at her. Her almost-angry glare puzzled those who saw it.

In Chicago, Garner got the Vice Presidency. "Politics is funny," he said.

The next day Roosevelt set out in a Ford trimotor plane to Chicago to accept the convention's nomination in person. It had never been done before. Custom demanded that weeks or even months after the delegates voted a committee must formally apprise the selected candidate of the fact of his nomination. Nor had important politicians, let alone potential Presidents, been known to trust themselves to an airborne craft. The audacity of the two novel acts caught Chicago's fancy, and hours before the candidate was due, crowds assembled at the municipal airport, which, the New York reporters noted, was fenced off, unlike the Long Island airfields, which were entirely open.

The plane took nine hours to fly from Albany, with stops at Buffalo and Cleveland for refueling. Low-hanging clouds covered most of the route. When the plane's announced arrival time came and went, the reporters speculated on whom the delegates would choose to take Roosevelt's place in the event of a crash.

Word spread, wrongly, that there were thirteen passengers on board (there were ten) and Roosevelt was asked by radio if the number bothered him. He radioed back, "What of it? There were thirteen states in the Union," and the joke, traveling through the twenty-five thousand people waiting at the airfield, made the crowds laugh. Laughing with them were Franklin, Jr., James, the nominee's daughter Anna, and his daughter-in-law Betsy. They did not stand off by themselves but chatted with anybody who came up. Jim Farley was there, of course, and Louis Howe, clutching the speech he had written for Roosevelt to deliver to the delegates.

Al Smith was not there. Alone of the men who had been potential candidates, he had failed to announce his support of the nominee and instead left Chicago on the Twentieth-Century Limited for New York. The reporters asked him whether he would eventually come out for the party's candidate, if he would make speeches, his future plans.

"Not one word," was his gruff response. The shades on his

drawing room were pulled tightly shut. The once Happy Warrior was sulking, thought the journalist F. Raymond Daniel.

When the plane touched down the crowds rushed over the fences and for a moment it seemed as if the propellers might cut someone down. Then the craft halted and the Roosevelt party emerged. Young John, green with airsickness after his first flight, staggered. Mrs. Roosevelt, tall, thin, homely, was in a dark blue suit with low heels and a straw hat. Then came the nominee. His two sons, his daughter and his daughter-in-law rushed up to him and he embraced and kissed them one by one.

Roosevelt shook hands with Farley and cried, "Grand work, Jim!" Louis Howe rushed up to push his speech into Roosevelt's hands. People were cheering on all sides; mingled with their applause were cries of, "Make it up with Al, Frank."

Roosevelt grinned, winked, cocked an eyebrow, waved, threw back his head and laughed. The crowds jammed in toward him and his hat was knocked off and his glasses pushed sideways on his nose. He pulled a face of pretended anguish and comically let his lips form into a little "O" of surprise; then he laughed to indicate he had only been fooling. He got into a limousine provided by Mayor Cermak, the tall and strong James Roosevelt deftly lifting him into it, and led a cavalcade toward the Chicago Stadium where the delegates waited. As he rode he grinned and waved his hands and tossed his great leonine head with laughter that was returned by the people on the sidewalks.

Before the flight and during it he had worked on the acceptance speech, drafted and reworked and polished by those of his backers who shortly would be termed the "Brains Trust"—later the "Brain Trust." But Louis Howe did not know or perhaps care about that. Between waves Roosevelt looked at Howe's manuscript and took the first page and put it on top of the Brains Trust speech. First he would read out Howe's page and then the Brains Trust speech. Everybody would be kept happy.

He went up before the delegates to say that he dismissed tradition as an obstacle to the country's salvation—"Let it be from now on the task of our party to break foolish traditions." He said, "Our Republican leaders tell us economic laws, sacred, unvariable, unchangeable, cause panics which no one can prevent. But while they prate of economic laws, men and women are starving." He looked the picture of confidence and strength.

"I shall vote for him as in duty bound," wrote H. L. Mencken. "Anything to get rid of Hoover! I'd vote for a Chinaman. . . . Even a Methodist bishop."

Roosevelt said in his great booming voice, "I pledge you, I pledge myself, to a new deal for the American people," and the delegates gave him moderate applause. The phrase did not catch their attention in that moment. Anyway, it had been used before, most recently in the current *New Republic* by the author Stuart Chase, who called for "A new deal for America," and, earlier in the year, by the *New York Daily News*, which on January 1 said, "Depression? Ha! Ha! This is a brand new year! 1931? Bah! 'Twas a terrible year. Who cares? Here's a brand new deal. 1932."

Roosevelt said, "Let us all here assembled constitute our-selves prophets of a new order of competence and of courage. This is more than a political campaign; it is a call to arms. Give me your help, not to win votes alone, but to win in this crusade to restore America to its own people."

He went away, waving one hand while with the other he clutched his son's arm for support. Shortly he and James, Franklin, Jr., John, and two other young men, one a cousin and the other a friend of James, went sailing in Eastern coastal waters aboard a forty-four-foot yawl, *Myth II*. The stories filed by the reporters trailing along in power boats had the smiling and sunburned nominee as "Cap'n" Roosevelt and "Skipper" Roose-velt; he and his young crew were depicted as rollicking and frol-icking and tickled to death to be out on the waters where he handled the boat with very great skill. His greatest interest had always been ships and the sea.

Now and again political leaders flew to where the boat was anchored for the night; they all returned to say that the nominee and all hands on board were in great spirits, telling jokes, joshing each other. The Skipper would praise the dispatch of the boys shinnying up the mast to untangle a fouled jib; they would compliment his coolness and nerve as he steered through a nar-row channel. He was always represented as gay and at ease, welcoming the spray kicking over the gunwales, loving the sun and the slapping of the waves on the hull, a man without a worry in the world.

In Washington the President faced the Bonus Army.

PART IV

The Bonus March

Chapter Thirteen

IN 1924 the American Congress passed the Adjusted Compensation Act. It was aimed at reimbursing the country's servicemen for the time they had spent away from home and high-paying wartime jobs, and it required the government to give each man an endowment insurance policy which would be cashable twenty years after its 1925 issue—in 1945. Each man would be given a policy for an amount arrived at according to various conditions of his military career. The average sum was around five hundred dollars. To this would be added 4 percent interest, which would result in a 1945 cash-in value of, on the average, one thousand dollars. The act was considered extremely generous. None of the Allies, let alone Germany, offered their veterans anything like it.

All through the early years of the Depression there were rumblings from veterans who wanted the bonus to be paid now. Their argument was that they had saved the nation in 1918. Now they were hungry. If the money was not paid until 1945 it would be of little use save to buy flowers for the graves of men who had starved to death.

Congressmen began getting substantial numbers of letters from ex-soldier constituents, and in May, more than a month before the Republicans and Democrats met in Chicago, the House Ways and Means Committee opened hearings on the sub-

ject. The Administration was against the bonus. It would completely unbalance the budget and thus jeopardize the financial
stability of the country. It would benefit a class of men in the
prime of life while ignoring the tens of millions of Americans
who were not veterans. It would open the way for a mass rush
on the Treasury. Secretary Mills appeared before the Committee
to say that the bonus meant inflation, and inflation was the
direct descendant of the dishonest and unscrupulous prince or
sovereign who defrauds his subjects by debasing their currency.
Worthless paper was the next step, and the saver, the bond-
holder, and the insurance policy holder would lead the suffering,
to be joined in short order by the working man. Germany was
the example.

"It involves," Mills said, "the courage, the character, and
the financial integrity of the United States. I can imagine a poor,
bankrupt people, at the end of their resources, and as a last act
of desperation, resorting to the debasement of their currency.
But for a great, powerful nation . . . it would constitute moral
bankruptcy."

If this was what was wanted, Mills asked, why not just get
paper and ink and set the printer to work? Any country "suffi-
ciently mad and imprudent" enough to begin might not, moreover, have the "character to stop. . . . In several countries that
I could mention, bales of currency have been peddled in the
streets."

After Mills came Dawes, Senator Hiram Johnson, Representative Fiorello La Guardia, Secretary of War Hurley. Their
arguments were the same as Mills's. But in the galleries were
men who saw everyone but themselves as War profiteers who
got rich while the troops were away. During the War it was
"We're behind you, boys." But now? When a minister and
former Army chaplain testified against the bonus the men in the
galleries hissed, booed, and shouted, "Throw him out!" Witnesses
came to say the bonus would "degrade the patriotism of war
service and make the word veteran synonymous with panhandler
and grafter," but the veterans jeeringly said that, having gotten
all these to speak against the bonus, the President would next
ask the deposed Wilhelm II to appear. When the head of the

American Legion wrote the President that he was against the bonus, he was bombarded from many Legion posts. A telegram from North Carolina said, "The veterans, as distinguished from the titular leaders, are becoming aroused. They will no longer sit idly by while pussy-footing, lying, hypocritical politicians plunge the country, which the veterans saved in 1918, into hell."

Representative Wright Patman of Texas, who had attempted to impeach Andrew Mellon, was the veterans' champion. Patman said he would get a bill passed to pay the bonus immediately and that the President would never "dare" to veto it. The President issued statements saying that the bonus would imperil the steady return of the economy, but Patman pressed for a vote on the issue.

And in the public parks across the country, sitting in the warming sun and reading papers plucked from trashcans, men of thirty-three or thirty-seven who once had been told they were their country's pride, the subjects of "Over There" and of The War to End War, of The Right Is More Precious Than Peace, began to see that it was possible for Washington to put hundreds of dollars into their empty pockets. The newspapers had told them at the time of the President's 1931 Moratorium that the Europeans were being exempted from paying millions of dollars owed to the United States; now the same papers said that the President stood firm against payments of debts to United States veterans. It made no sense to them. Let the Europeans welsh and then refuse to pay the heroes of the War? What had they fought for? To have a place in which to starve?

One of the veterans was Walter Waters of Portland, Oregon. In 1916 he had gone with a National Guard unit to the Mexican border to participate in Pershing's fruitless search for the bandit Pancho Villa. During the War, he went to France with the 146th Field Artillery. Waters arrived at the front in July of 1918. He fought through the summer and fall at Meuse-Argonne, St. Mihiel, Aisne-Marne, and then went to Germany with the army of occupation. Mustered out, twenty years of age, an ex-sergeant, he wandered into and out of jobs as a garage mechanic, bakery helper, automobile salesman, and farmhand in the Western harvest fields. He ended up in a cannery near Portland where he worked his way up to assistant superintendent. He had a wife, two little girls, a car and a home and a thousand dollars in savings. In December of 1930, a year after the crash, the cannery laid him off. He went around seeking work, back to Idaho, where he was reared. There was no work. He and the family moved to a tiny two-room apartment in a rundown section of Portland which he left each day to seek any kind of employment. Everywhere he went he saw men whose faces now bore the look that was on his—partly hope, partly bewilderment. His thousand dollars began to give out, and with the new year of 1932 it had vanished along with his hope that he could ever get work. He and his wife started pawning what they had, and soon they had nothing left but a little clothing. For food they relied on the local charities of Portland and whatever their friends could give them. By March they were completely broke. Only a compassionate fellow-veteran who managed the building in which they lived prevented their being cast out on the streets. Yet in his pocket Waters was carrying an obligation of the United States government promising to pay him money.

On March 15 Waters got up at a meeting of the National Veterans Association in Portland and said they ought to take a freight train to Washington to ask for their money. The weather was getting warm; it wouldn't be so uncomfortable a thing to do. Big business went to see Congress, he pointed out; why not the veterans? It was no good to send letters or sign petitions—they could be filed away. His speech fell flat. The men thought the bill would be voted on soon anyway.

He went back to searching for a job, thinking of the bonus as the substitute for that long-dreamed-of new start: work. Without the bonus there was nothing to look forward to but the shiny shoulders of the man in front of him in the breadline.

At the end of April at an outdoor meeting of ex-servicemen he spoke again asking for a march on Washington. No one was interested. Then in May the bill was shelved by the House Ways and Means Committee. From then on the ex-servicemen held meetings every day, and every day the crowds got larger. The

thought or desire for revolution was never there. It was rather
that the years after the War had been so prosperous. They'd
had cars, their own places, suits, ties, electricity, running-water
toilets, it was all so different from the lives of their turn-of-the-
century youths. The papers, the *Saturday Evening Post*, the
American Magazine, the radio had said in the great years that
they could be rich. Now they were shuffling through the breadlines. On May 10, 250 men from the Portland area voted to go
to Washington and tell Herbert Hoover and those birds in Congress that the doughboys wanted what was coming to them, and
wanted it now.

The veterans got a sign reading "Portland Bonus March—
On to Washington" and a drum. Carrying their sign and marching to the drum in the manner in which they had been taught
fifteen springs before, they paraded to the Union Pacific freight
yards. The 250 men had a total of thirty dollars. All through
the evening they waited for the night train out, joking and
horsing around like the young rookies of 1917 they once had
been. But none of the trains stopped. The engineers had been
ordered to go on through by the railroad officials. At midnight
the taillight of the last freight East disappeared into the distance.
The men did not disperse, but bedded down in empty freight
cars standing by the right-of-way. When they got up in the morning five of their number canvassed restaurants in the area for
enough coffee and bread so that everyone got a good breakfast.

They agreed that anyone who might sign on as they headed
East had to show evidence of wartime service and swear to
"uphold the Constitution of the United States to the best of my
ability and swear an unswerving allegiance to its flag." More
than one hundred professions were represented in their ranks:
clerks, lumberjacks, railroad men, a sign painter, a prizefighter.
When the sun was up a train halted in the yards and the men—
their number increased now to 280—lined up silently on each
side of the cars. The Union Pacific people were reluctant to argue
with them and indicated they could occupy, if they wished,
several empty stock cars. The animal dung was still there from
previous runs, but they clambered on board. It was like the

"Forty and Eights" of France, they said to each other, the forty men and eight horse railway cars that had borne them toward the sound of the German guns. And they were off.

At Pocatello, Idaho, the cars were shunted to a dusty siding, and there in a vacant and gale-blown lot on a windy spring day the men considered more carefully what they were about. Waters made a speech from the top of one of the cars, and the men elected him regimental commander. He made the ex-fighter Mickey Dolan leader of six military policemen, and appointed a regimental supply officer who would take charge of contributions. They voted that there would be no drinking, no panhandling, no "indulgence in talk attacking the government or engaging in any actions unbecoming a gentleman and a soldier."

In Pocatello, with the permission of the city authorities, they staged a parade through the business district, the mass of men marching down the center of the street to the beat of the drum, four of their number walking on the sidewalks with hats held out. They got twenty dollars.

They went over the mountains and down to the prairies in a series of boxcars, veterans' groups at the stops giving them food, with parades staged in the main towns. Their numbers swelled, with each new man—"recruit," they said—being carefully checked for evidence of his wartime service. At Cheyenne, Army kitchens from a local unit were drawn up at the tracks, the young soldiers serving out hot food to those who had preceded them in the service. A week out of Portland the mayor of Council Bluffs told them a little girl in the local hospital needed a blood transfusion. Waters had the bugler sound general assembly. He told the men about the little girl and asked for volunteers. The entire group stepped forward.

The veterans went to the yards of the Wabash Railroad and asked the trainmaster for a hand in making up the night train. He said there positively would be no empty boxcars. Waters argued with him and finally he said that if the men rode at all they would have to ride on the tops of filled cars, even though the roadway ahead was rough and winding and that it would be very dangerous to ride on the roofs. As he spoke the trainmen on the tracks were waving go-ahead signals with their lanterns and the engineer was answering with whistles. But when the train tried to start there was a great hissing of air. Waters' men had uncoupled the cars. The trainmaster called the police, who refused to intervene. The sheriff's office would not send help either. Nothing could be done but allow the men into empty freight cars.

At St. Louis the train halted before a mass of police armed with riot guns. The police seemed amazed to find the men were not the hooligans and roughnecks they had evidently expected, and the chief gave Waters five dollars. The men lined up and marched twelve miles to the Baltimore & Ohio yards in East St. Louis, Illinois; there was a river toll booth en route but the collector made no move to ask for money.

In the yards they found food contributed by the American Legion and the Veterans of Foreign Wars. They also found fifty railroad police and the chief special agent of the B & O who told them they could not ride on. The railroad crews were under orders to confuse the men, and shifted trains and engines back and forth. But Waters' transportation committee was able to see through the various stratagems. Finally the word came that a train was leaving on the third track; Waters blew a whistle and the men followed him in military columns of two up onto the train, into the coal gondolas, and on the boxcar roofs. The train did not move and the men got down from it and fell asleep on the track cinders.

From all up and down the B & O line railroad police gathered, about one hundred and fifty of them, and people drifted out to watch—"civilians" to Waters and his men.

A day went by and nothing moved East. Perishable freight and rush consignments piled up, and the first big stories started appearing in newspapers all over the country. Suddenly the men became "the Bonus Army." And with the name and the newspaper stories there sprang up new segments: four hundred men in San Francisco organized into two regiments; one hundred men in Sacramento; three hundred men walking from Slidell, Louisiana, to Bay St. Louis, Mississippi, to grab a freight North; a group of Texans with a burro trained to shake his head from side to side at the question, "Do you like Hoover?" and nod it vigorously at "Are you in favor of the bonus?"; and a group from the South holding prayer meetings in swaying boxcars.

In East St. Louis the impasse continued. The men of the Bonus Army were unshaven and covered with dust, but each had with him some little reminder of War days: an overseas cap, a tunic, a medal pinned on his shirt, old leggings. They were United States veterans carrying, one out of each twenty or thirty men, an American flag. Neither the railroad nor the regular police wanted to move against them. So for a day and a half they sat in the yards until the sheriff's office produced cars, dump carts, and trucks, and took them to the Indiana line, a heavy escort of Illinois State Police traveling alongside. At the line the Indiana State Police took up the task, depositing them at four in the morning at Washington, Indiana. At eight the men were up and waiting by the railroad tracks, eyeing the long lines of railroad police standing ten feet apart, each with a long club in his hands.

But as it turned out they did not need the railroads. For each governor of each state that the various segments of the Bonus Army crossed wanted desperately to see them over the line to the neighboring state. And so the Indiana National Guard appeared with trucks to move them into Ohio. At the line Ohio Highway Department trucks were waiting. By that time the movement was practically doubling in size every few hours, with men gathering everywhere and reports coming in that soon one million veterans would be assembled to demand their money.

In Washington the Deputy Chief of Staff of the United States Army said to the Chief of Staff that they were faced with revolution and that the Bonus Army must be stopped. The Deputy Chief was Brigadier General George Van Horne Moseley. Moseley was an exceptional soldier. In the eyes of such junior officers as Major Dwight D. Eisenhower, who worked in the office next to the Chief of Staff, Douglas A. MacArthur, Moseley was "dynamic," "always delving into new ideas," "an inspiration to the rest of us." Moseley, like Secretary of War Hurley, had studied the work of the Communists' "Unemployed Councils" which sprang up in every area where there was severe unemployment, and whose demonstrations appeared invariably to end in riots.

He had decided that the Bonus Army was the outgrowth of the councils, or at least their spiritual inheritor. Brigadier General Moseley went to Major General MacArthur and told him that the U.S. Army should move on the basis that the Bonus Army men were delaying U.S. mail trains. He suggested that federal troops intervene in all sections of the country where segments of the Bonus Army appeared. MacArthur did not agree, saying the matter had nothing to do with the U.S. Army, which in any event consisted of only one hundred and fifty thousand men, the thirteenth army of the world.

Moseley gave his plan to Secretary Hurley, who told him that it was a good idea but bad politics. The question went up to the President, who rejected Moseley's solution, saying the whole thing was just a "temporary disease." General Moseley brooded about it, but there was nothing he could do for the time being. He worked away on plans aimed at dealing not only with the Bonus Army but with all dissidents.

"Without regard to the mere technicalities of the law," he wrote the journalist Herbert Croly, "properly constituted authority would be able to deal directly with crime" and bad elements, including "those of inferior blood." Malefactors would be sent "to one of the sparsely inhabited islands of the Hawaiian group not suitable for growing sugar. On such an island, in a fine climate, they could stew in their own filth until their cases were finally disposed of with the return of normal conditions. We would not worry about the delays in the process of law in the settlement of their individual cases." He saw "carefully selected military governors installed in all our States and the District of Columbia"; he saw, in fact, an American five-year-plan which in name if not in kind would be similar to that of the Soviet Union. His plan, he often remarked to his friend Assistant Secretary of War Frederick H. Payne, would contain only five words: "five years of martial law." Thus the "Augean stables" would be cleansed.

Brigadier General Moseley was not the only person who viewed the Bonus Army as similar to the Blackshirts whose entrance by train into Rome in 1922 had put Mussolini in power. "I hope," wrote a friend to Presidential Secretary French Strother, "the Administration fully realizes that the movement of these groups of vagabond veterans toward Washington has in it the possible seeds of Revolution." Strother wrote back that the letter had impressed him so much that he had handed it on to the President.

Two and a half weeks after leaving Portland the main segment of the Bonus Army went through Ohio. They were bedded down in a park at Zanesville when a Secret Service man appeared asking for Commander Waters. "Our job is to protect Mr. Hoover," he said. He asked that Waters not leave the men, as he had planned, for a conference with Representative Patman, who was already being referred to as the father of the Bonus Bill. Waters still thought of himself as a soldier and a veteran and he obediently wired Patman that he would not be leaving the main body of troops. So he was with the men from then on, at state line after state line from where official trucks and police escorts rushed the men on. At Cumberland, Maryland, on May 28, they slept on the floor of an old skating rink, and the next day entered Washington, where they were led to a vacant building, once a department store, at Eighth and I streets, Northwest. Pelham Glassford, the commissioner of the metropolitan police, a former brigadier general and the youngest general officer in the American Expeditionary Force in 1918, asked Waters to come and see him. The two men got along well, although their positions were clearly defined not only as trim policeman opposed to seedy down-and-outer, but as officer and enlisted man. Perhaps neither of them thought of Waters as an unemployed and unemployable superfluous being, for he was still an ex-sergeant of American artillery; it was that which had brought him to Washington. After they talked, Waters, dog-tired, asked if he might rest somewhere until "my troops" followed, and Glassford told him there was a courthouse lawn opposite the police headquarters. So the commander of the Bonus Army, only thirty-four, capable of stirring a nation and, indeed, a Europe whose newspapers were now filled with news of the movement he had championed, lay down with Washington's unemployed all around him until Glassford told him his men were arriving.

In a matter of days there were twenty-three separate camps of the Bonus Army in Washington, in dumps, parks, and abandoned buildings. Glassford was constantly in and out of the camps, collecting money and foodstuffs, joking with the men and talking about the good old times. There was that and companionship, discipline, and the word of a boss who was called sergeant and got his orders from the captain, who got his from the colonel, who received his from Waters, all of them telling the men they were indeed men again, with a job to do. They asked Police Commissioner Glassford if he would be their treasurer and he accepted, setting up feeding stations to receive contributions of food and money. Glassford desperately wanted them out. He begged the governors of the states bordering Washington not to send any more men by official transportation. He pleaded with the American Legion and VFW posts across the nation to stop collecting money used to dispatch new units of the Bonus Army to Washington. But the governors and the veterans ignored Glassford's pleas, and as twenty-five thousand men moved in he managed to find places and food.

The commissioners of the District of Columbia were terrified by rumors that a million men would soon descend on Washington. They continued to press Glassford, who tried to keep on the good side of the men while still working to get them to leave. But the men quoted to him that section of the Constitution concerning "the right of the people peaceably to assemble and petition the Government for a redress of grievances." He sent Army bands to play songs that he thought might make them homesick—"California Here I Come," "Georgia on My Mind," "Along the Wabash"—but they thanked him and then had the bands play the old Army tunes.

The biggest camp was in Anacostia Park where the Camden, New Jersey, group had been the first contingent to settle. The men from Camden were led by Joseph Angelo, who had won a Distinguished Service Cross, second only to the Congressional Medal of Honor. Angelo had saved the life of an officer wounded by shellfire in the Argonne. A riveter, Angelo had been out of a job for two years. Within a few hours of the Camden group's arrival, Anacostia Park, which the men called "the Flats," was set up with Armylike company streets and latrines. Soon Angelo's men were joined by over eleven thousand veterans: by those who had blocked the Pennsylvania Railroad yards in Cleveland until the line took them to Pittsburgh and then to Washington; by the Illinois marchers escorted by police as they filed into boxcars; by the Texans whose mascot was a goat named Hoover; by the contingent from Little Rock sent on in a special train furnished by the Missouri Pacific; and by thousands of other marchers waving flags as they arrived in Washington. They represented not only themselves but the ten million unemployed, their wives and their children.

In order to have the Bonus Bill taken out of committee for consideration by the entire membership of the House of Representatives, 145 signatures of congressmen were needed, and in a matter of days the men of each Congressional district were swarming all over the Capitol Building to talk to their representatives, to watch them as they ate in the House dining room, to gather about them as they went to their cars in the evening and to receive them when they came to work in the morning. It was now, the papers said, a matter of an open palm. But that palm might clench into a fist.

Nor did the news from abroad quiet Washington's nerves: "Santiago, Chile, June 4: The first Communist republic in the Western Hemisphere was in process of formation here tonight after the overthrow of the Government of President Juan Esteban Montero." Pictures of President-Elect Hoover touring the Chilean Presidential Palace in 1929 were dug out of newspaper files. There was a red flag flying over that building now.

The men lived on Mulligan stew, beans, coffee. Glassford was feeding them at a cost of six cents per day each. There soon were more than twenty-five thousand, most of them ex-enlisted men, but also some former officers, including one who carried his military field glasses and another wearing his twenties golfing plus-fours. The men uniformly carried reminders of a better past: country club membership cards, pictures of the cars they had been forced to sell, bank books showing good balances in "popped" banks whose assets were now worthless.

Waters, who wore a pair of boots and breeches, was saluted by his men. The men—always "troops" to him—lived in the wrecked cars they had hauled into the camps, in chicken coops hammered together into rooms, in fruit crates and tarpaper shacks, packingboxes, tarpaulin lean-tos and wigwams and wicki-ups with windows made of isinglass from old touring cars. The Army of No Occupation. He decided they ought to be more like soldiers. So he ordered daily marching drills. The former sergeants who once in choker collars and multicolored campaign hats had shouted, "Ready, front!" and "Dress it up!" again flung those commands across this strangest of drill fields.

The troops began to march in front of the Bonus Expeditionary Force's sentry boxes where the military policemen stood at parade rest wearing old helmets and white brassards, past the little hospital contributed by a woman whose brother had died in France, past where the bugle calls summoned them to mess. And into their thinned faces streaked with the dust of Washington's summer there came, it seemed to those who watched, a look of pride. They had been youngsters when they learned these things, John Dos Passos thought, a goulash of faces and dialects; now there was a sameness about them, "hollow cheeks off breadlines, pale-looking knotted hands of men who've worked hard with them, and then for a long time have not worked." Dos Passos thought, in these men's faces, as in Pharaoh's dream, the lean years had eaten up the fat. They drilled and those of their fellows—"buddies," they said—who were on detail found their eyes growing misty. There were tears in Commander Waters' eyes. "To think of it—after fifteen years," he breathed.

Flies settled over their latrines—"Hoover villas"—and the heat was oppressive. A great fog of dust and foul odors hung over their camps. But still new men kept coming. There was a formation to salute as Old Glory came down the pole. They had chaplains for services and in the evenings they watched sporting events: Pep O'Brien, who had fought Benny Leonard and Lew Tendler and who had been lightweight champion of the Atlantic Fleet, boxed exhibitions. Also there were speeches. "Here's a plant that can turn out everything every man, woman and child in this country needs, from potatoes to washing machines," John Dos Passos heard, "and it's broken down because it can't give to the fellow who does the work enough money to buy what he needs. Give us the money and we'll buy their bread and their corn and their radios. We ain't holding out because we don't want those things; can't get a job to make enough money to buy 'em, is all." Next to Dos Passos a man said, "Now, I'm not a Red, goddamn it. . . ." They sang "Where Do We Go from Here, Boys?"

General Moseley constantly pressed General MacArthur to make some move toward meeting what might be an emergency. When intelligence sources indicated to MacArthur that the speeches were becoming progressively more angry—one man, MacArthur was told, had advocated hanging him on the steps of the Capitol Building—MacArthur ordered Moseley to take some precautionary steps. Moseley secretly had Army Reserve tanks transferred from Fort Meade, Maryland, to the nearby Fort Myer. Trucks also were made ready for the quick transport of troops into Washington from both posts. The Bonus Expeditionary Force continually held court-martials to drum suspected Communists out of camp, "We're Americans and we want nothing to do with the Reds," Waters told the reporters. But as time went by the city grew progressively more tense. Glassford was bombarded with orders from the district commissioners and the White House that he get the men out, but there were no recommendations as to how he should go about it with a force of police perhaps one twenty-fifth the size of the BEF, which was popularly supposed to have supplies of dynamite and guns.*

At first the camps had been something of a tourist attraction for District residents, who came down on weekends, very often bringing food or cigarettes for the veterans. But donations began to fall off as the BEF began looking like a permanent fixture in the city. ("We'll stay here until 1945 if necessary to get our bonus," Waters announced in what he called a communiqué.) Despite the BEF rule against panhandling it soon became impossible to park a car for more than a moment in any part of the District without a veteran coming up with a rag and an offer to clean the windshield. Housewives took to answering their

* There were no arms of any kind.

doors with the safety chain in place. "Dime, lady? I was overseas." The men were never belligerent but always unsettling.

On June 7, a week before the Republican convention, at
twilight, the Bonus Expeditionary Force paraded up Pennsylvania Avenue, twenty-five thousand strong. They massed at the
Ellipse in columns of four formed into six regiments. They carried hundreds of American flags and the local American Legion
and VFW posts sent bands and bugle corps. They had signs:

THE BONUS OR THE BREADLINE
OUR WIVES AND CHILDREN ARE CRYING FOR OUR BONUS
FOOD AND CLOTHING NOW, NOT A TOMBSTONE LATER
CHEERED IN '17: JEERED IN '32
WILSON'S HEROES, HOOVER'S BUMS
1917, BERLIN OR BUST. 1932, BONUS OR BUSTED

During the war days some of them had paraded the other
way, from Capitol to Ellipse, and at the funeral of the Unknown
Soldier in 1923. Now as they tramped they looked over toward
the White House, but they could see no one looking out of the
curtained windows.

They went up the avenue, their faces set with concentration as they kept step. And in fact they marched very well, the
turns executed with snap and precision and the lines dressed.
As they swung up Pennsylvania Avenue in their shabby ranks,
night began to fall; and when they were finished it was entirely
dark. A reporter for the *Washington Star* thought back to the
parade of the First Division in 1919, the War's last great parade,
the equivalent of the Grand Review of the Union Army in 1865,
and it seemed to him that these men now, who had then
marched behind Pershing, were coming back not to tear down
the Capitol but to ask of it shelter for the night. From the
White House there was no comment and no sign of the President's attitude or reaction, save for an increase in the number
of policemen seen in the building's vicinity. Rumors spread in
the BEF that since their arrival the President had never ventured to come below the second floor.

Back in camp, Joe Angelo, the New Jerseyite with the

Distinguished Service Cross won for saving an officer's life, dug a hole six feet deep into the dust and soil of Anacostia Flats and had his buddies shovel the dirt back over him with only a stovepipe sticking up in order that he might breathe. His buddies charged a dime to allow Washington's citizens to approach and talk with the man in the ground, the "living corpse."

"This is a swell country where you got to be buried alive if you want to eat," Angelo called up through his stovepipe.

Inevitably he was asked how long he would stay down there.

"Till they give me my bonus. You tell them to put that in the papers. If they don't vote the bonus they're going to have to erect a monument here where a wearer of the DSC starved to death."

On June 9, as the Republicans gathered in Chicago, Glassford mustered up a fleet of trucks and had them call at the various BEF camps with an offer of free transportation out of town. No one took him up on it. "No force on earth except death is going to get us out of Washington until the bonus is paid," Waters said. "Let everybody in this country know that we simply are not going to move an inch from our encampments until we get the bonus. That's simple and easy to understand, isn't it?"

Official Washington vented its frustration on Glassford, saying he was making the city into a "hotel for bums." With money donated to him in his capacity as Treasurer of the Bonus Expeditionary Force, he bought 200 old tents for the men, and arranged for them to shower now and then in the armories of the District of Columbia National Guard.

They needed the tents and showers, for conditions at the camps were vile. The journalist Sasha Petrovna wrote of how in Russia in 1907 he had asked for water in a small village and had been given it in a sardine can. It was the only vessel the village had, salvaged from the garbage of a rich landlord. Now, Petrovna wrote, sardine cans and tomato cans were used as cups by United States veterans, who wore them hooked on their belts. "Nineteen thirty-two," Petrovna wrote. "In Washington. I feel sick to the stomach."

On June 11 they celebrated the day the Marines and doughboys took Belleau Wood, the first of many celebrations of the great moments of fourteen and fifteen years earlier, the first draft call, the push into the Argonne. In the House of Representatives debate began on the bill. The arguments against it drove the men mad with frustration. "What do we care about the gold standard?" they cried. "The government's got plenty of printing presses. Use them to print us some money so we can get some food for our families and pay the rent." The representatives opposing the bill said there could be nothing for the Bonus Army.

In the evenings at the camps speakers got up on improvised platforms set in the mud. To roars of applause they pointed out that they weren't even asking for a loan, just what was due them.

In the House they had their champions. One was Representative Edward Eslick of Tennessee. "I want to turn from the sordid side," he said, then hesitated, put out his hand and fell heavily to the floor. His heart had stopped by the time the other congressmen reached him. It was the first death on the floor of the House in a century. Three days later, under a blistering sun, each man hatless and grimly impressive in his silence, eighteen thousand veterans escorted Eslick's coffin to Union Station for its last trip home. They marched four abreast with no banners or placards, only American flags.

Washington that June was hot and humid as always, and also wet. It rained almost every day, drenching the men and turning Anacostia Flats and the other score of encampments into seas of mud. The men began to spread out all over the District; no one could be sure whether when he came to work in the morning he would find half a dozen veterans sleeping in the entryway of his building or store. Rumors spread that the War Department had ordered local high school drill teams to remove the bolt assemblies from their rifles out of fear that those weapons might find their way into the hands of ex-soldiers who knew how to use them all too well. And there were rumors that military police batons were being issued to all troops at Fort Myer, that tear gas squads were being organized and that the White House police were holding practice sessions in grenade-throwing. The harried congressmen facing the vote on the bill quickened their pace when they saw ragged veterans approaching them, and then almost ran as if the devil were at their heels.

The number of men kept growing at the rate of one thousand a day and an increasing number of them brought their wives and children to make the squalid camps more like cities than the military bases they attempted to emulate. In California Royal Robertson set out with a large group of veterans and their families traveling in dilapidated jalopies and relying for gasoline upon filling station owners intimidated by the sight of a hundred grim and hungry men. Robertson led his caravan across the desert into El Centro, California, where he was greeted with fifteen tons of watermelons contributed by the populace, plus seven private airplanes flying in circles overhead. He was tall and thin and wore a neckbrace that held his head in a straight and unmoving and somehow menacing angle. He told the reporters he expected to enter Washington with fifty aircraft at his disposal. His words frightened everyone in the capital from senator to post office clerk.

Beyond the currents of sudden unrest that would without warning set five thousand men to shouting, "We want shelter!" or "Let's march on the Capitol!" there was a growing hatred of two men: Mellon and Hoover. Mellon was in England as ambassador but the men still spoke and thought of him as the representative of the rich and powerful who somehow had failed them, or, worse, had deliberately reduced them to this. The *BEF News*, put out from an Anacostia Flats shack equipped with one old typewriter, spoke of the personality of the President and said, "Millions of people feel that they are thwarted by the President himself. They are convinced he is hostile to their welfare, and thus have no hope that he will ever lead them out of their misery."

At Anacostia and the other camps tiny miniature cemeteries containing two tombstones appeared.

On June 13 the House voted to pay the bonus immediately. There remained now the Senate. Eight thousand veterans massed in front of the Capitol to await the Senate's vote. At Anacostia ten thousand more prepared to join them, but the police raised

the 11th Street Bridge connecting Anacostia with Washington
and so isolated the men at the Flats. A minesweeper was
brought up the Potomac and docked outside the camp, its guns
trained on the tin shacks, junked cars and chicken wire. The
men at the Capitol did not know their buddies were unable to
join them.

The men crowded every square inch of the area in front of
the Capitol Building, spilling over into the plaza before the
Library of Congress. They moved up the Capitol steps, the police
managing to keep open only a thin lane for the senators arriving
to vote. But few senators cared to brave the thousands of
ragged men; those who did heard menacing cries of "We want
the bonus!" and taunts of "Did you get your orders from Wall
Street?" The great majority of the senators used the tunnel
connecting the Capitol with the Senate Office Building in which
Glassford had hidden every available policeman and detective
from the District's force.

Glassford had also arranged with the Army for a band to
come and serenade the men; and as the debate before the vote
drew to its close inside, the men sang along with the tunes of
the War, but with new words:

> "Pay the bonus,
> Pay the bonus,
> Pay the bonus everywhere, everywhere,
> For the Yanks are starving,
> The Yanks are starving,
> The Yanks are starving everywhere."

The songs and the spontaneous bursts of cheering and boos
could plainly be heard inside the Senate Chamber: three cheers
for Waters, three cheers for Glassford; three boos—far louder—
for Hoover. The sun went down as the senators ended their debate; outside in the twilight a young girl got up on the steps and
sang for the veterans. Her voice reached out to them where
they stood or sat on the steps where Presidents are sworn in and
beyond into the park:

"There's a long, long trail a-winding
Into the land of my dreams."*

The last sunlight caught at a locket on her young breast. Looking at her curly brown hair and young face, men thought of how it had been when she was a baby and they were flocking to the recruiting stations. It had been a long time ago.

"Till the day when I'll be going down that
long, long trail with you."*

At nine-thirty the senators voted. A messenger came and whispered to Waters, "They want you inside." After five minutes Waters came back. The veterans were all on their feet waiting for him to speak. "Prepare yourself for a disappointment, men. The bonus has been defeated, sixty-two to eighteen." Some of the veterans shouted and waved their fists. But most of the eight thousand remained silent.

"This is only a temporary setback," Waters called. "We are going to get more and more men and we are going to stay here until we change the minds of these guys." His voice turned husky. "You're ten times better Americans than the senators who voted against the bill."

Inside, in the bright chamber, the senators sat wordlessly in their seats, afraid of what might be coming, afraid to leave for fear the streets would be unsafe.

But the Bonus Expeditionary Force stood silent, Waters thinking that if one wrong word was said, the eight thousand men would storm the Capitol. Pale in the harsh spotlights, he shouted, "Now go back to your camps. There is no more to be done tonight."

Nobody moved. A group of reporters standing by Waters broke, turned tail and ran.

Inside, Senator Hiram Johnson said, "This marks a new era in the life of our nation. The time may come when this folderol— these trappings of government—will disappear, when fat old men like you and me will be lined up against a stone wall."

Outside Waters cried, "We are not telling you to go home. We are just asking you to obey the law and not antagonize the authorities."

The men stood silently. The reporter Elsie Robinson thought to herself that in the bitter faces she saw a menace she had never seen before, that with it was an emptiness deeper than a hunger for food.

"Tell them to sing 'America,' " she whispered up to Waters. He did so and some of them obeyed. Then the whole of the mass took up the song: "America, America, God shed His grace on thee . . . thy amber waves of shining grain . . . from sea to shining sea." Then they marched away.

Chapter Fourteen

THE LAST HOPE for the bonus was gone, but the men hung on, talking about the mud of Amiens, the Argonne Forest's German sharpshooters, Camp Gordon in the sunrise, and just one break, the bonus.

With the President's expressed approval the Senate passed a bill offering free railroad tickets home to any member of the BEF, the amount of the trip to be deducted from the man's bonus in 1945. Many of the men took the tickets. Then they hung around Union Station, selling the tickets cut-rate to travelers. Waters repeatedly said that they would never go home until they got their bonus. And the men moved farther and farther from the boundaries of their now stinking and fly-infested camps. They took over abandoned buildings, the sidewalks, Washington's parks.

The avowed Communists of their number set up their own camp, pariahs of the main body of the BEF. From it they sallied forth for a march on the White House, where Glassford's police met them. For more than an hour downtown Washington was a battlefield, with nightsticks rising and falling on the Communists' heads, and thick layers of police with a tear gas canister on each hip standing in front of the White House. "Hoover Locks Self in White House," said a *New York Daily News* headline.

In a sense it was true, for the President had indeed locked himself away from the BEF, turning down Glassford's repeated requests that he meet with Waters and a few of the other leaders, that he reach out, give them something to cling to, say to them that he was their Commander-in-Chief, that they were still America's soldiers in heart if not in fact, that he regarded them as his own, but that the country could not do what they asked. Glassford said he could even go to their camps in "perfect safety and dignity." He need only go for a little while, inspect their lines, receive their salute. But he would not go.

Speaking through the voice of the District of Columbia commissioners, the President ordered the men to leave in two weeks or be sentenced to six months in the workhouse on charges of vagrancy. Waters told the reporters in reply, "We didn't ask Hoover if we could come here, and we won't let him tell us when to leave." The Communist leader John Pace said, "Hoover is lucky if we don't decide to move into some of those spare bedrooms in that chateau of his. He'd better not crowd us." The men of the BEF grew more menacing, refusing to move out of a Treasury-owned building with shouts that when the Treasury paid the bonus they'd leave.

Washington was a sleepy Southern town, not unlike the provincial capital of a minor European power. The men, very much in evidence in its uncrowded streets, frightened the people, the congressmen and senators; they frightened the Vice President, Charles Curtis. The butt of jokes, he had made himself particularly laughable by social pretensions which appeared to demand that he dine out each night at the behest of whatever group asked him, no matter how obscure its origin. On July 14, the day the mobs stormed the Bastille in the French Revolution, Curtis looked out of the window of his Capitol office and saw a group of BEF men. He convinced himself that they were bent on destruction and ruination. On his own authority, which existed only in his own mind, he called out two companies of Marines. They were borne to the Capitol in trolley cars and debarked wearing trench helmets and with bayonets fixed. The BEF men somehow thought that, like the Army bands, the Marines had come to entertain them with fancy drills or a small parade. They broke into cheers and dipped their soiled American flags. Enraged, Glassford ordered the Marines withdrawn, adding that he was fed up with "meddlers."

Another meddler soon appeared in the form of Major General (Ret.) Smedley Butler. He had spent his life in the Marine Corps but had left under a cloud after slandering Benito Mussolini by saying the Italian dictator was a hit-and-run driver. General Butler was a flamboyant man of great personal leadership qualities but limited restraint. He drove up to Anacostia Flats and when he got out of his car a former Marine cried, "Hi, buddy! Remember that time in France you took a cigarette out of my mouth and smoked it?"

"Sure do!" shouted Butler and went up to a rickety platform to cry out, "I'm here because I've been a soldier for thirty-five years and I can't resist the temptation to be among soldiers. If you guys don't hang together, you aren't worth a damn!"

They roared out their approval of a former general officer telling them what they wanted to hear.

Shortly the child of a South Carolina veteran died in a local hospital of pneumonia; the attending nurse said, "the poor little fellow was nearly starved when he was brought here."

Waters told the reporters, "Starvation killed Johnny Greer and it's going to get some more of us, too, if we're not fed. Here we are, the defenders of a nation, in the capital of the richest country in the world, and we are not getting enough to eat. There is something wrong with the picture. I can't understand it, myself. We were heroes in 1917, but we're bums today."

Congress headed toward a July 17 adjournment and as it did so the Californian in the neckbrace, Royal Robertson, arrived with five hundred men, the final group to join those who had been in Washington for two months. His threatened fifty airplanes did not materialize. But even without them there was something menacing, even terrifying, about the man, his tall, skeletonlike form, his head held rigidly pointing toward the sky. His men camped around the Capitol and went to sleep on the lawns. The police turned on sprinklers to drive them away. They got up, formed in a line and began to march around the Capitol. Within hours their slow shuffling parade was called the

"Death March," and even the other, earlier members of the BEF watched it in awe. Robertson, with his head held in grotesque jutting position, led them as they went slowly and noiselessly in their circling trip. Many of the men wore the spiral leggings of 1918 and those leggings came undone and trailed behind them. Their feet swelled in Washington's heat which even at midnight stood at ninety degrees, but they did not stop. Some were barefoot, their shoes put aside on the curb, but they continued on, as utterly silent as were the crowds that came to stare.

The whole of the Bonus Army, perhaps thirty thousand strong, were gathered by the Capitol, and the men of the Death March shuffled noiselessly through the lanes when on July 17 the Congress met to adjourn. Two days earlier the Lord Mayor of Weimar, seat of the German Republic, was beaten almost insensible by mobs invading the Rathaus chanting, "Hunger . . . Hunger . . . Hunger." In New York the 106 members of the Italian Olympics team arrived for the games in Los Angeles dressed in Fascist uniform and massed on the decks of the *Conte Biancamano* singing the Fascist anthem "Giovinezza."

The senators and representatives arrived for the final proceedings of the Congress literally trembling with fear at the ominous roars that arose from the packed masses of veterans. Congress must not adjourn, the men shouted, and became disorderly, pushing up against the solid lines of police trying to hold them back from the steps. Commissioner Glassford leaped off the motorcycle sidecar in which he traveled and ran in his high boots to fling his weight against the pushing veterans. The police line held for a moment and then parted as the BEF rushed through and up onto the steps.

"Don't shoot, don't shoot, don't shoot!" Glassford yelled over and over again to the police with their hands on the butts of their revolvers.

The wires flashed with calls for police reserves, and someone telephoned to Fort Myer for cavalry but Glassford countermanded the order.

Secret Service men were everywhere; it had been announced that the President would attend the final session of the Congress to sign last-minute bills. His limousine was drawn up in the White House driveway and recurrent rumors spread that he was en route. In the end the senators and representatives voted to adjourn and then ran to cars and taxis where they sprawled on the back-seat floors so as not to be seen by the jeering and cursing Bonus Expeditionary Force. The President never came.

In the area between Pennsylvania Avenue, Missouri Avenue, Third Street and John Marshall Place stood a number of partly demolished buildings. They were owned by the government—technically by the Treasury. Pennsylvania Avenue, upon which they fronted, was shabby in that area, with quarter-filled hotels, cheap gift shops selling replicas of the Capitol and the Washington Monument. In the plans drawn up by Andrew Mellon's architects, all this would shortly disappear in favor of grandiose new government buildings. To this end leveling work had begun. The fronts of the buildings had been ripped away, exposing the staircases that had once led up from the display floor of an automobile agency. Into these half-wrecks reminiscent of shelled dwellings in France moved the Sixth Regiment of the BEF. In mid-July Glassford's police told the Sixth Regiment to evacuate the buildings so that the planned work might proceed. The men shouted back that they knew damned well that Mills and the Treasury owned the buildings and that when Mills and the Treasury put the bonus into their pockets they would leave the buildings. Not before.

On July 22 the men were flatly told to leave or be evicted by force. The men refused to move. Glassford went to the district commissioners and told them the situation. Three conversations with the President followed, and the order was rescinded. At once a rumor spread through Washington quoting Glassford as saying he would resign rather than order the forcible evacuation of the buildings; he did not want to be responsible for bloodshed. A representative of the commissioners told the press that Glassford had written the commissioners a letter on the subject but that it would not be made public because it made "certain references to the possibility of riots."

On that day, July 22, the President signed an act allowing the lending of one hundred and twenty-five million dollars of government money for loans to homeowners unable to get loans from private sources; money also was made available to building and loan associations and other institutions involved in construction projects and the holding of mortgages. The previous day he signed a bill allocating more than two billion dollars for loans to states and municipalities for local relief and for the financing of public works.

With the signing of these bills, which he called the last great cog of the reconstruction machine he had created, all the indices suddenly shot up. Dinner pails for hundreds of thousands of workers were packed for the first time in years as the shifts were called back to work; silent machines were made to hum again. The newspapers said jobs for two million men would be created by the President's measures; editorials said that perhaps it was bad luck to say so, but that perhaps it was all over now. President Hoover had said many times before that the Depression was over. What else could he do, he asked his aides, say that it would go on forever? But this time he completely believed the thing was finished. Wheat prices went up in a straight line, and with them went the hope of the long freight trains filled with grain going across the prairies. Roosevelt would become a footnote in history, the defeated and discredited frivolity who had lightly thought to do away with traditional America, the America of the Fathers, of the dreams and songs. It was now just a question of advancing on all fronts and rolling back the nightmare. And a part of that process involved the rebuilding of the area around Pennsylvania Avenue and Third Street. So the Sixth Regiment must go. And the Bonus Expeditionary Force must go. To that end, Secretary of War Patrick J. Hurley sent for Waters.

Waters came with an aide and was shown into a room where the Secretary and the Chief of Staff awaited him. Hurley was straightbacked and brisk in a military fashion, and Waters thought him an attractive man. MacArthur was in civilian clothing—officers of the War Department wore mufti by Army regulations—and seemed to Waters as "prim and affable as a teller in a small-town bank." The men began their talk and as they did so MacArthur began to pace the floor. The talk went on for five hours, and during the entire period MacArthur never once ceased his walking up and down. He smoked cigarettes continually, using a long ivory holder, always a fresh holder for each cigarette, new ones coming from a batch on the desk.

Waters' aide was Doak Carter, who held the rank of major in the BEF and who, like Waters, still thought of himself as a soldier for all his tattered clothing. He spoke formally, like an officer addressing a superior. "I would like to convey to you, Mr. Secretary," Carter said, "on behalf of the veterans in Washington the fact that in case any serious upheaval develops from the activities of Communists or others inimical to our government, the BEF would be proud to serve in the front line of defense. We still love our country and will fight to preserve it."

The idea exasperated Hurley. Hurley loved the military service, liked to be referred to by his wartime rank of colonel, and believed entirely in the President and the Administration. He was a self-made millionaire living in the house that had been Charles Dawes's when Dawes was Coolidge's Vice President, and it was upsetting to him to have these two shabby men talking to him as if they were something other than the menace he conceived them to be.

"Under no circumstances would we accept such an offer," he said. "We have plenty of troops to protect this government. We don't need you and we don't want you." It was a cruel way to put it. "The American Army, yours, mine, and every citizen's, can take care of that."

"Well, Mr. Secretary, I don't mean to be insolent, but I must remind you that such a feeling did not exist toward us a few years ago."

"I was not Secretary of War in 1917. I was one of you."

"Well, your predecessor didn't feel that way."

Hurley talked of how there was no suffering in the country, no excuse to be homeless or broke.

Waters said, "I don't know where you get your information from, Mr. Secretary."

"I have recently taken a journey across America . . ."

"You must have talked to the wrong people."

Hurley began to speak about how anyone who wanted to work could amass a fortune. This was America. He himself, he pointed out, had begun with a cow and a pig and a few acres of land and was now a millionaire. It was beyond comprehension what these men were doing here. "I implore you to lead them out," he said. But if Waters would not do so, he had better keep in mind the fact that troops were ready for any emergency.

Waters did not need to be told. For days past rumors circulated that the officers of the District of Columbia National Guard companies were sleeping at the armories, that planes loaded with gas bombs were fueled and ready for action at the nearby military airports, that all leaves for the Regular Army had been canceled. To Waters it seemed that the Secretary's reference to troops indicated a willingness to use those troops. Waters turned to MacArthur. "If the troops should be called out against us," he asked, "will the BEF be given the opportunity to form in columns, salvage their belongings and retreat in orderly fashion?"

MacArthur halted his patrolling of the floor for an instant. "Yes, my friend, of course."

His answer reassured Waters. At least they would not be driven out like rats, he thought to himself. He agreed to order the men out of the Pennsylvania Avenue and Third Street buildings. But the BEF as a whole would not leave Washington.

At nine-thirty in the morning, July 28, Waters had assembly blown before the buildings. When the men formed up he told them they must leave. A chorus of shouts arose: "By God, Waters, have you lost your nerve?" "How much did you get for selling out to Hoover?" "What about 1945?" Waters shouted back that he had made an agreement and that the men must stick to it. They grumbled but after some more talk agreed to accede to his order. At that moment the New York Stock Exchange was beginning its best day of the year, stocks leaping up in response to the economic uprise that was manifest all over the country. On that day, also, Ambassador Mellon was landing in New York from London, home for a vacation. The men were turning back into the buildings when a messenger arrived with an order from Mills that the area must be evacuated in the next ten minutes.

The abruptness shook Waters. He read the men the order and said, "You're doublecrossed. I'm doublecrossed."

One hundred policeman began running a rope barrier around the buildings, and federal agents came to back them up. Prodded, the men started getting their things together. The atmosphere was reasonably good; nine-tenths of the policemen were fellow veterans who only a couple of hours earlier had been tossing baseballs back and forth with the members of the BEF. For an hour or so the evacuation proceeded calmly.

It was two months from the day when the BEF had arrived in Washington. In that time the men had committed no crimes beyond panhandling and sleeping on the sidewalks. They had gone across the nation with no criminal act other than riding the rods. Their first major crime was the throwing of a brick which came arching from one of the buildings to strike a policeman and knock him down. Instantly the air was filled with flailing nightsticks and more bricks. Glassford rushed up a flight of stairs exposed to the street because the wall had been torn down, and yelled at the men to stop fighting.

The police already had their guns in their hands. Shots sounded and William Hrushka, thirty-seven, eighteen months overseas, gassed and shellshocked, dropped, mortally wounded. Another man fell; he would die in the hospital. The veterans battered at the police and seemed to be driving them back but Glassford, his gun in its holster, shouted as a policeman fell from a blow, "Hey, you fellows, you've just knocked out a Distinguished Service Cross man." The fighting went on; the air filled with bricks. Glassford yelled, "Those bricks are pretty hard, boys! Let's call off those bricks." The fighting slackened for a moment and his voice could be heard clearly. "How about let's stop for lunch?" The men put down their bricks and the police put away their guns. The fighting had lasted for perhaps five minutes.

Afterward the men went back to evacuating the wrecked buildings. But it did not matter now. Riot, thrown bricks, a dead man, policemen in the hospital—all this immediately reached the three District commissioners. Along with the first reports came word of a great crowd gathering near the spot where the flurry had taken place—veterans who had trudged up from Anacostia mingling with citizens of Washington who alighted from trolley cars to see what was going on and remained to speak in hushed voices.

The instinct of the commissioners was to ask the President for troops. On Secretary Hurley's advice, the President asked them to put it into writing. The commissioners dutifully responded:

It will be impossible for the Police Department to maintain law and order except by the free use of firearms which will make the situation a dangerous one; it is believed, however, that the presence of Federal troops in some number will obviate the seriousness of the situation and result in far less violence and bloodshed.

As soon as he had the message in his hand, Hurley told the Chief of Staff to order out troops. That was at 2:50 P.M. Hurley had written the orders out in advance, days or perhaps even weeks before:

To: General Douglas MacArthur,
    Chief of Staff, U.S. Army
The President has just now informed me that the civil government of the District of Columbia has reported to him that it is unable to maintain law and order in the District.

You will have United States troops proceed immediately to the scene of disorder. Cooperate fully with the District of Columbia police force which is now in charge. Surround the affected area and clear it without delay.

Turn over all prisoners to the civil authorities.

In your orders insist that any women or children who may be in the affected area be afforded every consideration and kindness. Use all humanity consistent with the due execution of the order.

                                    Patrick J. Hurley,
                                    Secretary of War

By three o'clock MacArthur had troops assembling at their posts. As the men formed up Hurley and the President held a hurried consultation. The President said the entire Bonus Army should be rounded up and penned in so that the names of all the men, along with their fingerprints, could be taken. That would establish exactly who they were and what their records were. Then the ringleaders could be tried. The whole matter could be reduced to charges, indictments, facts, figures—the President could deal with them then.

Hurley listened and thought to himself that an attempt to pen up this large force might well result in the defeat of his United States Army by mob action in the streets of its own capital. It seemed to him the wrong way to go about the matter. Hoover had no military experience, after all; and Hurley had been an officer.

Hurley was also under the influence of the brilliant Chief of Staff. Douglas MacArthur was the son of a Civil War general officer; he had been First Captain at West Point and something of a legend in the war. Lieutenant Colonel Hurley had a decent enough record, including decorations. But Major General Mac-Arthur had walked around wearing a soft cap in place of a helmet—the Germans had not made and could not make the bullet which would hit him, he said—and had gone over the top at the head of his troops with nothing but a riding whip as a weapon. And MacArthur, spurred on by his deputy chief, Moseley, believed that the Bonus Army was collecting machine guns and armed men, that its creation signaled the beginning of a Communist rebellion all over the country. Hurley listened when MacArthur spoke, and remembered his words even as the President talked. Hurley decided to pen nobody up, but to let MacArthur drive them away and scatter them.

Within two hours the Fort Washington and Fort Myer troops were assembled at that Ellipse from which weeks before the Bonus Army had begun its twilight march up the Avenue— the Third Battalion of the Twelfth Infantry Regiment, the Second Squadron of the Third Cavalry, the First Platoon of Company B of the First Tank Regiment, the Headquarters Company of the Sixteenth Brigade. Units to be held in reserve were on the move to Fort Myer from Forts Meade and Howard in Maryland and Fort Humphreys in Virginia.

At four o'clock the commander of the Sixteenth Brigade, Brigadier General Perry Miles, the officer in charge of the operation, reported to MacArthur in his War Department office.

"We are acting on the order of the President of the United States," MacArthur said. "The cavalry will make a demonstration down Pennsylvania Avenue. The infantry will deploy in line of skirmishers in the rear of the cavalry. You will surround the area on Pennsylvania Avenue and Third and Fourth streets and evict the men in possession there. Use care and consideration toward all women and children who may be in the area."

Major Eisenhower's office was next to that of the Chief of Staff, with only a slatted door between them; MacArthur simply raised his voice when he wanted Eisenhower to come to him. He told Eisenhower the situation was so serious that now at the last moment he had decided to get into uniform and take charge of the operation. He spoke of himself in the third person, as he always did, saying, "MacArthur has decided to go into active command in the field."

Major Eisenhower remonstrated, saying the matter could easily become a riot and it was highly inappropriate for the Chief of Staff to be involved in "anything like a local or street-corner embroilment."

MacArthur said there was "incipient revolution in the air," and therefore he would take the field in uniform and that Major Eisenhower, also in uniform, would accompany him as a special aide.

MacArthur lived in Quarters Number One at Fort Myer, where all his uniforms were. He had none at the War Department. One of his uniforms was sent for,* including breeches and English boots and field tunic with rows of ribbons from the left breast pocket to the epaulet. The two men got into their "pinks" complete with Sam Browne belts.

A few minutes after four the troops moved out. There were some eight hundred of them. The cavalry, commanded by Major George Patton, came clattering down the avenue with sabers drawn. Then came the infantry with bayonets fixed. New-style baby tanks brought up the rear. It was the first action the Amer-

---

* An abiding legend has it that Major Eisenhower personally rushed to Fort Myer for the Chief of Staff's uniform and that the entire operation was held up for the time consumed for the errand.

ican Army had seen since the conclusion of the intervention in Russia just after the War.

From the White House the previous night the President had telephoned the Republican Senate leader, Watson of Indiana, to say the Bonus Army was taking up position on Pennsylvania Avenue; that their staying there was preventing the implementation of construction contracts totaling millions of dollars; that there thus existed a grave question of property rights; that the veterans being there made those property rights insecure; and that "life would soon become so" and that he was thinking of calling out the troops.

Watson reminded the President that he was a candidate for reelection and that to call out troops to disperse the Bonus Army would be a stupendous blunder. Were he in the President's place, Watson added, he would invite Commander Waters and a few aides over for dinner, talk over the situation and ask that they leave peacefully. Then there would be no need for force. That was what a Watson would do and could do. He would have told the men a few jokes, handed out cigars, given them a shot of bootleg alky. But Hoover was not Watson. With an inward sigh Watson told the President that if he had to do it, then at least to do it in as nonaggressive a manner as he could, and with as little bloodshed as possible.

And so the big bays of the Third Cavalry who once, a long time before, had led President-Elect Hoover to his inauguration, came pirouetting down Pennsylvania Avenue, Major Patton shouting orders, the heavy sabers weaving through the air. The cavalrymen went by halted trolleys crammed with homeward-bound government clerks whose eyes popped as they stuck their heads out the windows. Then the cavalrymen were upon the Bonus Expeditionary Force. "Get on, you sons of bitches! Move on! Get out! Get going!"

A dazed veteran staggered down the middle of the street. "I don't have to—" A cavalry saber held flat flashed down and whacked him. "Beat it!" "I don't have to—" Whack! "I want to—" Whack! "Get over there where you belong!" The horse reared in the man's face. "I want to—" Whack!

Crying with rage, the men filled the air with flying bricks.

Some of the missiles hit home and cavalrymen rocked in their saddles, many falling to the pavement. Major Patton was using mounted couriers for communication with his superior officers seventy-five feet away. One of the messengers rushed up—hoofs kicking up dust as the rider reined in—begged to report and said tear gas was about to be fired. The cavalry in extended order parted for the infantry companies to come through, then sheathed their sabers for a moment in the scabbards under their right legs so that their hands might be free to adjust their gas masks. The infantry came through, throwing tear-gas canisters.

A gentle wind blew blue vapors toward the BEF and into the faces of spectators along the sidewalk. Senator Hiram Bingham in a white Palm Beach suit and panama hat covered his face with a handkerchief and ran. Some of the onlookers cursed the soldiers: "Shame! Shame!" "You goddamned bums!"

The cavalry clattered up onto the sidewalks, the troopers yelling, "Clear out! Clear out!" Everyone ran from the plunging horses save for little groups of veterans who stood fast with their flags, tears pouring out of their eyes from the gas, but screaming as they shoved the flags forward, "Yellow bastards! Now hit us!"

The younger cavalrymen grinned sheepishly and hesitated to attack men holding the American flag, but the older non-coms showed impatience. One of them spurred his horse directly at a man carrying a banner, but an officer shouted, "No, no, no!" The infantry came up and wrested the flag away. "You crummy bum," one of the infantrymen said to a former sergeant. The boy was young enough to be the ex-sergeant's son and the older man felt like tearing his uniform off him. But he had that bayonet.

A spectator cried out, "The American flag means nothing to me after this."

MacArthur heard, and snapped, "Put that man under arrest if he opens his mouth again."

The infantry kept pushing on, the tear-gas tins pfutt-pfutting on the pavement. The veterans were moved back into a park. Some of them climbed trees and clung to branches. Below the cavalrymen prodded them with swords and the infantrymen pinked them with bayonets.

The veterans shouted, "Jeez, if we had guns! If we had guns!" Ambulances went up and down the streets picking up prone forms. In the alleys bordering the main streets the cavalrymen routed out veterans trying to hide; now and then a few tried to make a stand, throwing bricks and shouting, "Hoover's Cossacks! Where were you in the Argonne?"

The result was always the same: The young soldiers herded the veterans back toward the river and the bridge to Anacostia Flats. One Negro climbed a tree with a flag and waved it back and forth, chanting, "God that gave us this here country, help us now! God that gave us this here country . . ." A trooper flung a gas tin at the base of the tree and the veteran fell from it to the ground, his flag fluttering. Another veteran grabbed it. "God will avenge us!" men shouted as they ran, their cries mixing with the yells of "Tin soldier! Tin soldier! Yellow, yellow, yellow!" Down the cobblestone streets leading toward Anacostia fled the Bonus Expeditionary Force.

In a couple of hours they were gone to the Flats and with them went the odor of the tear gas slowly blowing away on a southerly wind. The tanks clanked up and took positions with the other contingents on the Washington end of the Anacostia bridge. Field kitchens arrived with rations and as evening came on the troops stacked their weapons and sat down to eat supper.

In the War Department, Brigadier General Moseley, in charge of communications to the troops at the bridge, received a call from Secretary Hurley, who was dining with the President. The President, Hurley told Moseley, absolutely did not want the troops to cross the bridge into Anacostia. Moseley left his office and went to see MacArthur personally. MacArthur got out of his open staff car and in shining boots with spurs walked with Moseley for a few minutes. He was enraged at the message and said in the most emphatic way that he did not want his plans interfered with until they were completely executed. Moseley answered that he had been told to deliver the message and had done so. Now he would ask the Chief of Staff if he might be excused to go back to his War Department office. Shortly after Moseley returned to his office Hurley telephoned again from the White House to ask if the message had been delivered. Moseley told him it had.

Awhile later Hurley called once more to order that the message be repeated to MacArthur: the troops must not cross the bridge. Moseley dispatched Colonel Clement B. Wright, the Secretary of the General Staff. Wright went to the bridge but did not get to speak with MacArthur, the Chief of Staff saying to Major Eisenhower that he was "too busy and did not want either himself or his staff bothered by people coming down and pretending to bring orders."

By then the entire country knew of the battle. The streets of Washington were tensely silent and deserted, but the windows of the War Department and White House blazed with lights. There was no certainty that the veterans might not attempt a counterattack, and a thousand rumors said they would do so with weapons given them by friends in the service, that the Marines had refused to march against the BEF, that the guardhouses were filled with soldiers who would not follow orders, that if the BEF counterattacked the troops on the bridge would march with them to the heart of the city. MacArthur ordered heavy machine guns brought up. Caravans of Army trucks arrived and made U-turns so that the guns in the back might be taken off and emplaced to fire across the bridge. Darkness fell and the fire department brought lighting equipment that shone beams over the lounging troops and horses tethered in picket lines.

At twenty minutes past nine MacArthur ordered the troops into formation. He positioned himself at the head of the column, with Major Eisenhower at his side. He ordered, "Forward march." The troops moved off out of the lit-up Washington side and into the complete blackness of the Anacostia side where the Bonus Army, their wives and children, waited. "Here they come," breathed voices in the darkness.

When the infantry crossed the bridge an order was given and the men stepped off to left and right in files of two. The reporter Thomas Stokes tensely waited for the first shot from out of the silent night, thinking to himself that this moment might one day be recalled as the end of the country as he had known it. It was an experience different from all others of his life. All the misery and suffering, he thought to himself, had finally come to this—soldiers with their guns marching against American citizens. His thoughts at that moment were on the President. He would not try to put himself in the President's position, he thought; he was not able to figure out what he might have done in the President's place. "But this—"

The troops moved forward into the silence and the darkness. Behind them came the cavalry and the clattering tanks. A reporter for the *New Republic* thought to himself that it was absolutely essential that the men stand where they were, essential for their own spirit. But for a moment nothing happened. Fire trucks rode across the bridge, their searchlights reaching out to illuminate all that Anacostia Flats was: rotting half-eaten potatoes, cook-shacks with improvised ice boxes, rusty pots and pans, baskets of onions, kettles of cabbages, a pair of women's worn pink mules and black satin slippers in the straw of a dugout in the ground. There were bits of clothing, ratty-looking mattresses, junked cars with bedding in the rear seats, magazines, greasy and bulging overstuffed furniture from the city dumps jammed into the corners of teepees, rocking chairs, a broken-down hatrack, slotted tin cans for the tobacco fund, a thousand ancient bedsteads, the unit signs from Georgia, Brooklyn, San Francisco—all the states, all the cities—the latrine gullies, the flagpole, the tin sheet-metal hovels and wickiups.

Then the men of the BEF were making their last charge with their sticks and stones. Tear-gas canisters jumped from the infantrymen's belts and arched off into the light from the fire trucks which caught the gleaming fixed bayonets.

And then the Bonus Expeditionary Force was running away, crying, but with a few of its members still trying to fight. One of them threw a brick; it caught Major Patton and he went down in the mud. MacArthur's troops charged and, as they did, someone who remembered France and the rules of war from fifteen summers ago stumbled forward with a white flag. But the real soldiers chased him away with bayonets and sabers.

The men ran and the young soldiers threw their gas bombs. One veteran fled with his baby in his arms; he ran into a cloud of tear gas. His baby would die from that. As the men fled, the shacks began bursting into flames, and soon the flames were two hundred feet high, blocking the men from going back into Washington, even if they could slip through the Army's lines. The leaping flames turned the skies red so that the shipping in the Potomac and the airplane hangars at Bolling Field were put into bold relief; the light could be seen from the Lincoln Study where the President sat.

The BEF fled up Good Hope Hill toward Maryland. A Washingtonian whose father was legal adviser to Glassford thought to himself that it was like the sacking of a defenseless town by Russian Bolsheviks. "There were perhaps a few radicals among them," Frank Easby-Smith wrote a friend, "but who isn't somewhat radical in times like now. . . . Refugees we saw during the War did not equal that pitiful sight."

Europe's sufferers of those days also came into the mind of a member of the BEF who, wandering past the burning huts, came face to face with Glassford. "Mr. Glassford," the man said, "you know what the Belgian children used to say? 'They have burned our beds. They have even burned M'sieu Jesu Christ.' "

Glassford said, "Those were the Germans."

The veteran's wife was along. She said, "These are tin soldiers who dared to come only by night."

"No," Glassford said sadly. "These are the Regulars."

The flames burned on, bidding to consume all of Anacostia Flats. The fire trucks stood by unused but ready for action if the conflagration should spread from the Flats. Something about the fires struck at Major Eisenhower's heart. Secretary Hurley came out to the smoke and shadows and said, "It was a great victory. Mac did a great job. He is the man of the hour." But Eisenhower wondered if indeed all this were so. He told the Chief of Staff he should not return to the War Department, for there would be reporters there and it would be best not to see them. Let the political officials talk, not the soldiers.

MacArthur did not agree and told the press, "It is unnecessary to describe what took place. . . . You all saw it, I think. That mob down there was a bad-looking mob. It was animated by the essence of revolution. The gentleness, the consideration, with which they had been treated had been mistaken for weakness and they had come to the conclusion beyond a shadow of a doubt, that they were about to take over in some arbitrary way either the direct control of the government or else to control it by indirect methods. It is my opinion that had the President not acted today, had he permitted the thing to go on for twenty-four hours more, he would have been faced with a grave situation which would have caused a real battle. Had he let it go on another week I believe that the institutions of our government would have been very severely threatened. I think it can be safely said that he had not only reached the end of an extraordinary patience but that he had gone to the very limit in his desire to avoid friction and trouble before he used force. Had he not used it at that time, I believe he would have been very derelict indeed in the judgment in which he was handling the safety of the country." MacArthur called the men of the BEF "insurrectionists" and said that "if there was one man in ten in that group today who is a veteran it would surprise me."

When the Chief of Staff concluded, a mimeographed sheet was handed out. "The President said: 'A challenge to the authority of the United States government has been met, swiftly and firmly. After months of patient indulgence, the Government met overt lawlessness as it always must be met if the cherished processes of self-government are to be preserved. We cannot tolerate the abuse of Constitutional rights by those who would destroy all government, no matter who they may be. Government cannot be coerced by mob rule.' "

The commander of the cavalry, Major George Patton, knocked out of his saddle by a brick, was treated and returned to duty. Joe Angelo of Camden, New Jersey, who led the first contingent to Anacostia Flats, and who later buried himself in the ground and spoke to the world through a stovepipe, ran up Good Hope Hill into Maryland. Flapping from his shirt was the Distinguished Service Cross given him in 1918 for saving George Patton's life.

PART V

We Have Nothing to Fear

Chapter Fifteen

GOVERNOR ROOSEVELT, smiling, came back from his sailboat to plan his campaign. On July 29 he called his aide Rexford Guy Tugwell, a house guest at the Governor's Mansion, and asked Tugwell to come into his bedroom. Tugwell found Roosevelt sitting up in bed with *The New York Times* on his lap. Photographs of the rout of the Bonus Army the day before dominated the paper.

The governor's wife had felt a spasm of horror when she heard of the Bonus Army's fate; something of that horror made Roosevelt cover the terrible pictures with his hands. He said to Tugwell that they need not talk about Hoover as they had planned. As for himself, he apologized for having suggested him as a Presidential candidate in 1920.

There was nothing left inside the man but jelly, Roosevelt said to Tugwell. Maybe there never *had* been anything. Why hadn't Hoover offered the men coffee and sandwiches instead of letting Pat Hurley and Doug MacArthur loose? He himself, he said, had often been importuned to call out the New York National Guard for various disturbances; he was proud that he had never done so.

Tugwell ventured the thought that perhaps people would consider the President's use of force justified, but Roosevelt said nobody would. He himself might feel sorry for the President if he didn't feel more sorry for the Bonus Expeditionary Force. They must be camping right now on the roads leading out of Washington. They would be in terrible shape, and their families also. He repeated to Tugwell that there was no need to go on analyzing Hoover. The man had been turned inside out. Everyone could see what was there, and wouldn't like it. Roosevelt himself did not like it. He wouldn't feel sorry for Hoover even on Election Day.

Tugwell thought to himself that if Roosevelt had had any doubts about what the result of the election would be, they vanished when he saw the *Times*. He left the room with that conviction. As Tugwell was leaving the room, Roosevelt said that either Hoover had been very different during the War years, or that he hadn't known him as well as he thought. There was something wistful about the way he said it, Tugwell thought.

There was another story in the papers that day. It concerned the reply of the mayor of New York City to the charge of a legislative committee that he was guilty of gross malfeasance of office. The reply was directed to Governor Roosevelt. "Since the day of my birth," Jimmy Walker wrote, "I have lived my life in the open. Whatever shortcomings I have are known to everyone—but disloyalty to my native city, official dishonesty, or corruption form no part of those shortcomings."

The legislative committee said otherwise: that he had accepted what he called "beneficences" from a series of rich men, some of whom owed their fortunes to contracts signed with the city. Walker, the legislative committee charged, had let people give him money, letters of credit for European tours, and the use of private railway cars. Other men had paid his hotel, tailor and florist bills.

So Governor Roosevelt would have to sit in judgment. He did not look forward to it. He had known Walker since 1912, when Walker was a New York State assemblyman and Roosevelt a state senator. He liked Walker, as everybody did, but Assemblyman Walker rebuffed Senator Roosevelt's attempts to be friendly. Roosevelt of the great estate at Hyde Park was, in what Walker called his sidewalks-of-New-York eyes, too high and mighty.

Then Roosevelt came to the governorship of the state and

Walker to the mayoralty of the first city of the state. But the two men grew no closer, although Roosevelt and Roosevelt's wife wished it otherwise. Mrs. Roosevelt asked Walker to come to the Governor's Mansion every time he was in Albany. Mayor Walker, however, preferred the company of his former cronies in the State Assembly and Senate to dining in the mansion with those he called career-seekers. Walker was always like that, neglectful of the great, late to appointments, forgetful. He was not interested in politics, but in songs (his earliest and most abiding ambition was to be a song writer; his most lasting composition was "Will You Love Me in December As You Do in May?"), clothing, prizefights, nightclubs, and, of course, women.

Jimmy Walker was perfect for the New York of the twenties. He wore New York in his buttonhole, they said, with his Irish blarney charm, his smile which no one could resist, his deadpan remark that the speakeasies ought to close earlier because it might make for class hatred when the milkmen saw the drunks coming home in evening clothes. He carried a gold-headed cane and wore a top hat; he was the prize specimen of a big spender of the happy-go-lucky days of the golden bubble, with hundred-dollar tips for hatcheck girls, dates with Ziegfeld Follies beauties at Montauk's casinos, trips to Paris, Bermuda, Louisville for the Derby, Havana, Cannes, Berlin, Los Angeles, Florida. (He took 143 days of vacation during his first two years of office.) "Peter Pan," said Gene Fowler. His friends were Cohan, Jolson, Cantor, Jessel, Fanny Brice, and the mothers of his friends, whom he kissed and made blush. He was the *beau ideal* for greeting visitors to the city and escorting them up the Great White Way under confetti clouds and amidst the cheering of the hundreds of thousands.

His permanent girl was the musical comedy actress Betty Compton, whom he unaccountably called Monk. She was appearing in *Okay* at the Imperial with Gertrude Lawrence and Victor Moore when he met her on opening night in 1926. She was twenty-three; he was forty-six. Mrs. Walker had long grown accustomed to his dalliances, but she loved him none the less for his sweetness, his lightness. She looked the other way and Betty Compton left the stage and lived in style.

But it cost money. Walker raised his salary from twenty-five thousand a year to forty, but it was far from enough for him. So he took "beneficences." Al Smith was against all this, a Catholic flying in the face of the Church, a public official not coming to the Hall on time to do his work right. But Smith could never stay angry with Jimmy. Nobody could. So in 1928 even as Roosevelt placed Smith's name into nomination for the Presidency, it was Walker who nominated Roosevelt for governor. Smith lost; Roosevelt won; Walker went on as mayor. Then came the crash and the breadlines.

Jimmy Walker was wonderful leading a parade of citizens demanding the end of Prohibition; he was the right man in the right place sitting on the tonneau of an open touring car next to Lucky Slim Lindbergh going up Broadway; he was Beau James. Then there came a time when New York could not afford him. He was still immaculate in his spats, still the "darlin' boy"; but men were selling apples on every corner.

So Roosevelt ordered him to Albany in early August to face the charges brought against him by the legislative committee. Walker sat before the governor and the governor's cold Irish-Catholic Special Counsel (Roosevelt was taking as few chances as possible with the big-city Eastern vote) and his defense consisted of "I don't remember" and jokes. His testimony showed he knew nothing of government, and perhaps it was not surprising, for he had never had the patience to read more than one page of typed material at a sitting. Samuel Seabury, the counsel to the legislative committee, was straightlaced, rigid, Protestant, painstaking, all that Walker was not. The contrast between the cases developed by the two men was spectacular, and Seabury's presentation was such that Roosevelt's Special Counsel, Martin Conboy, could only tell the governor that Walker was guilty of all the charges. Nothing so much worried Roosevelt and his advisers as the problem of whether or not to remove Walker from office, but Roosevelt could not make up his mind about what to do.

"How would it be if I gave the little mayor hell, and then kept him in office?" Roosevelt asked his aide Raymond Moley, and then quickly added, "No. That would be weak." Moley was certain from that moment that Walker was finished.

After a dozen sessions before Roosevelt in the Hall of the Governors in Albany, Walker was given a brief recess. The following day his brother George died. After the funeral Walker went to a meeting of Democratic leaders at New York's Plaza Hotel. Smith was there. He said, "Jim, you're through. You must resign for the good of the party." That night Roosevelt sat with some friends and mused aloud about what he should do. The men generally agreed he should not remove Walker, but just reprimand him. As it was, Al Smith's Catholic supporters in the great Eastern states resented Roosevelt. The destruction of Walker, a Catholic, might drive those states out of the Democratic column. Roosevelt said he did not know what to do and indicated that perhaps it would be best to remove Walker, for really that would be the right thing to do. Louis Howe, who had just lit a cigarette, furiously hurled the lit match at the governor. "So you'd rather be right than President!"

Roosevelt said, "Well, there may be something in what you say."

At that moment the telephone rang. Walker had resigned.

Walker went off to tour Europe with Betty, came back, said he might run for mayor again, and then went back to Europe to walk alone on the Croisette at Cannes, to sit on Italy's beaches, telling the few visitors from Broadway, "I wish I were home again." He bore no grudge against Roosevelt, and no one ever knew what the governor had intended to do: remove him, reprimand him, let the whole thing blow over. But it did not matter and Roosevelt kept Tammany Hall and the Catholics on his side, for he had not beaten Jimmy into the ground. The South and the Protestants stayed on his side, too, for he had not let Walker go off scot free.

In the last days of August Roosevelt went West to visit crippled children in hospitals and tell them that he also had been "bitten by a little bug" and could he go swimming with them? His smile dominated the pictures that the photographers took: always a smile, the head thrown back, always tickled to see the people, to introduce "my little boy Jimmy" who stood nearly six-foot-four, and who held his father's arm on the back of the Special or as they made their way to the podium in the hall. His reference to "my little boy Jimmy" was his best line, the reporters thought, and his best way of presenting himself, a man gallant yet joking, intent and yet self-deprecating. "My friends—" he cried; and the people believed they were his friends. For he waved, grinned, seemed happy to see them. His speeches were vague and often self-contradictory. He pledged himself to cut federal spending 25 percent even as he said it was the right of all ten million unemployed men to expect a job from the government. Somehow the people accepted it, thinking, as *Time* said, "He might not know the specific solution. But his heart appeared to be in the right place."

But for all his jokes and the ever-present smile, the governor was shocked by what he saw as he crossed the country. It was far worse than he had thought: the men living under the railroad trestles by the river banks, the hungry, inquiring faces. It seemed to him that it was like Europe just after the War, when, along with Wilson, he had seen the streets filled with yearning adults who had the look of lost children. Roosevelt had read in the eyes of Europe's women the belief that Wilson somehow would save their children from the war and hunger they had known. Now it seemed to him, a decade and a half later, America's women were saying, "We are caught in something we don't understand; perhaps this fellow can help us out."

The governor went to Topeka and talked about the farm problem, and the men who came to hear him shocked Roosevelt's aides. The reporter Lorena Hitchcock, who was very close to Mrs. Roosevelt, thought to herself that the men in their ragged clothes looked like Mongolian peasants seen in the rotogravure sections of the Sunday papers. They stood under a broiling sun in utter silence. It was hard to know what they thought of his speech. But the train had to make two unscheduled stops in Kansas because people from one hundred miles around jammed the tracks to see Roosevelt. Breckinridge Long, Roosevelt's assistant floor manager under Farley at the convention, circulated at the edges of the crowds to hear what they had to say. Long was rich, aristocratic, international-minded. But the people got through to him. Long asked a man if he would support Roosevelt and the man said solemnly and quietly and in an entirely un-demonstrative way, "We are going to change."

They went West and Long saw a cowboy trade 116 cow-hides for one pair of boots. He saw miles of fields filled with rotting potatoes. It did not pay to bring them out of the ground. In Washington State he saw apples, with culls out, selling for eleven dollars a ton; in California the prune crop wasted under the trees. On the way back, in Omaha, big onions sold retail for one penny a pound, and Iowa corn was going for ten cents a bushel and on its way down to seven. In the cities they all noticed how no smoke came from factory chimneys. Back in New York a giant Hooverville flourished along the slaughter-houses near the East River. There were others: in Central Park and along the railroad tracks of Riverside Drive. People went to look at the men on Sundays, staring at them with a strange, in-different curiosity. Most of the men accepted their fate, but some sat with their faces in their hands or with their caps pulled down as far as possible. "Is Hoover going to drive me out of here? He drove me out of Washington."

Breckinridge Long cried, "He has set his face like flint against the American government's giving one cent to starving Americans. He insists that the American way is to unload the responsibilities for their living or starving upon private charity. He calls this individualism. It is an individualism so rugged, to use a favorite word of Mr. Hoover, that it includes even the right to starve."

At the same time Long denounced the "saturnalian expendi-tures" of the Hoover Administration. It was a theme echoed by other Democratic orators. Governor Ritchie declared the Demo-crats, unlike the Republicans, would balance the budget. Carter Glass protested Hoover's mandates by which "the minions of federal bureaucracy are given full sway to distribute huge sums of money picked from the pockets of the American people." John W. Davis, the compromise candidate of '24, cried that Hoover was "following the road to socialism at a rate never before equaled in time of peace by any of his predecessors."

The flood of books denouncing Hoover increased in number

and in vituperation. Dogs instinctively disliked him. He had made millions for himself out of Belgian Relief. He had not played a hero's role at all during the Boxer Rebellion in China, but hid under a bed, dressed in women's clothing. Hoover, said the rumors, had engineered the kidnapping of Charles Lindbergh, Jr., in March, and also the child's murder. He had done it to distract the public's eye from the worsening economic situation. (Even people sympathetic to the President were disturbed by the argument that Hoover's doctrine of rugged individualism and doing-for-oneself had logically resulted in someone's kidnaping the only son of the greatest American hero of the twenties.) Most damning of all, he was not really an American, but a Britisher. Louis Howe enjoyed embellishing this last theme. He created a comic-strip character, with the cartoonist F. Opper doing the art work, and had millions of copies of the character's adventures distributed. The character was a round and tubby creature called "'Erbie." 'Erbie's best chum was a European-looking individual named "'Ropy." 'Erbie forgave 'Ropy his debts and cuddled him while callously shoving a poverty-stricken soul identified as the American taxpayer into a corner with orders that he stay there and starve quietly. There were those who, squeamish, asked Howe if he didn't think the thing was a trifle too subtle, but Howe gaily replied, "Why, I don't expect to do a thing, my dears, but appeal to their blind prejudices."

Howe was having the time of his life in the campaign. The newspapers harped endlessly on his strange appearance but it did not bother him. He took to announcing his telephone calls with a sepulchral "This is the Medieval Gnome speaking." A breathless reporter asked if it were true that he and Governor Roosevelt addressed each other by their first names, and Howe replied, "Yes, and sometimes worse than that." He delighted in reading the letters that came in with advice on how to win the election. ("Get bunches of children to stand on every street corner singing 'Mama, Are All the Hot Dogs Dead?' This will show the people that under the Republicans all the little children are hungry.") Howe heard that the Republicans might launch a whispering campaign to the effect that infantile paralysis eventually affects the brain. He responded by getting a leading polio expert to draft a statement saying that it was not so, with the information included that even so illustrious a figure as Sir Walter Scott suffered the disease as a child. Howe waited for the Republicans to make the charge officially, but they never did, which must have saddened him. He printed millions of little booklets which pointed out that only two years earlier insurance company doctors had certified Roosevelt to be eligible for $500,000 in life insurance.

Grimmer men joined in the fight against Hoover. One was the nominally Republican Senator Hiram Johnson of California. Gritting his teeth, as he always did when he spoke, he said, "When a miracle man fails and a mystery man explodes, instinctively we turn to one who knows and understands and feels with us. . . . In the present cataclysm with eleven million unemployed and suffering, and want on every hand . . . I cannot and will not support Mr. Hoover." Hoover's Administration, Johnson said, was "inept, futile, ineffective, inefficient, disastrous and un-American." Another of the Senate's Republican "progressives," William Borah of Idaho, did not come out for Roosevelt. But more important, he did not come out for Hoover. "William the Silent," the reporters called him. In 1928 he had spoken in fourteen states for Hoover.

Roosevelt visited the autumn state fairs, where he was always "immensely tickled" to see the cowboys and cowgirls, and "delighted" to see the plowing contests. The heat did not bother him, nor the dust nor the interminable parades nor the endless waving of his battered old gray felt good luck hat. Legion bands played War songs for him and sometimes he would sing along, a Presidential candidate throwing his head back and mimicking the crooners' mannerisms as he laughed at himself and they told each other, he and the crowd, to pack up their troubles in their old kit bags.

As before, the governor's speeches were entirely contradictory. Roosevelt would begin by espousing the most conservative policies and end by hinting at a wholesale change in American life. Such fundamental contradictions bothered his advisers but not the voters, who only saw the head thrown back in the confident way.

But others had great reservations about him. The journalist Jay Franklin wrote, "There is a widespread conviction that Franklin Roosevelt lacks guts, that he can't force the pace, and that when cornered he will play dead dog. He is not regarded as a fighter. If he gets into the White House it will be as a blank check. . . . No one knows if he is a statesman or a name." Rabbi Stephen S. Wise of New York's Free Synagogue wrote his friend Professor Felix Frankfurter of Harvard Law School, "I do not mean to argue about Roosevelt with you. You think you know him and evidently you believe you can trust him. I know him and I know how utterly untrustworthy he is the moment any problem arises, decisions or tactics touching which may adversely affect his own political fortunes. I have nothing but horror at the thought of what Roosevelt will be for four years at Washington. . . . I say to you as a liberal and a progressive and a Democrat— you will rue your decision to give your support to him. . . . There is no basic stuff in the man. There are no deep-seated convictions. He is a tremendously agreeable and attractive person, but there is no bedrock in him. He is all clay and no granite."

Frankfurter replied, "I am supporting Roosevelt fundamentally because I think the most urgent demand of the hour is to turn Hoover out. . . . Politics, perhaps you sometimes forget, is a choice of the second best. He is not my ideal of a President, but I do not expect my ideal to become President. Not the least important thing in this world, as I see it, is to do what we can with the meager tools at hand."

The Communist candidate William Z. Foster declared capitalism was doomed. The socialist Norman Thomas said that when men and women searched garbage cans in competition with rats for food the choice was between socialism or catastrophe, which Thomas described as the Democrat Roosevelt and the Republican Hoover. Will Rogers summed it up: "The way most people feel, they would like to vote against all of 'em if it was possible."

Chapter Sixteen

On THE EVENING of the September day when Maine voted for senator and governor (it was Maine's traditional day for local elections) Roosevelt left Albany for another Western tour. Just before the train pulled out the first reports were brought to him. Three precincts in Androscoggin County indicated an enormous Democratic plurality. There must be some mistake, Breckinridge Long decided. The next day, in Cleveland's railroad station, they learned there had been no mistake. Maine had elected a Democratic governor and two senators. No such Democratic sweep had occurred in Maine since before the Civil War.

The night that Roosevelt headed West President Hoover was told about the results in Maine. "It looks pretty dark," the President said to Secretary Theodore Joslin. "I am afraid we are in for real trouble." But the next day he had composed himself. "What's happened has happened. It is a catastrophe for us. It means we have got to fight to the limit." He ordered Joslin to make a study of the actual truth of the concept that as Maine goes, so goes the nation.

Hoover's office had originally indicated that he would make almost no campaign for reelection. Traditionally, Presidents conducted front-porch presentations limited to a speech or two. The public should be able to judge them by the work done over the previous four years. Moreover, it would be undignified and out of character for the President to barnstorm about praising his own work. So Hoover's schedule, his aides said, would consist of perhaps one address in New York and another in Chicago. But after Maine it was announced he might make more than two speeches. Still, the main labor would be carried by others.

To this end the Cabinet members went to work, Mills kicking off the campaign in Boston. The Secretary of the Treasury declared Hoover's men were veterans in fighting this peacetime war, and that it was no time to send raw recruits to the front. Secretary of Agriculture Hyde warned that "if Roosevelt is elected the homes and lives of one hundred million American people might be in jeopardy."

But the issue was Hoover, not Roosevelt. All over the country signs appeared—"Buy Here or We'll Vote for Hoover"— and hitchhikers carried placards—"Give Me a Ride or My Vote Goes to Hoover." Jokesters said the country was well governed only on weekends when Hoover was off fishing along the Rapidan.

Hoover aides embarked on a campaign to "humanize" him. For the first time in three years the reporters and cameramen were asked to visit the President in his Virginia retreat along the Rapidan River. For their eyes and cameras the President, wearing riding boots, got on Billy, a Marine Corps mount, to ride up and down the trails. But what he thought of it all showed unmistakably in his unsmiling face. (In addition, he hated horses. Long ago as a fledgling engineer prospecting in the Western mountains he had come to the conclusion that the horse was one of nature's mistakes, that it was designed with its body too far from the ground, and that it were better equipped with multiple sets of legs, like a centipede, so that the ride would be smoother.) After the newsreels had filmed the grim exercise in horsemanship, he put on high boots and went casting for trout in the streams. Throughout he wore a buttoned collar and a tie. Afterward he sat out of doors in the sunlight with Mrs. Hoover. She sat with her knitting while her husband held an open book in his lap. If nothing else the pictures clearly showed that he was not reading and that he was bored, irritated, even humiliated. All that he wanted was for the men to be gone. Then he could go back to his work.

That September the President, at long last, could begin to see the fruits of his labors. Buoyed by the reconstruction program his Administration had fostered, all the indices were rising. The stock market virtually doubled from its low earlier in the year; electric power production and carloadings increased sharply. A million and a half men went back to work that fall and tens of millions of dollars of gold withdrawn by frightened foreigners began to flow back.

Hoover decided he would not allow himself to lose the Presidency by default. He did not decide because of Herbert Hoover, who, with whitened hair and drooping shoulders, appeared twenty years older than he had been in 1928. Nor did he do it for Lou Henry Hoover, for she was worn, nervous, exhausted. Rather he would do it for the American nation. He shocked Secretary of State Stimson when he told him that he would use the great recovery program in a partisan manner to bring about his reelection. The President repeated it even as Stimson replied that he could not believe the President meant what he said. Hoover did mean it. In his eyes Roosevelt was a lightweight experimenter, irresponsible. Roosevelt's people were not part of traditional America. Now America was on the very verge of going the last half mile to victory. It came to the President that he had succeeded in his task. Or half-succeeded. He would need more time. Another term.

So at the continued urging of his aides he finally consented to "human-interest" interviews that irritated and affronted him, even though the interviewers were uniformly sympathetic. Christian Gauss came to do a piece for the extremely important *Saturday Evening Post* and wrote in a flattering way of how the telephones were constantly ringing outside the President's office, about the reporters who gathered to await news. In contrast, the President's own office was spacious and restful with no new-fangled gadgets on the large flat-topped desk, only a telephone. Sitting at that desk was a calm and resourceful Chief Executive.

Gauss asked what qualities of character, training and education might explain the rise of this Iowa farmboy, "this spectacular, this truly phenomenal career," but the President offered him no exciting memories, no drama. Only hard work and the engineer's persistence were involved, he said.

Gauss mentioned the President's Swiss ancestors landing in Delaware and then making their way to Maryland, North Carolina, and finally to West Branch. "I could not persuade the President that this Odyssey indicated a particularly energetic pioneering spirit. According to him there was nothing unusual about it."

Gauss wrote of how perhaps it was all explained by the President's objectivity, his impersonality, the fashion in which he clothed his "private life and personal qualities in Quaker gray. . . . To him, war, disaster, excitement and crisis are an interruption of sober and constructive action; they may be romantic, but his job has been to cure, not create, such events."

Gauss anticipated what his millions of readers might say, although perhaps he was kinder than they would be: "I had never seen so much romance buried in the course of a single afternoon."

Will Irwin came to do a piece for *Liberty*. Irwin had known Hoover and Miss Lou Henry since their student days together at Stanford; he had been a house guest in London when the immensely successful engineer had paced the floor debating with himself whether he should take over the job of bringing relief to the Belgians. Irwin tried to counter what people were saying about the President. The journalist wrote of his friend of forty years that he owned a quiet sense of the comic, told stories, liked to have people around him; that he wasn't a machine, but a man who read history, biography, science, economics, fiction, poetry. "Surrounded by yes-men," Irwin wrote, and then told how the President had said, with a low, agreeable chuckle, "Last Sunday, having a little time to myself, I applied the scientific method to this burning yes-man problem. I reviewed the events of the past week and I found that only three men who came into my office had anything agreeable to say to me."

It was true. After Maine, and after the first straw polls, people came constantly to report on developments that no incumbent President had ever faced, for conditions were so bad that the early summer rise in employment and other indices were hardly visible to most people. Men from the Great Plains said the farmers were saying, "It cannot be worse," and "anything is better than this." In one day seven Republican leaders told him the same thing and the President cried out in anguish, "If only they would leave me alone and let me work perhaps I could help to change the situation."

The plan to "humanize" the President fell into discard, and the emphasis of the campaign shifted to discussion of his programs. A series of popular magazine articles were prepared by Presidential aides under Presidential supervision for the signature of Cabinet members. At the same time Republican headquarters for the election was in effect shifted from Chicago to the White House.

The Chicago headquarters was floundering. Money was not coming in. Even more painful, the local state chairmen and local candidates were shunning Chicago. Assistant Secretary of State William R. Castle wrote friends that the leaders there seemed to think it amusing that the deskman in the Palmer House, where they had an entire floor, did not know which floor it was.

Castle had met with Everett Sanders, chairman of the Republican campaign. It was soon obvious that Sanders was not interested in talking with him. Sanders terminated the interview by saying a state delegation was waiting. Castle left. On his way out he saw no one waiting.

Everett Sanders had been a questionable choice as chairman, but it was a choice they had had to make. He was a former secretary to Calvin Coolidge, whose name was reminiscent of the great days. Coolidge's role in the election was endlessly discussed. The national committeeman for California, M. L. Requa, wrote Presidential Secretary Walter Newton that Coolidge must campaign: "I think you ought to tie the old gentleman up as definitely as possible and as soon as possible."

Newton wrote back, "Attention is being given this matter by Chairman Sanders himself." Sanders was not the only person besieging the former President. The Olympic games were opening in Los Angeles, and throughout the country Republican candidates were hoping that Coolidge would come to inaugurate the festivities. (The last person they wanted to see was Hoover.) If Coolidge should stop in their states they might get on the train and ride with him for a time and be photographed with him on the back platform. But Coolidge's asthma was bothering him, as it always did when he was under stress. Hopelessly he tried to understand how it had happened that everything had slipped away. In Washington the President permitted himself, sometimes, to think that Coolidge had seen it all coming and had run out, leaving someone else to face the debacle.

Coolidge clung to the rise in carloadings and the price of steel, hoping against hope that the collapse was not as serious as it seemed. But all of Northampton faced ruin—the banks, the insurance companies, the fathers of the Smith girls. The great men Coolidge had invited to the White House were toppling down, all those for whom he was supposed to have said, "The business of the country is business."

His anchor was gone, thought William Allen White: working, saving, the simple life, courage, honesty, common sense, all the foundations. His barber said to him, "Mr. Coolidge, how about this Depression? When is it going to end?" Coolidge said, "Well, George, the big men of the country have got to get together and do something about it. It isn't going to end itself. We all hope it will end, but we don't see it yet." He did not have the faintest idea of what the big men should do. And he never said he did.

At fifty-nine he looked as his late father had at seventy. When people asked him to go places and do things he almost always declined. "It's too much of an effort." There had to be police escorts and fanfare and crowds, all of that. He smiled a bit and said, "It's my past life that makes all the trouble. If only I could get rid of my past life!" His asthma worsened, and not a night of the summer passed without his using a spray. He let it be known that he would write an article on the Republican case for the *Saturday Evening Post*. But that was not enough for the desperate people afraid of losing their positions in the great world, and a flood of letters poured in asking that he do more.

Instead of Coolidge, Vice President Curtis went West to open the Olympics. There had been a movement during the convention to replace Curtis with Dawes on the ticket, but it had died a-borning, for Dawes was deeply involved with the Central Republic Bank and not at all interested in Curtis' office. Curtis hugely enjoyed his meaningless office. He played not the slightest role in the Administration, save for his incessant party-going, which saw him dine out night after night for weeks on end. Dolly Gann, his sister and the reigning queen of Washington's parties and receptions, desperately wanted the Republican ticket returned to power. She volunteered to go about delivering speeches largely drafted by the President's secretaries. Surprisingly, she was very good at it, except for those times when she injected her own thoughts—as once when she announced that the Depression was entirely over. "Dolly Calls It Off," the newspapers headlined. After that she checked with the White House by telephone as often as three times a day before going up to a podium or speaker's table.

Her brother went to the Olympics to the accompaniment of frequent heckling by people gathered at the railway stops where he traveled by Pullman accommodations. (Gone were the private cars of '28.) Often he lost his temper. In Iowa he shouted that the average voter was "too damn dumb" to understand the President's programs. At Las Vegas his speech was interrupted by someone yelling, "Why didn't you feed those ex-soldiers in Washington?" He exploded: "I've fed more than you have, you dirty cowards! I'm not afraid of any of you!" The crowd began yelling, "Hurrah for Roosevelt!"

He went into the Olympic stadium lifting his hat at entirely imaginary applause to announce, "In the name of the President of the United States I proclaim the Olympic games of the Tenth Olympiad." Ten trumpets sounded at the foot of the great column of the peristyle over the east gate. Seventy-five-millimeter guns pumped out a salute while thousands of pigeons were released to fly past in two huge flocks, the juxtaposition of the birds of peace and the artillery making everyone think of the War. As always Curtis enjoyed himself shaking hands with the people. He reminded them of Throttlebottom, the character in the year's Pulitzer Prize musical *Of Thee I Sing*, who passed his Vice Presidential years feeding birds in the park while trying to get two references so that he might have a library card. His trip to Los Angeles disastrously demonstrated that he could not be relied on to bring in votes.

The White House turned instead to the bearer of a famous name, Theodore Roosevelt, Jr., governor-general of the Philippines. Lawrence Richey wrote Roosevelt that a speech-making tour could be arranged for him. Instead, Roosevelt made a radio address from Manila beamed at the mainland.

Of all the speakers Secretary Mills was the best. He had personality and an excellent radio voice. But in the end there was only one thing to do. The choice was Hoover's alone.

Chapter Seventeen

SHORTLY AFTER MOVING into the White House the First Lady discovered that the original furniture and chairs that had been in Abraham Lincoln's study were sitting forgotten in a White House storage room. She had them taken out and, using an old picture of the study, reconstructed the room so that it would look exactly as it had in Lincoln's time. In that room of personal destiny, as opposed to the official business offices in the Executive Wing, President Hoover would make his fight.

The President must take the field in his own behalf. It was his own decision, suddenly arrived at. Even in late September Secretary Mills was writing a friend that the President had "no thought of making any stumping trip" and would simply "make two or three speeches between now and Election." But in fact he would make two hundred speeches. Once decided, he threw himself into preparation of his first one. It would be on October 4 in Des Moines, Iowa, in that place of his yesterdays where surely they would understand.

Within a short while the Lincoln Study, once immaculate, became cluttered with memoranda, suggestions, and drafts and redrafts of his speech.

"Talk right out," he said to the men coming to advise him on what he should say. "Don't mince words at all. Say just what you think and mean." The most astonishing transformation took place as he spoke to them. In only a matter of weeks, incredibly, he changed entirely. Suddenly he was looking his callers in the eye, and his endless doodling ceased. He did not sit stiffly in his chair as before, but lounged backward, appearing relaxed and almost at ease, quicker in his movements, easier in his manner. And now upon occasion he smiled.

"One learns," he said laconically to those who commented on the change. To the journalist Anne O'Hare McCormick he was suddenly like the companionable man whose assistants and friends held him in reverence as The Chief, the man whom, she wrote, the public had "never seen or believed in."

Roosevelt was a simplifier who decided things quickly and went swiftly and lightly; and the first draft of Hoover's October 4 speech at Des Moines was seventy-one typed pages. There followed fifteen rewrites. Proofs were run off and sent to a dozen people for their suggestions. And the corrected copies marked with the hundreds of suggestions poured back into the Lincoln Study. They covered all the tables and chairs and overflowed the wastebaskets, and the President, who had so often worked alone, now sat with Mills, Joslin, Newton, Hurley, and anyone else he thought might help.

Amid the spectacular disarray so utterly unfamiliar to those who had known him in the past, he said to his callers, "It is unnecessary to tell me that Kansas, Missouri, Iowa, Minnesota are lost today. I know it. I have been given that information forty times. But this fight isn't over yet. We have just started. I shall fight every inch of the way. If you have any advice, I want it."

Des Moines was not going to be an apology for his Administration and his life and his view of things, but a proud affirmation of what he had and had not done. He wanted to finish the job, he told Anne O'Hare McCormick, he wanted to defend the American tradition.

For hours on end he dictated to his stenographers, rewrote with his stubby pencil (a typewriter or smooth pen encourages glibness and this was a time for the truth, for an appeal to the American people who with reason would endorse their President while rejecting a candidate who pandered to them). At night he got up to rewrite some more (daytime was for official government business) and then rewrite again.

Joslin said that the President had a message for the people which he would deliver at Des Moines. But the tremendous work load got at Joslin, and he faltered and finally went off for a respite of a couple of weeks. As a reporter covering the President, Joslin had, along with others, cursed the President's secretiveness and standoffish ways, but once appointed to the staff he had dedicated himself to the President and his methods; and for that his former fellows hated him. He was the subject of derision: "Nobody could approach his desk without being told that the place was a madhouse, that he never imagined there could be so many and such exacting duties, and that there was scarcely time for a long breath between early morning and twilight." Sometimes he flung himself on a couch and could hardly be awakened; during his vacation at a Massachusetts resort he fainted twice in the public dining room.

To replace him during his vacation the President brought in Edward T. Clark, Coolidge's old secretary. Clark could not get used to the change in the White House since his days with the President's predecessor. "The Executive offices have become imbued with the policy of efficient business management," Clark wrote Coolidge. The secretaries, who physically saw each other at least every hour, communicated by means of written memoranda. There had to be written records of everything. It was all so different from the Coolidge days when people were told that they were earning good money and not to bother the White House with problems.

It was astonishing to Clark to see how the President personally ran his campaign for reelection, something no President had ever done before. "The President is not only willing, but determined to share the responsibility," he wrote Coolidge. "His telephone rings endlessly with questions as to this release and that speech and who shall reply to Roosevelt and what he shall say, and who shall be taken care of on the payroll and who shall not. Every speech by his Cabinet is half written in the President's own handwriting."

Both Mills and Undersecretary of the Treasury Ballantine

told Clark they could not understand how the President carried on, for he allowed not a single factor of government or political policy to be in any other hands than his. Clark told Coolidge, "Not only is he burdened with what comes to him verbally or in letters, but he persists in attempting to follow public opinion through endless reports of editorial comment all subdivided into the nature of the comment and how much each comment means in the way of circulation, geographic locality, and other details which I cannot remember.

"I think he feels, too, depressed and hurt by the absence of public commendation in the campaign. It is hard to realize, but nevertheless it is true, that whereas the publicity directors in past campaigns would bring out each day some new testimonial, some new expression of support and confidence, there is not today one Republican leader in banking or in industry whose support would not bring jeers of derision. In 1924 Henry Ford's support meant a great deal. Today it would lose Mr. Hoover thousands of votes in Detroit, and so on down the line."

On the fourth of October he went to Des Moines. If he were going to win the election he had one month and three days in which to do it. The night before he left, he was awakened at three in the morning by a noise in the fireplace. A mouse was rummaging around. Hoover got up, turned on the lights, chased the mouse away. After that he could not get back to sleep, so he dressed and worked through the rest of the night. Joslin had recently returned and as they headed West in the Presidential car *Marco Polo*, the President seemed to his secretary to be groggy and in an uncertain state.

Hoover was not the only person aboard who was nervous and unsettled. The Secret Service men were, Joslin noted, "very jumpy"; their chief, Edmund Starling, was facing the trip "panic-stricken, with fear and trembling." He ordered the most elaborate safeguards ever devised.

In Iowa that fall the farmers were in revolt. At the October foreclosure sales the farmers came to bid a dollar or two dollars for the farms of their dispossessed neighbors; anyone who bid a higher amount risked his life. When the farm was knocked down for a ridiculously low price, the deed was presented to the former owner. But there were too many farms going on the block that fall, hundreds in each county, and it was impossible for the men to menace each potential buyer. So they took to invading courthouses to get the judges who sat in foreclosure proceedings. They dragged them from their benches to trees outside the courthouse where there were ropes draped from tree branches and a hundred men saying one of those ropes would be around the judge's neck if he foreclosed on a neighbor.

They were also in rebellion against the disastrously low prices for their produce. The farmers lined up on the roads leading into the central distribution point of Council Bluffs with clubs and rifles, and, their women alongside, forbade milk trucks to pass until the price was raised. Sheriffs swore in War veterans as special deputies to clear the roads, issued weapons, and then hesitated to order those weapons used.

The farmers who tried to run the blockade were stopped by exploding shotguns. While children went hungry in the cities, the trucks were turned over and milk poured out into the ditches. "To hell with Hoover, to hell with the Department of Agriculture, and to hell with you," the farmers told the reporters. Their leader was Milo Reno, and to many he seemed to be leading an American peasants' revolt, which could end with burning homes and armed mobs running amuck over the countryside.

As the President's car left for Des Moines, rumors came in that Milo Reno would mobilize thousands of farmers, each armed with half a dozen rotten tomatoes and half a dozen rotten eggs. Two terrified Iowa Republican leaders told Joslin the President must not come to the state of his birth; it would be far too dangerous. Joslin told them there was no more chance that the President would call off the trip than there was that he would try to jump over the Washington Monument. The very much respected *Literary Digest* poll predicted an overwhelming victory for Roosevelt, but the President remained calm, saying, "It is not the crushing blow I had feared." Joslin wondered what he considered a crushing blow to be, for in Joslin's view there were not more than half a dozen states safe for him. But Hoover had the fire of combat in his eyes, something that had never been there before, and the prospect of the trip to Des Moines somehow lightened him. He seemed actually anxious to go.

As the President's train pulled out of Altoona, Pennsylvania, a Secret Service man took Joslin aside and said, "You know things are not nice. . . . The President must make a real effort to win. The stage is set against him. He has got to loosen up more than he ever has before. Wherever we stop, he has got to show himself. That means he must go to the rear platform, shake hands, receive gifts, write autographs, do any number of things."

The Secret Service man was discussing a professional problem, and he said to Joslin that the people up close need not be worried about, nor the ones on the outskirts of the crowd. It was the people fifteen or twenty feet away that had to be watched. "Things are worse some times than at others. This is one of the times when they are mighty bad. We have got to hope for the best and be prepared for the worst. . . . Now, I am not telling you what to do, but I am telling you what I shall do if it's necessary. If anyone makes a false move and I can't get to him, I shall give the President a shove to the back of the platform and stand directly in front of him. They may hit me but they can't hit him."

But as they went West it was hard to believe the reports that he would lose every state he passed through with the possible exception of Pennsylvania. For the crowds were enormous, consistently larger than those Joslin had seen when as a reporter he toured with Wilson, Hughes, Harding, Cox, Davis, Coolidge. At each stop and at every crossroads people were standing, waiting.

Joslin looked at them and wondered to himself if the usual rule that the size of crowds meant nothing could be discarded. Anne O'Hare McCormick wondered also what those great crowds meant. She had also seen them gathered for Roosevelt, and it astonished her that both for the President and his challenger the audiences had been greater than in pre-radio days. But the people were so oddly quiet and painfully attentive. It seemed to her that they represented a nation in waiting, in suspense and uncertainty, that they seemed to reflect a "strong conviction that the action of the government in the next two or three years will determine the course of the nation for generations." She was a reporter; and she saw a great story, a great moment, a climax that was "one of the grandest in the great American thriller."

And so Hoover came to Des Moines, to Iowa. He was old in that moment. His shoulders drooped. The lines around the eyes were very deep. The round babyface of 1928 had grown firm. To his enemies he looked a discredited man out chasing votes, a beaten man, but to his friends he was a very marvel of fortitude. He drove past one hundred twenty-five thousand people standing in the Des Moines streets (there were no rotten eggs or tomatoes) to the Governor's Mansion. After a short rest there he went to the Des Moines Coliseum. When he came in the audience rose and wildly cheered him and he waved and smiled his shy smile, perhaps unknowing of the fact that each and every person there had been hand-picked for attendance in that place in that time, each one certified by Republicans all over the state to be "safe" and personally involved in the reelection of the President. "Heckle-proof," in short, said *Time*. He went up to the podium and began, and as he spoke his voice rose and fell in sing-song fashion, not unlike that of a preacher at an outdoor meeting. He was still Herbert Clark Hoover, no Wilson, no Teddy Roosevelt, no Bryan, no flash or brilliance in his delivery; but as he spoke his clumsy and awkward sentences, even the reporters who hated him found themselves moved.

"I have every confidence," he said, his voice going up and down in solemn cadence and now and then striking a tremulous note, "that the whole American people know in their hearts that there has been but one test in my mind, one supreme object in the measures and policies we have forged to win in this war against Depression. That test was the interest of the people in the homes and at the firesides of our country. I have had before me but one vision: that is, the vision of the millions of homes of that sort which I knew as a boy in this state." The reporter Thomas Stokes thought to himself that the words bore unmistakable evidence of Herbert Hoover's constricted and inhibited struggle with the English language, that a literary adviser might have turned a phrase and polished a sentence to stir an audience. But also that from the printed page of the next day's paper something from the heart would cry out.

His voice devoid of trick or artifice or subtlety chanted on in the hall, and he cried, "I wish to speak directly to those of my hearers who are farmers of what is on my mind, of what is in my heart, to tell you the conclusions I have reached from this bitter experience of the years."

He said, "That agriculture is prostrate needs no proof. You have saved and economized and worked to reduce costs; but, with all this, yours is a story of distress and suffering." He said to the Iowa farmers that he had done the very best he could. In his high-button shoes and vest and stiff collar he stood before them and said that if in their wisdom they chose to return him to office he would once again do what he could for them. But there could be no promises.

"I come to you with no economic patent medicine especially compounded for farmers. I refuse to offer counterfeit currency or false hopes. I will not make any pledge to you which I cannot fulfill." The people cheered him, the sound going out over the nationwide radio hookups costing seventy thousand dollars, and raised only by virtue of the President's personal telephone calls to Republican contributors who, wildly generous in 1928, were now reluctant to write a check for even a single dollar.

He talked about the terrible battle he had fought in the dark and in silence, of the earthquake whose destructive force striking forty nations could not be revealed at the time of the cataclysm for fear of the panic its revelation might have engendered, of his fears for a universal bankruptcy of his country which might have cost twenty-five billion, five times the federal budget for the year, of homes and farms and businesses which would have literally been worth nothing. He said people had asked dictatorship from him, unrestricted use of the printing press for money, suspension of payments on government bonds, but that he had had none of these, nor would he have. For something finer, greater, more important was involved. That was moral integrity.

"We determined we would stand up like men," he said. "The American dollar rang honest on every counter." Something of the long lonely years came through, the unsmiling man working through the terrible days. "I have been talking of currency, of gold, of credit, of bonds, of banks, of insurance policies, of loans. Do not think these things have no human interpretations. The happiness of one hundred and twenty million people was at stake in the measures to enable the government to meet its debts and obligations, in saving the gold standard, in enabling five thousand and five hundred banks, insurance companies, building and loan associations, and a multitude of other institutions to pay their obligations."

He was giving the greatest speech of his life, and those who heard him remembered in that moment that once he had been the Great Humanitarian, the Great Engineer, the Great Liberal, the Great Progressive, that once upon a time he was considered the finest man ever to stand before a Chief Justice and take the oath of office, that he was then considered in that moment of his pledge-taking to be the most perfect American who ever assumed this highest of all offices within the gift of his people.

"We held the Gibraltar of world stability," he cried out. "The world today has a chance. It is growing in strength. Let that man who complains that things could not be worse thank God for this victory."

He went down from the platform leaving all who heard him moved. The *New Republic* man thought his speech, his defense, his fight, was like the climax of a Greek tragedy. "It represents, as in Aristotle's definition, the struggle against inexorable fate of a good but not wholly guiltless man. Elected four years ago on the flood tide of success and fame, he now faces certain and probably overwhelming rejection because of the misfortunes which have overtaken him and his people. Though he still thinks of those misfortunes as being undeserved, their origins are inextricably interwoven with his own past. He was a part of the Administration which led the country up the mountain and to the brink of the precipice and he took credit for the ascent. . . .

He himself was an Iowa farm boy, nurtured in the spirit of pioneer individualism; he has done what any such boy of sufficient character and intelligence would have been expected to do. What is the matter?"

The President went to speak to a meeting of Iowa newspaper editors. No talk had been prepared, and he asked Joslin what he should say. Joslin told him, talk about West Branch. So he spoke about homemade sleds for Iowa's winter, the willows in the water under the railroad bridge where the children swam, how the Ritz had never yet provided game of such wondrous flavor as the birds plucked and half cooked over boys' fires in Iowa. Joslin thought the Des Moines speech to be brilliant, all that one might want, but he knew his President and realized there would be no more speeches like that, for Hoover had only one in his soul. So the secretary esteemed the talk to the editors more highly, thinking, If only the President would throw away all his planned speeches on weighty subjects and reveal himself to be what Joslin saw him to be: human, kindly, considerate! But of course Herbert Hoover could not do that. But he charged in with plans for new speeches and acted as though victory were certain.

Roosevelt with his corps of speechwriters was saying the Administration had encouraged the orgy of stock speculation— "The Horsemen of Destruction of the Republican Administration." He charged, too, that the Administration had lied to the people about the seriousness of the crash, that it and Hoover had done nothing. "My friends," Roosevelt cried, "all that I can tell you is that I deplore, I regret, the inexcusable, the reprehensible delay of Washington, not for months alone, but for years. . . . I want to say with all the emphasis I can command, that this Administration did nothing and their leaders are, I am told, still doing nothing. . . . The crash came in October, 1929. The President . . . did absolutely nothing to remedy the situation. . . . It is a leadership that is bankrupt, not only in ideals but ideas." Roosevelt was forceful in his delivery and colorful in his words. When he compared the President to Humpty Dumpty the reporters had something they could work with.

And there were constant informal press conferences, some conducted with the governor and the newspapermen in bathing suits in the pool at Hyde Park. Mrs. Roosevelt never referred to him as "the governor" or "my husband"; it was always simply "Franklin."

Hoover went to Fort Wayne and in his sing-song and formal way said, "I wish to take the occasion . . . to say a word to . . . all the people of the great Midwest. During my public life I have believed that sportsmanship and statesmanship called for the elimination of harsh personalities between opponents. On this journey, however, I have received a multitude of reports as to the widespread misrepresentations which have been promulgated."

He cried out, "I regret that the character of these personalities necessitates a direct word from me. I shall say now the only harsh word that I have uttered in public office. I hope it will be the last I shall have to say.

"When you are told that the President of the United States, who by the most sacred trust of our nation is the President of all the people, a man of your own blood and upbringing, has sat in the White House for the last three years of your misfortune without troubling to know your burdens, without heartaches over your miseries and casualties, without summoning every avenue of skillful assistance irrespective of party or view, without using every ounce of his strength and straining his every nerve to protect and help, without using every possible agency of democracy that would bring aid, without putting aside personal ambition and humbling his pride of opinion if that would serve—then I say to you that such statements are deliberate, intolerable falsehoods."

That day, October fifth, Roosevelt and Smith met at a Democratic meeting. It was the first time they had seen each other since the convention. Al stuck out his hand. The cheering as he did so and the exaltation on the platform were such that Jim Farley, standing between the two men, could not hear what they said to each other. A reporter standing perhaps six or eight feet away dictated to his stenographer his idea of what it was likely that Al had said. The report went out all over the country, making the President's speech the secondary story of the day behind the imagined description of Al with his red face and big cigar shaking Frank's hand, saying, *"How are you, you old potato?"*

Chapter Eighteen

HOOVER WENT on separate trips to Cleveland, Detroit, Indianapolis, New York, preaching. The speeches were models of intelligence and logic, emotional only in his appeal for the preservation of the traditional American way, in his faith in the future.

The audiences listened to him in the auditoriums and coliseums, for they were all hand-picked. But in the streets where no selection could be enforced, the crowds booed and cursed him, the only President ever to hear these sounds, not Lincoln in Richmond during the last days of the Civil War, not Wilson in the German neighborhoods. "I've been traveling with Presidents since Roosevelt," a Secret Service man from Teddy's day told *Time*, "and never before have I seen one actually booed, with men running out into the streets to thumb their noses at him. It's not a pretty sight."

Detroit was the worst, with a raging mob at the railroad station held back only by mounted police with batons and guns. The Secret Service delayed letting the President off the halted train around which resounded the terrible calls of "Hang Hoover!" When Secretary Joslin ventured out into the station entrance someone flung a large lightbulb at him. It crashed on the pavement like a bomb. Joslin winced. People screamed, "Hoover—baloney and applesauce!" The mounted police charged the mob, and as they did so the Secret Service double-timed the President into a waiting limousine. Armored cars patrolled the four-mile route to the Olympic Stadium which the Secret Service chief, Edmund Starling, had carefully chosen with the aim that only wide and straight streets be used. They sped by at top speed, but even so it was, the reporter Thomas Stokes thought, a Calvary for the President. Through block after block they flashed past tens of thousands of men and women utterly silent and grim save for those who could be glimpsed shaking their fists and shouting unheard words and phrases. Edmund Starling glanced at the President and saw a man who looked bewildered and stricken.

At the hall the carefully screened faithful Republicans waved flags and cheered. Hoover all but staggered up to the podium, his face ashen. His hands, hanging limply by his sides, were shaking. "In this Depression as never before the American people have responded with a high sense of responsibility to safeguard and protect . . . there is the future well-being of the future generations of our children. . . . I hope . . . I wish . . . I can remember . . . I have sought . . . I have urged. . . . If you will study what happened in Germany, or France, or Austria. . . . I have in my desk a five-million-mark note which before would have been worth one million dollars, and yet which I bought for actually one dollar. We have fought a great battle to maintain the stability of the American dollar, the stability of its exchange, in order that we might protect the working people of the United States."

At St. Paul he said that the people might well thank God that there was a government in Washington that knew how to deal with a mob and the audience thinking of the Bonus Expeditionary Force snarled back in such fashion that Starling found himself suddenly covered with perspiration. The President's voice that day was weak and shaking as he chanted on: our race, our traditions of the century and a half, our ways. Listening on the radio in Washington Joslin knew as soon as he came on the air that The Chief was not right. The long nights without sleep were taking their toll, and he lost his place in the manuscript several times. A Secret Service man stood behind him holding an empty armchair so that if he collapsed at least he would not lie sprawling on the floor.

He went from speech to speech, his Special halting on the way back to Washington and more work and then out from Washington to more speeches: a hundred short speeches at the railroad depots, with a million Americans seeing in the flesh this most desperate fight ever staged by any President. "Why don't they make him quit?" an important Republican asked Starling. "He's not doing himself or the party any good. It's turning into a farce." But it was not a farce. And suddenly the newspapers which had universally conceded the election to Roosevelt a few weeks earlier were saying it was a tossup. There had been no question that the President would have been defeated in September or even on October first, Joslin thought, but when the election was two weeks off the President suddenly looked as though he would win. Employment was up by a million and a half; the Roosevelt lead once so massive appeared to be falling away; and the professional politicians who had given state after state to the Democrats began to hedge their predictions.

Hoover walked alone in the campaign, and he did not ask for help. Except from Coolidge. A stream of people, a friendly reporter—one of the few—the head of the Republican Speakers' Bureau for the East, continued to go to Northampton to ask in the President's name that Coolidge speak out. But Coolidge did not know what to say. "I know little about what the government is doing or what the results of it have been," he told his callers. Empty, he fought off the appeals by saying the people would expect something of importance and he was unable to offer it. Mills went to Coolidge's old secretary, Edward T. Clark, and said it would be well for Coolidge to say that the President's actions had prevented the closing of every bank in the country. Clark sent Mills's request to Coolidge. Coolidge replied his throat was bothering him and repeated, "I find it terribly hard to know what to say."

Clark wrote Coolidge of what the President stood for in this fight: "That there can be no recovery by a miracle of Federal intervention; that he will not adopt these plans calling for billions of dollars which have been advocated by the Democrats in Congress; that he will not make false promises; and that upon this platform he stands even if it means his defeat." Only two people could change the sweep toward Roosevelt, Clark wrote— the President himself or the ex-President. "Mr. Hoover is so obsessed with the idea that all that is necessary to insure his re-election is the proper presentation of the real issues by one to whom the country will listen, that it is hard to refuse to present again his side of the case."

At last Coolidge agreed to speak out. On October 11 he went to a cheering crowd in New York's Madison Square Garden who shouted for him upon his introduction for so long a period that he took out his pocket watch, held it up, and pointed to the microphones of the radio chains whose rental for the period of his talk had demanded the very utmost from the party's few contributors. "That's Cal," somebody shouted.

He talked in generalities and for a long while made no mention of the fact that he had once been President. He came to a point where he said in his twang, "When I was in Washington—" and the audience burst into laughter. Coolidge hesitated. They seemed to him to be in a strange mood, their behavior incomprehensible. He shook his head. He had never talked to an audience which laughed. Mrs. Coolidge listened over a radio placed in the back room of the store in Plymouth, Vermont, where her husband had been born. She thought he was in good form, although it was apparent to her he was using his voice with great care so that it would hold out. He went home determined to do no more.

For he did not understand anything anymore, he said; he was "burned out." It was the Depression which had done it, and made him, his friends saw, a different being. "I feel I no longer fit in with these times," Coolidge said to those close to him. "Great changes can come in four years. These socialistic notions of government are not of my day. When I was in office, tax reduction, debt reduction, tariff stability and economy were the things to which I gave attention. We succeeded on those lines. It has always seemed to me that common sense is the real solvent for the nation's problems at all times—common sense and hard work. When I read of the newfangled things that are now so popular I realize that my time in public affairs is past."

The tide was going the President's way. Al Smith went off speechmaking ostensibly in behalf of the Democratic ticket, but the things he said hardly helped. For he indulged himself in the most reckless fashion, hashing over his crucifixion of 1928 and condemning all who voted against him as bigots. Nothing could have been more worrisome to Roosevelt, for Smith in the name of the Democratic Party was bidding to drive millions of voters into the Republican camp.

Each week the President rushed for a train heading out of Union Station and braced himself up to deliver his talks. In Cleveland they turned the public address system up several times as he staggered through a speech, but his voice was so weak that it faded away despite the amplification. His eyes were red around the edges and his hands shook, but he fought on and somehow the shyest office seeker of his time blossomed in the battle. "This fight has not been lost for a second," he said. His face tightened.

He went to Newark: "The Republican Administration has built up a series of unprecedented measures through which we have warded off disaster and chaos. . . . We have begun to see positive and practical results through the return of men to work, through the increase of prices, through increased carloadings and in many other fundamental indications of recovery in our national life. We are in the midst of a great economic battle. We have carried the front-line trenches. Any hesitation, any halting of the battle for changes of policies cannot do otherwise than to stagnate progress and bring disaster."

But even as he spoke the indices were beginning to go the wrong way. He was sure he knew why. It was the Maine election of September that had indicated that Roosevelt was likely to win in November. Such a victory meant men like Garner, Huey Long, Raymond Moley, Rexford Tugwell—experimenters, innovators, wild men. They frightened the businessmen and the businessmen held back their expenditures and took as few risks as possible.

He turned wild at what was happening and something like

desperation seized him. For he had seen it through and won the battle, carried the front-line trenches, and now it seemed to be vanishing—the victory, the vindication of all he stood for. He turned again to Coolidge in these last days of his fight, thinking Coolidge could make them see.

Clark wrote the ex-President, "I know it is utterly unfair to you, but he believes the success or failure of his campaign rests on one more speech."

Coolidge wrote back, "My throat is in such shape that I cannot make speeches. I was barely able to get through the short one I tried to make in New York but of course my delivery of it was so restrained as to be almost ineffective."

Under the pressure of the incessant requests Coolidge turned peevish: "If the Republican Party is not producing the best speakers in this campaign it is the first time this has been so and I do not think it is so now. If it is a fact it means that the Party has been reduced to a one-man government." He repeated he could do no more. Northampton's bank crashed; Coolidge found his law partner sitting in the office with his face in his hands. Silently he put a check for five thousand dollars on the desk. He wandered past the trees around his home, unseeing. Three months later he was dead.

Everything seemed to be tumbling down. The men who had gone back to work for so brief a time returned to their homes and to the parks where they lounged away the deadly hours.

Roosevelt cried, "It is unfair; it is unjust; it is not American! . . . The Horsemen of Destruction rode into every town and every county." And some of the things he said appeared to hint at great revisions in the way things would be—Federal planning, collectivism. He was, as always, vague; but as always he could reach out.

"I tell you, lady," a cab driver said to Anne O'Hare McCormick, "the day Roosevelt is elected will be a national holiday—like Armistice Day, you know. I figure out that if we can get rid of Old Gloom and put in a feller that can laugh and act human, the Depression will be half over."

The President worked and reworked his speeches late into the night, revising them on the trains and telephoning endlessly to raise the money so that they might be broadcast. On the last day of October he went to New York's Madison Square Garden. The police held back thousands of people chanting, "We want bread."

He listed the array of men behind Roosevelt and some of their proposals: Huey Long shouting that every man was a king and that the nation must "share the wealth," Senator Norris calling for the socialization of important industries. The President warned, "If they are brought in this will not be the America we have known in the past." He said Roosevelt's people, his speechwriters, all aimed at a great federal government, and that it must not be. He spoke of courage, of initiative, of liberalism, Democracy, ideals.

"I am not setting up the contention that our American system is perfect," he said. "No human ideal has ever been perfectly attained, since humanity itself is not perfect. But the wisdom of our forefathers and the wisdom of the thirty men who have preceded me in this office hold to the conception that progress can be attained only as the sum of accomplishments of free individuals.

"My countrymen, the proposals of our opponents represent a profound change in American life—less in concrete proposal, bad as that may be, than by implication and by evasion. Dominantly in their spirit they represent a radical departure from the foundations of one hundred and fifty years that have made this the greatest country in the world."

He raised himself to say that if Roosevelt were elected it would be something like doom itself: "Grass will grow in the streets of a hundred cities, a thousand towns; the weeds will overrun the fields of millions of farms."

That night he decided he would cross the entire country to vote. He would go home, to California.

Chapter Nineteen

His FACE DRAWN and with circles around his eyes, he headed for Palo Alto, the train halting at the waystops wherever there was a crowd to whom he might say, "I deeply appreciate the generosity and the courtesy of your greeting. It is heartening, it is encouraging, and it is an indication of where you will stand on the eighth of November."

He went out to the sections of the nation he had not seen since coming to Washington to take the oath of office of his Presidency. Along the roads paralleling the tracks he saw the fires of the hundreds of thousands of people who were aimlessly traveling the highways by day and sleeping near them at night. Most of them were young boys and girls who drifted along picking up a day's work in a gas station or at a roadside eating house. They washed in the tourist camps, huddles of tiny cabins each with two cots and a washbowl and renting for a dollar a night. None of the young tramps were launched on a workaday life; they did not think of getting real jobs and having real careers, for there were none to be had.

"Where are you going?" the reporter Morris Markey asked a young girl.

"Going?" she said. "Just going. You ain't dumb, are you? I just keep going."

In Illinois the President visited Lincoln's tomb, and his

backers revived the Civil War image of not changing horses in the middle of a stream. ("Don't change barrels when going over Niagara"; "Don't change engineers in the middle of the wreck," jeered Roosevelt's people.)

Out in the old gold country of the Far West people were prospecting by the weed-grown holes of the abandoned strikes of fifty and sixty years before. The area was crowded with people to whom the Mining Division of California had frankly said that the likely value of the most painstaking efforts would not exceed fifty cents a day. "The invariable retort," wrote Samuel G. Blythe, "was, 'Well, that's better than nothing, ain't it?' " So they labored up the mountain roads and camped along the streams and piled up fresh rockpiles by the old ancient ones: "the Argonauts of '32."

At Carlin, Nevada, on the day before election, the train halted for a moment and the President huskily explained that he would be unable to say anything, for his voice was almost gone. That night he was scheduled to speak, for the last time in the campaign, over nationwide hookups.

"Oh, raspberries," someone yelled.

Hoover said, "If the man who made that remark will step forward I will tend to him."

There was silence. He turned and went back into the car and the people broke into cheers.

That evening the train rolled into the Nevada Valley mountain town of Elko and stopped. Twilight was coming on. He was to have ten minutes of radio time for his last appeal. The population of the town was three thousand, and most of them stood outside the car looking at the drawn shades—cattlemen, sheep herders, miners. The station was dreary, surrounded by white earth sterile with alkali stretching off to the mountains. Inside his coach were a bank of microphones and floodlights, a dozen of his friends and aides, some reporters.

"Weariness shows in his slumping torso," wrote William Allen White. "His eyes lack luster and are red-rimmed with care. And over the radio to his friends and supporters in the Nation, his voice comes tired—how infinitely tired!—and his words, how hollow and how sad. . . ." He stood before the microphones: "I have been fighting that the wrong course may not be adopted, not by appeal to destructive emotion, but by truth and logic. I have tried to dissolve the mirage of promises by the reality of facts. . . ." And he finished.

The next day, election day, at 6:30 in the morning, the train crossed into California, into the land of the Argonauts of '32 and into the place where he had begun his career. They stopped at Colfax and he went out to talk. He was haggard and his rasping and broken voice carried only a few feet from the rear platform of the car. There were substantial numbers of boos mixed with the cheers. (Earlier tomatoes and eggs were flung at the train.)

He began in his usual formal way: "My friends of Nevada County: I am deeply affected by your welcome." But then he began to speak more naturally, and entirely extemporaneously. For he was back home in the California which he had never seen since leaving it to take the oath of that Presidency which had begun so gloriously. "It is difficult to formulate phrases to express the feelings of one's heart," he said, and then, incoherently, "on that part of a touching recollection."

Then he gathered himself and in the dim light of the chilled dawn said, "I recollect the full facts and I recollect Nevada County with a particular vividness because at that age and that time in life one remembers everything that happens. When you are from fifteen to twenty-two or thereabouts, everything is an adventure and everything is an event. As we get along in life we don't mind, so much, some of us, what happens this month or next month." His lips were trembling. "But at the time I spent in Nevada County, I remember everything: the Harmony Mine, and I remember the Grass Valley and the Mayflower and the mine where I worked at one time. All of it I remember and I remember the road all of the way from here to Nevada City and back again." It had been forty years. He went on toward Oakland and San Francisco and home, talking and campaigning all the morning long as he violated the tradition against doing these things on election day.

At Oakland at the Mole he took a ferryboat decorated with flags and bunting and crossed the bay. Fireboats blew jets of water into the bright sunshine, and the naval station at Yerba Buena Island fired a twenty-one-gun salute. At the Embarcadero, at the Mission Street Pier, autos were waiting to take him to the Civic Center. "I proudly say to you there has been no time when the esteem of the nation for California and its ideals have not been upheld by my representation of the state—" His shattered voice chanted on, almost lost sometimes in the volume of shouted curses and catcalls.

He headed for Palo Alto, stopping frequently to offer a few more desperate words, even though there could be no real chance of his doing much to affect the decision which already was on its way to being irrevocably made. It was shocking to most of the reporters that he would continue to fight his cause at this last moment. His advisers asked him to have done, but he could not be stopped. He talked on, telling the people the stakes, the meaning, the ultimate end of the concerns of this day, this choice.

"Mr. President, will you say at this time what your plans are after voting in Palo Alto—go right back or take a little rest?"

"I would like to have a short rest. I haven't had one for more than two years. It all depends upon whether some crisis develops that I have to go back to take care of. If not I would like to have just a week at my own home. I would like to catch up a few hours' sleep if it were possible."

"Will you vote at Stanford University this year as you did in 1928?"

"Yes, it is the only place I can vote."

"At the Stanford Union?"

"The Administration Building—in the club. I don't know whether it is there this year or somewhere else. In any event, in that precinct."

"Is that on the university grounds, somewhere?"

"The university itself is a precinct."

They came to the end of the long campaign journey, the eleven thousand miles, so much more than any other President had attempted. He had written out and had typed on a special large-letter machine: "This afternoon I greet you as cherished friends and kindly neighbors. I know that some thoughtless person has said I am not responsive to these demonstrations of human friendship. No more cruel thing was ever said. My heart flows and my soul is nourished by your handclaps and your smiles of welcome."

But there at home, too tired, or perhaps too genuinely touched, he did not read his set piece but simply said in a husky, breaking way, "My friends, I am just glad to come home. I have brought back everything with me except my voice. I can tell you the emotions of occasions like this are too much for expression. I just thank you."

They went through lines of Stanford students to the polling place illuminated by the lights of the waiting photographers. The clerk asked him his name and address: he gave it, and then, handed a ballot, marked it on a drafting table draped in awning cloth curtains and returned it to the inspector of elections, who put it into the ballot box. Then they went to his low-roofed Moorish-Pueblo home overlooking the Santa Clara Valley. The grandchildren were waiting, Peggy-Ann and Peter taking his hands into theirs, Joan in the arms of his youngest son's wife.

There were telegrams awaiting him:

WE WANT YOU TO KNOW THIS DAY GREATEST HONOR THAT CAN EVER COME TO US IS PRIVILEGE YOU HAVE GIVEN US TO SERVE YOU AND COUNTRY IN THIS TIME OF STRESS STOP UNEXAMPLED SERVICES YOU HAVE RENDERED YOUR FELLOW MEN PLACE YOU FOR ALL TIME AS ONE OF OUR GREATEST AMERICANS STOP YOURS WAS MAGNIFICENT FIGHT . . . WHICH HAS MULTIPLIED CON-FIDENCE AND RESPECT OF YOUR FRIENDS AND WON ADMIRATION OF ALL THOUGHTFUL PEOPLE STOP. WITH OUR DEEPEST AFFEC-TION

THEODORE H. JOSLIN.
WALTER NEWTON

Soon there were other telegrams:

RETURNS SO FAR INDICATE OPPOSITION WILL WIN MINNESOTA WILMINGTON DELAWARE FIRST RETURNS FROM FEW EARLY DIS-TRICTS INDICATE FALLING OFF OF REPUBLICAN VOTE

After that as evening came on the reports were shattering. In that hour just four years earlier he had put up a blackboard to chalk in the results of the race against Al Smith which had seen him carry forty states. He called Joslin in Washington to discuss what to say if it should be necessary to announce a capitulation. Then he retired to the same room in which he had sat in 1928 and waited there alone as the scope of the debacle became clear.

When he went down to circulate among the people Mrs. Hoover had invited in his appearance shocked them. His neighbors had not seen him in four years and could hardly believe this man with the sagging shoulders and whitened hair and stunned look was the man they had known. Nor had the Washington people ever seen him look so ghastly. He seemed in a daze as he read the telegrams from all over announcing an unparalleled disaster. Bewildered, he appeared entirely to lose his orientation, so much so that he shook hands with one man three times in a short period. The wife of his old friend Secretary of the Interior Ray Lyman Wilbur thought that the incredible defection of entirely safe Republican states took him entirely by surprise, and that he had fully expected to be reelected. He seemed to her about to collapse.

At nine o'clock Presidential Secretary Lawrence Richey came out to the reporters and said, "We have conceded nothing yet." Mrs. Hoover was downstairs supervising the preparation of a buffet supper with a fixed gracious-hostess smile on her face; the President had returned to his upstairs study. The unbelievable telegrams showed clearly that where he had once carried forty states he would now carry six.

He called Joslin and asked what Joslin thought. Across the three thousand miles Joslin forced himself to say that the last chance was gone. The President said, "All right, that's that. I'll give out the message right away and get myself a good sleep."

In New York, at the Biltmore Hotel, Roosevelt in evening clothes sat silently by a battery of telephone and telegraph operators. Farley said, "Sheffield, down in the Carolinas, goes for you one hundred and eighty-eight to one. That Hoover vote came from the postmaster." Everyone exploded into laughter, but

Roosevelt showed no emotion at all, his brooding eyes gazing into space.

John W. Davis, the defeated candidate of 1924, came in. "Frank, it's wonderful," he said. Roosevelt did not smile. His wife did not smile, but sat alone, abstracted. Jack Dempsey came in and shook hands and headed for the door.

Outside, Al Smith appeared. None of the people who had been with him for years would go in. A man said, "There's a new champion, eh, Al? Roosevelt's the new champion."

Al looked at him blankly. "Huh? What does that mean?" He did not wait for the man's answer but pushed on by. Dempsey was just coming out.

"Hello, Jack Dempsey," Al said, clapping the fighter on the shoulder. Then, "Hyuh, Frank." For the first time Roosevelt smiled.

In a hotel room nearby Louis Howe, suddenly frightened, repeated over and over that losers always spurt in the beginning. Grace Robinson of the *New York Daily News* went to Mrs. Roosevelt and asked if she was pleased.

"Pleased?" the governor's wife asked. "You can't look at an election this year just that way, can you?"

There was a long silence. Mrs. Roosevelt had always admired her friend of War days, Lou Henry Hoover, for her activities for the Girl Scouts, for the way she had established a life for herself apart from that of the President's Lady. Eleanor Roosevelt doubted that she could do the same thing, she was so shy, so awkward and ill at ease. She thought that she would take a couple of horses down to Washington and ride, and try to keep in the background of a situation in which she could not possibly find a place. Grace Robinson was waiting for her to say something. "If it was going to be, it was going to be. . . ." She had nothing more to say.

It was 9:17 P.M. California time when Jack McDowell, the Stanford Alumni Secretary, came out on the steps of the President's house and announced that Herbert Hoover had conceded. It was his own California that made him see the truth. For at that point, with only a fraction of the state's precincts reporting, he was behind nearly half a million votes. Reporters bowled over the Stanford students and ran to the phones; in New York Louis Howe took out a bottle and said, "I put this sherry away in Albany twenty years ago. I said then he'd be President some day and I made up my mind never to open this bottle until that time came.

"To the next President of the United States."

Hoover came out on the front terrace of his home, through the French windows. At once the photographers' floodlights on the roof came on. Mrs. Hoover was just behind him. Below them swarmed the Stanford students. "Sis-boom-bah! Hoover!" They repeated their cheer. In New York Roosevelt quieted the screaming exaltation that had greeted the flash of the announcement of capitulation in Palo Alto and said, "I want to say just a word. There are two people in the United States more than anybody else who are responsible for this great victory. One is my old friend and associate, Louis Howe, and the other is that splendid American, Jim Farley."

He went to his townhouse on East 65th Street. His mother was waiting for him in the doorway. She put her arms around him: "This is the greatest night of my life."

The reporters rushed up to ask if she was proud of him.

"Why, yes. But then, I've always been proud of him."

At Palo Alto the cheering went on and on and the college choir began to sing Stanford's songs. A half smile came to the President's lips and stayed there—faint, faraway, bittersweet, thought Erwin D. Canham of the *Christian Science Monitor*. The moonlight was very bright, joining with the floodlights to illuminate the President and his wife, who stood just behind him, also with a rueful, sad smile. The students cheered and sang, the girls' choir finishing with "Taps," and Robert Gros, head of the Stanford Students for Roosevelt, found himself thinking that the country owed this man in front of him a very great debt. Given his best, his all, for the country, Gros thought. History will remember.

The students gave one more cheer: "Sis-boom-bah! President and Mrs. Hoover! President and Mrs. Hoover!" Flares made the scene as light as day and sent smoke swirling upward. The cheering ended and the silence was so complete that the hissing of the powder candles and the clicking newsreel cameras could clearly be heard. She was smiling a misty smile behind him and it was reflected on his face also. He said, "All I can do is thank you for this demonstration of fine loyalty. Thank you." And immediately turned away. It would not have been like him to let them see the tears running down his face.

In New York James Roosevelt helped his father into bed. He bent over and kissed him. The President-Elect looked up and said, "You know, Jimmy, all my life I have been afraid of only one thing—fire. Tonight I think I'm afraid of something else."

"Afraid of what, Pa?"

"I'm just afraid that I may not have the strength to do this job."

Chapter Twenty

GOOD MORNING. I don't know that I have got anything to say to you. No doubt you are ravenous for news, and I haven't got it. I just got up from the best night's sleep I have had in a week."

"What are your plans, Mr. President?"

"I think I shall probably leave here Saturday night and go straight back to Washington."

"Mr. President, I imagine you are receiving a great many telegrams?"

"Literally thousands of telegrams. All very fine in their tenor."

GRATITUDE AND THANKFULNESS IN YOUR PRESIDENCY IS THE BURDEN OF THIS MESSAGE STOP THAT THERE ARE THOSE WHOSE EYES HAVE NOT SEEN DOES NOT IN A WHIT ALLOY OUR FEELINGS STOP AND IT IS THE FULL HUMANITARIAN RECORD THAT IS STRIKING HOME PASADENA CALIFORNIA

INTELLIGENT DETROIT VOTERS STILL BELIEVE IN HOOVER AND HOOVER POLICY AND CAN ONLY HOPE THE COUNTRY CAN SURVIVE ROOSEVELT. . . .

"Mr. President, have you heard anything from Roosevelt yet—any acknowledgment of your telegram?"

"Yes, a very pleasant acknowledgment. I don't recollect what the terms of it were."

"Mr. President, is there anything you want to say to the people who supported you? I noticed you didn't say anything last night."

"I haven't had time; I just got up. I probably will say something."

He had about him, thought J. Russell Young of the *Washington Star,* a certain strange wistfulness, particularly when he smiled. They had never seen him smile so much before. He was calm and philosophical, but always there was that wistful smile. And the manner in which he handled his long cigar suggested to Young a nervousness and suppression of his real emotions. There was a great silence around his home as he conducted the press conference with his back to the fireplace in his ground-floor living room, with only the sound of his grandchildren at play in the swimming pool. After he talked with the men he went out on a balcony and watched the children, still smiling, and then at twilight walked around the hillside in bloom with Christmas berry trees, California oaks and pepper trees. Mrs. Hoover was stricken numb, taking it far harder than her husband. She had never doubted he would win.

His aides, calling him "the tiredest man in America," wanted him to go back by sea via the Panama Canal. But he decided to take the train, and so they set out for the East in that manner. The trip back was far different from the one out. Now there were no boos and no hecklers, and he was easier with people than he had ever been before in his life. (The older reporters remembered back to Taft, who had been like a growling bear just before the day of his defeat, but who afterward had gone out and played golf and rumbled with laughter in his appealing fat-man way.) When those around the President talked with fear and contempt—perhaps more of the latter—of the oncoming Roosevelt Administration (how strange it sounded to say that! for Teddy had been dead thirteen years) he smiled in a sad, quizzical way and said, "It will work out some way." He told his aides they would all work on as though there had not been an election at all, that they would fight the Depression until the last minute of the last hour came before Roosevelt's inauguration. The reporters asked if he would take up residence in Washington and he said, "Oh, I would not live in Washington after the fourth of March. I will come back to California, I am sure."

"In that connection, Mr. President, have you any announcement to make concerning your plans after you return to California?"

"Not the remotest. I haven't thought about it."

"Does this mean the end of public life for you, Mr. President?"

"I haven't given consideration to anything of that sort. I will probably have to earn something of a living. I have been in public service now ever since 1914 and it is a long drain on one's resources."

"Mr. President, would you care to give any comment on your philosophy of—"

"No."

He had no comment, but perhaps his shattering and unprecedented defeat was comment enough. "Curiously enough," wrote William Allen White, "no one knows today exactly what it means. This story may be the prelude to a new era. . . . Possibly it is the triumphant struggle of the American spirit to survive and move forward to a rebirth of power. When, in the perspective of the decade before us, we shall really know how to read the meaning of the spectacle of these most recent four years, we shall know whether this battling figure of the President is an emblem of futility crushed by the onrush of new times and strange new ways of men, or whether he is the hero who went down with the blazoned banner that shall rise victorious before the battle ends. Then men will know whether, in the campaign of 1932, Herbert Hoover was the last routed defender of the old order or a leader born before his time."

The Hoover Moratorium of 1931, which suspended all debt payments between nations, was a one-year agreement. It was scheduled to end on December 15, when payments of hundreds of millions of dollars owed by the late Allies to the United States would come due. But in November the British ambassador, Sir Esmé Howard, handed Secretary of State Stimson a note which made Stimson immediately telegraph the President in the West. Sir Esmé Howard, like all British ambassadors to important powers, was urbane, genial, easy to get along with. Save for the President. In his years of being on His Majesty's Service in America Howard had met a great many Americans but none so hard to know or understand as the most important American of all. Perhaps it was that which accounted for the suddenness of the move; perhaps a British ambassador able to sit down with an American President might have worked it out somehow. But it could not be, and so Sir Esmé handed a curt note to the Secretary of State. The note was telegraphed West. It said that England wanted to review the entire question of the war debts. The implication was that England, in whose capital of London mobs of unemployed had run wild, did not want to pay. The War was long over. It was a different world. There ought to be a rethinking of those obligations whereby the British government, and the governments of a score of other countries, had contracted to pay unending millions of dollars to Uncle Shylock. But of course Sir Esmé did not put it that way to Secretary Stimson. Simply that England wanted to talk about the matter.

The telegram reached the Presidential train at Yuma, Arizona. There in the hot desert the President—"President-Reject," *Time* brutally called him—telegraphed the President-Elect asking him to come to the White House as soon as possible to discuss the British note. Roosevelt wired back, his telegram reaching the train at Hutchinson, Kansas, that he would telephone the President in Washington to make an appointment.

When the train pulled into Union Station a tiny crowd was waiting. Brigadier General Moseley thought bitterly of the contrasting scene when the President had gone West and all of official Washington had turned out. What a travesty, what a spectacle! Moseley said to himself, thinking also that the President was victorious in defeat, that the President's duty, firmness, integrity, was unwavering; that he had gone down with all flags flying for principle. The President drove to the White House and

Mary Randolph, secretary to the First Lady, looked at him and pitied him from the bottom of her heart for the difference between this entrance and that of March the fourth, 1929. There were no palm branches and laurels, no cheers, no music, "no air of bustle or expectancy . . . just a quiet, subdued White House; a laden desk in the Executive Office; and a heavy burden to be borne somehow until the inauguration of his successor."

Roosevelt telephoned on November 16.

"Good morning, Mr. President, how are you?"

"All right."

"They tell me you had a little rest."

"I have and I hope you have, too."

"I have been in bed for five days. I had a real case of flu."

"That is too bad."

"I got up today, for the first time came downstairs. I want to know if it is all right with you if I come on Tuesday next."

"That will be fine."

Roosevelt came on the ten-thirty out of New York and arrived at Union Station at three-thirty. An open touring car took him through large crowds to the South Grounds where he could take an elevator up to the Red Room where the President waited with Mills. Raymond Moley, the organizer of Roosevelt's Brain Trust, was along. Roosevelt's hair had gotten mussed in the ride and he tried to smooth it down in an embarrassed manner. But he cheered up when he recognized one of the doormen waiting to help him out of the car. "Well, John Mays, how are you?" he smiled, putting out his hand to someone who had shaved Wilson in the long ago and who had welcomed the young Assistant Secretary of the Treasury to 1600 Pennsylvania Avenue. The President-Elect's manner was so informal and friendly that word of it made the White House servants buzz excitedly to one another. The head usher, Ike Hoover, led him up to the Red Room.

"The governor of the State of New York."

"Mr. President."

"Governor. I'm glad to see you."

Mills stepped forward and greeted his Dutchess County boyhood chum and Harvard classmate, calling him by his first name. Roosevelt addressed him as "Ogden." (To Hoover he was always "Mills.") The two joshed each other about the Democratic campaign charge which showed a magnificent golf course and indicated it was Mills's private preserve. Then the four men, the President, the President-Elect, Mills and Moley, sat around a small mahogany table underneath pictures of Jefferson, Madison, Grant, John Adams. The President explained that he wanted Roosevelt's backing in a demand that the Europeans pay their debts on December 15, and also Roosevelt's cooperation in preparing the American position in the forthcoming World Economic Conference. As Hoover spoke, referring to detailed notes, he looked alternately at the Great Seal of the United States embroidered in the rug at his feet, or at Moley. He thought to himself that Roosevelt was amiable, pleasant, anxious to be of service, but very badly informed and of very limited vision. Therefore he concentrated on Moley.

The men were together for two hours, past dusk and into the late fall darkness. The President and Mills smoked cigars; Roosevelt and Moley cigarettes. They drank ice water and orangeade. The President as always was prepared with position papers and statistics and a point of view. He wanted Roosevelt to endorse these things, but Roosevelt was suspicious. And perhaps something of the President's opinion of him as a young man very ignorant and very much in need of education came through. Roosevelt was vague about committing himself to do the things the President wanted done, and after he left he summed up the whole war debt question to the reporters by saying he wasn't President yet and that therefore "It isn't my baby."

So the country went into something like an interregnum. Congress opened in early December amid scenes that made Washington look like the capital of a banana republic on the morning after a revolution, with police everywhere and demonstrators herded away from the Capitol and the White House. It was a Congress far more responsive to the President waiting in the wings than the one in the White House. It was also the most lame-duck of all Congresses, with Republicans who had been in power for years playing out their last days in office. They were sour, angry, and frightened of the future and hardly in a mood to pay heed to Hoover's State of the Union message which entirely ignored the results of the election and called for adherence to the principles that resulted in his winning 87 electoral votes as opposed to Roosevelt's 444.

In that cold, gray time New York grew irritated with the apple-sellers on every corner (HELP WAR VETERANS) and ordered them off the main streets, and the national income, eighty billion in 1929, dropped to forty billion. Yale beat Harvard before the smallest crowd ever to see that game in history, the end section of the Yale Bowl entirely empty. Every housewife in the country was buying cheap or unknown brands of goods she had never bought before, and people revived the half-forgotten crafts of the past—fruit drying, brewing medicines from herbs, soap making. One third of Iowa was foreclosed (Milo Reno and his men had collapsed and their movement was gone) and abroad the power of the Austrian agitator Adolf Hitler grew so that it was obvious that shortly he must assume the government of Germany.

The Confederate Veteran, subsidized since the Civil War by the United Daughters of the Confederacy, ceased publication. Less than half the usual number of marriages took place during the year; thrice the number of suicides. *Time* regularly ran stories under the heading "Destitution": A Boston graduate of Harvard Medical School, almost sixty, murdered his wife because he could no longer see her live "in abject poverty." He had been discharged from his job as an elevator operator. A Pittsburgh artist gave up his studio to seek work as a housepainter—"I'm tired of painting over canvases I've used before and I'm about out of paint. I want a job." Police in Babylon, New York, found a nurse who had ministered to the troops of the AEF starving in a maple grove. For two weeks she had been sleeping on a bundle of old rags and newspapers.

In Rahway, New Jersey, a man murdered his wife and took his own life. He left a note: "My brain just cracked. I have had many financial worries. I am terribly sorry." In El Monte, California, a prominent clubwoman killed her rancher husband and herself—"Finances." A woman left a two-month-old baby in the car of a stranger parked on Broadway. A note pinned on the infant's suit said, "His name is Billie. I have tried to keep him but I can't keep myself. I am a young widow almost starving." In Philadelphia a grocer shot and killed a man who tried to steal a milk bottle. The dead man's wife said he had been a mechanic long unemployed. He had gone out to pick up cigarette stubs in the gutter. In New York the writer Edmund Wilson saw a man idling along in front of half-empty apartment houses and thought to himself the man was typical of the millions: "His life had come under a shadow from which he can see no way of escaping and for which he has no method of accounting." A woman went to Washington's Animal Rescue League: "You put animals out of their misery. Why not my baby?"

At Hyde Park the President-Elect grinned when Huey Long came on the telephone screaming about this or that, and winked as he jollied Huey along. But afterward he said that something would have to be done about Long, for he was one of the two most dangerous men in the country. Who was the other most dangerous man? asked Rex Tugwell, and Roosevelt said, "Doug MacArthur." Hitler and Mussolini did not matter, Albert, King of the Belgians told an interviewer, for the end of civilization was being prepared elsewhere: in Russia. Julian Huxley said our civilization was dead or dying, and that its return must take centuries.

Roosevelt's old mentor in the Navy Department, ex-Secretary Daniels, wondered what to call the younger man, and Roosevelt wrote, "I am still Franklin to you." If Daniels exulted in his friend's victory, the greater mass of Americans did not. That Roosevelt viewed a pressing problem as "not my baby" encouraged the concept of him that most people had always held—charming, human, but irresponsible in the end. Roosevelt's wife thought him capable and energetic, but to her very closest friends she said it was possible that no one could do anything to save America now.

In the great Gothic movie theaters left over from the twenties, one heard a curious phenomenon in that December: They cheered Herbert Hoover in the newsreels. But of course that did not matter. Congress settled into meaningless and powerless argument about things that did not matter; Congress was afraid to do anything without the President-Elect's permission, and he was not yet in office to give that permission. Prices slid down to low points not seen in generations or even in centuries. The cost of wheat and corn was below what it had been in Colonial days; the price of other commodities was figured in actual value to be at the levels of the Middle Ages.

The President resolved to go away for the holidays. It was his first real vacation since taking office. On the night of December 23 he went through Union Station with a group of friends to two cars attached to the Southern Limited. Justice and Mrs. Stone were with him and the First Lady, Senator and Mrs. Warren Austin, the columnist Mark Sullivan, the White House doctor Joel Boone, and Secretary Richey. As they went through the station's concourse there was no applause from passersby; the cold and the slush and 1932's December hardly encouraged it. A few men raised their hats.

The somber vacation party had no set itinerary, but would simply head for where the fish were biting in the South. The reports of the sea trout off Savannah were encouraging, so they made for there. The Presidential yacht *Mayflower* was laid up, as were half the boats of all the world, so they took the Commerce Department lighthouse inspection boat *Sequoia*. On Christmas Day they went ashore at the Sapelelo Island home of Howard E. Coffin and had a holiday dinner of roast oysters. Back in Washington, the White House stood entirely dark. There was no Christmas tree. In the evening the fishing party put out to sea, the President wearing an old Panama hat, white duck trousers much the worse for wear and a shabby, worn blue sack coat along with the inevitable high collar and tie. They went south along the Florida coast past towering palm trees and little fishing villages dotting the shore every few miles and then into the passage between Fort Pierce and Lake Worth, eight miles north of Palm Beach. The ocean turned rough.

In Washington Louis Howe came to inspect the Executive Offices and order ramps placed on certain stairways so that Roosevelt's wheelchair might more easily be maneuvered there. The President-Elect, it was announced, would attend the Albany swearing-in as governor of New York of Lieutenant-Governor Herbert Lehman on the night of December 31, and then go by car to his home at Hyde Park. On the afternoon of that day Hoover hooked three sailfish from the deck of a sixty-five-foot sloop, *Orca*, which was put into use while the larger *Sequoia* remained in harbor at the landing of the Sailfish Club of Lake Worth in Palm Beach. The largest of the sailfish was seven feet eleven inches; had it been one inch longer he would have been eligible for the "Diamond Button" class pin the Sailfish Club awarded. Only eight had been given out in the previous four years. When the day's fishing was done, *Orca* went through the ground swells of the open sea and into the Palm Beach inlet and then into the harbor and the landing.

Intermittent showers and winds came up offshore as evening came on. Governor Roosevelt in Albany was asked how he would greet the New Year and he said he would probably be in a car heading home to Hyde Park—"I'll be curled up asleep in one corner, and the Missus in the other." In Florida the rain beat on, and it was cold and dreary. There would be no formal celebration at the landing of the Sailfish Club. At the White House J. W. Hunefeld, a housepainter who had been first in line at the annual New Year's Day reception just one year before, went there again as midnight approached. "Keep my record clear," he said.

Midnight of that year came.

Chapter Twenty-One

THE COUNTRY was six weeks into the new year when all its banks began to close.

It began in Michigan. Detroit's tottering Union Guardian Trust appealed to the RFC for help. The Union Guardian Trust was the bank Henry Ford used. He had poured millions into it. But the millions were gone. The bank had no collateral for a loan. "Let the crash come," cried Senator James Couzens of Michigan. "Why should the RFC bail out Ford?" He warned the RFC directors he would destroy them if they approved a loan virtually unsecured by any collateral.

Hoover called Couzens to the White House and told him he had prevailed upon General Motors and Chrysler to deposit money in the Union Guardian Trust. He asked that Couzens deposit one million dollars of his own money in the bank. Then, shored up with the new collateral, the bank could be granted the loan.

Astonished and angry, Couzens refused. The bank meant Ford to him. Twenty years earlier, as partners, the two men had put the Model T on every road. Then they broke up. Only hatred was left—that and the tens of millions each had. He would do nothing for Ford's bank. Hoover bitterly said, "If eight hundred thousand small bank depositors in my hometown could be saved by lending three percent of my fortune, even if I lost, I would certainly do it." Couzens walked out of the White House. He would fight the loan, he repeated.

The Union Guardian Trust was left helpless before the swarming depositors demanding their money; all the banks in Michigan suffered murderous runs. To save them, Governor William A. Comstock ordered a statewide close. He called it a bank "holiday."

Through the crisis, President-Elect Roosevelt remained silent. On February 17, three days after Michigan's banks closed, President Hoover wrote a letter begging the President-Elect to issue a statement that might help allay the terrible waves of panic sweeping over the country. He asked Roosevelt to announce that the new Administration would not tamper with or inflate the currency, that it would balance the budget and not destroy the public's belief in the sanctity of the government's word by issuing bonds which could not be backed up.

He wrote Roosevelt's name on the envelope, misspelling it "Roosvelt" in his haste. Then he told a Secret Service man to carry it personally to the President-Elect. The man hurried to New York and found Roosevelt in a hotel ballroom watching comic skits performed by a newspapermen's group.

Roosevelt opened the letter. "My dear Mr. President-Elect: A most critical situation has arisen in the country of which I feel it is my duty to advise you confidentially. I am therefore taking this course of writing you myself and sending it to you through the Secret Service for your hand direct as obviously its misplacement would only feed the fire and increase the dangers. . . ."

Roosevelt finished it, showed it to his people. "Cheeky document," he remarked. Who was Hoover to tell him what to do?

In Washington Hoover anxiously awaited a statement, or at least an answer to the letter. Almost a week went by. Roosevelt kept silent. He must be a "madman" to go on this way, Hoover cried out to Secretary of State Stimson. After ten days Roosevelt wrote saying the banking fire was "bound to spread in spite of anything that is done by way of mere statements."

Meanwhile banks closed and gold fled the United States. Every ship bound for Europe carried gold bars in its hold, the property of foreigners who feared what Roosevelt might do when he came to power, and of Americans who no longer trusted their country. Rumors spread that Roosevelt would establish a dictatorship in the fashion of Adolf Hitler, who had taken power in Germany on the President-Elect's birthday, January 30. Or that he would water down the dollar so that it would buy a dime's worth of goods.

Hoover thought of assuming the wartime powers that had been Wilson's in order to prohibit the flight of gold. But it seemed so futile. In a matter of days his term would be over. "We are on the verge of financial panic and chaos," he despairingly wrote Senator Simeon Fess.

He invited in Democratic leaders to ask that they back him in a move to get the federal government to guarantee at least a portion of each depositor's account. Senators Robinson and Glass told him nothing could be done without Roosevelt's approval. And that Roosevelt would approve nothing.

"Panic . . . Whirlwind . . . Fear . . ." He exhausted all the words. The country was grinding to a halt. Banks everywhere were closing their doors. He called Roosevelt on the telephone to beg for any kind of constructive action. Roosevelt repeated that he would wait until he had full power.

On the evening of March 2, Roosevelt came to Washington and a suite at the Mayflower. The next day he went with his wife, his son James and James's wife for the traditional call on the outgoing President.

Such a meeting was always a formal social call. But when the party arrived they found Secretary Mills and Eugene Meyer, head of the Federal Reserve Board, waiting with the President. With less than twenty-four hours of the Hoover Administration remaining, the President and his aides began to ask Roosevelt to join with them in some action against the bank closings.

Roosevelt gave the same answer he always had. Hoover with his charts and indices tried again. Roosevelt repeated there was nothing to be done. He made as if to straighten his leg braces preparatory to rising and said he would be getting along now.

Hoover got up and stood over him. He thought that now at

the very last he understood Franklin Roosevelt. Ten days earlier he had received a call from the industrialist James Rand. Rand told the President he had lunched with Roosevelt's adviser Rexford G. Tugwell, and Tugwell had said the men around the President-Elect fully understood the bank situation. It would undoubtedly collapse in a few days, Tugwell said. And the responsibility would be "in the lap of President Hoover."

Working on his braces and preparing to go before the President dismissed him, Roosevelt looked up at Herbert Hoover.

"Mr. President," Roosevelt said, "I know it is customary to do so, but you don't have to return our call if you don't want to."

"Mr. Roosevelt, when you have been in Washington as long as I have, you will learn that the President of the United States calls on nobody!" Hoover turned and headed for the door.

Roosevelt opened his mouth to lash back, but Mrs. Roosevelt jumped to her feet. "It's been very pleasant, but we must go now," she said. When her husband stood up, his fingers gripped his son James's arm with almost convulsive strength. James had never seen him so angry.

All through the afternoon and evening governors across the country ordered the banks closed before the Americans emptied and destroyed them. A Roman holiday, Hoover thought. Five days earlier Adolf Hitler had manufactured the Reichstag fire as an excuse to run amuck, arresting, imprisoning, slaying the Germany that had been. Roosevelt, Hoover thought, had learned from Hitler. The bank closings would be his Reichstag fire.

When night came, his last night, the President was still at his desk. Inauguration Day arrived at midnight. At four in the morning Governor Lehman of New York issued a decree forbidding his state's banks to open. Illinois followed his example shortly after.

When dawn came the Great Depression was in its climax. There was not one bank in America that would open its doors. Dull gray clouds covered the sky and occasional rain fell as Washington's leaden sky lightened somewhat with the morning hours. The country was in something like rigor mortis. Paralyzed.

Hoover looked across the desk at Secretary Joslin. "We are at the end of our string. There is nothing more we can do."

The morning papers reported that deafening, continuous cheering greeted a speech by Chancellor Hitler. In Manchuria the Japanese Army slashed ahead, its airplanes machine-gunning at will Chinese troops with no anti-aircraft guns. In America there was no money in circulation beyond what a man had in his pockets or a shop in its cash register. Bus drivers accepted IOU's; people wrote checks to get on New York's subway.

In the White House a Secret Service man came into Hoover's office. The man at the desk had heavy lines under his eyes. He seemed utterly weary. No one knew when, if ever, the banks would reopen. But whatever happened, in two hours the President would be a private citizen.

The Secret Service man explained that he had come to get Hoover's Presidential Flag. It would be packed away with the last things to be loaded on the U.S.S. *Henderson* addressed to Mr. and Mrs. Herbert Hoover, Palo Alto, California, c/o Commanding Officer, Twelfth Naval District. When the Secret Service man spoke, Hoover looked at him directly for the first time in their four years together. They began to chat. For a little while they were together, talking in an informal way. The Secret Service man left, thinking to himself, he told a reporter, that only now was he "seeing Mr. Hoover as he really is."

Other White House personnel came in to say good-bye. Someone told the President two Negro porters would like to greet him before he left. He had never spoken to them before. He had them sent in, one wearing a hastily donned suit jacket with his overalls.

Then it was time to go. Roosevelt's car drew up in the north driveway. Looking up, he took note of how shabby the White House looked because of the budget economies which precluded painting it. The President appeared. The Third Cavalry which had helped to chase away the Bonus Army came to a saber salute. Hoover mustered up a smile as he leaned over to shake hands with Franklin Roosevelt.

As they turned the corner of Pennsylvania Avenue and Fifteenth Street a very faint cheer reached them. Roosevelt took off his hat, waved it, smiled at the people along the curb. Hoover looked around him and uncertainly took off his hat. For an instant he held it a few inches above his head and then quickly put it back on. He did not raise it again.

They drove down the Avenue and at every sound of slight applause Roosevelt raised his hat. Hoover sat absolutely motionless, eyes down. For the first moments of the trip Roosevelt tried to make conversation. There was never a word of reply. They came to the skeletons of the new buildings coming up on the site of the Bonus Army's fight. "My, Mr. President," Roosevelt said, "what interesting steel structures." There was no answer. Roosevelt abandoned the conversation.

They went through the sunless gray streets of the capital of a stricken, beaten, nation; in the eyes of the journalist Arthur Krock, Washington on this day was like a beleaguered city in wartime. Russell Owen of *The New York Times* thought the gloom was such as could be physically felt. Four years earlier the crowds had been gigantic, boisterous, cheerful and noisy, carrying umbrellas of every color, gay yellows and oranges. Now the people wore dull dark suits and dresses that would not need frequent cleaning.

The caravan halted in the Capitol Plaza. *I had some nice talks with Herbert Hoover before he went West for Christmas*, Franklin Roosevelt had once upon a time written his friend Hugh Gibson. *He is certainly a wonder, and I wish we could make him a President of the United States. There could not be a better one.*

They went into the building by separate entrances. Hoover went to the President's Room, put a cigar in his mouth, and began signing last-minute bills. After half an hour, as noon approached, he arose and walked to the rotunda past the members of the diplomatic corps. They saluted him and, nodding, head down, he quickened his pace.

He came, alone, to the top of the Capitol steps and halted. His hat was in his hand. He stood motionless, gazing out at the crowds waiting for Franklin Roosevelt to take the oath of office. A silence settled over the great plaza as the people looked at him. For what seemed like a long time he stood there. It was very quiet.

Then Roosevelt, aided by his son James, came up behind the President. Hoover did not look back and did not move, but stood gazing out at the people.

A Secret Service man touched his arm and indicated he should step forward and take his seat.

Hoover went down the steps, sat down. He stared straight ahead. He was motionless.

Franklin Roosevelt took the oath of office with his hand resting on a Bible opened to Chapter Thirteen of Paul's First Epistle to the Corinthians:

Though I speak with the tongues of angels and have not charity, I am become as sounding brass or a tinkling cymbal.

And though I have the gift of prophecy and understand all mysteries and all knowledge, and though I have faith so that I could remove mountains, and have not charity, I am nothing.

President Roosevelt made his inaugural speech and said that what the nation needed was confidence. "The only thing we have to fear, is fear itself." His predecessor listened with no sign that would reveal his thoughts.

At the end ex-President Hoover rose quickly and went down the steps to a waiting limousine. He helped Mrs. Hoover enter and they curved around the Capitol to Union Station where a Special waited. At Philadelphia Mrs. Hoover got off and boarded a California-bound train. The ex-President went on to the Waldorf-Astoria hotel in New York. It was announced that he would stay there for a few days, "one reason being a desire to be available if President Roosevelt should want information."

In Washington, as the gray afternoon faded into evening, Eleanor Roosevelt, in a sitting room of the southwest corner of the White House, talked to a reporter about the people in Capitol Plaza. Their solemnity would always be her most abiding impression of the day. There was something terrifying about it, she said. "One has a feeling of going it blindly, because we're in a tremendous stream and none of us knows where we're going to land."

Night came. Mrs. Roosevelt and the members of her family went out to the Inaugural Ball, but her husband sat alone with Louis Howe in the Lincoln Study which Lou Henry Hoover had so lovingly decorated.

Later a friend said to Roosevelt that if he succeeded he would go down in history as the greatest American President and that if he failed he would live on as the worst.

Roosevelt replied, "If I fail I shall be the last one."

Afterword

HE STAYED IN NEW YORK for the first few days of the Roosevelt Administration, going on long drives in the limousine of ex-Secretary of the Treasury Mills, strolling on Fifth Avenue, waiting for President Roosevelt to telephone. The call never came.

He went back to California then. For twelve years, the period of Franklin Roosevelt's Presidency, he never set foot in Washington. He was entirely a private citizen, with no role in the life of the country save that of critical book- and speechwriter pointing to the faults of the New Deal and saying that it had prolonged the Great Depression in America until the Second World War, whereas it was considered to have been over in Europe by 1934 or 1935.

Very few people listened. Washington itself forgot Hoover almost at the moment that his train pulled out of Union Station. What replaced him was excitement, churning action, daring experiments taken up and dropped, a quick end to Prohibition—fun. Roosevelt's press conferences were a delight for the reporters and their readers, and Roosevelt's people were colorful and dashing. In the winking of an eye the country was involved with Blue Eagle, AAA, WPA, the CCC, TVA, a dozen other agencies and movements. When a second Bonus Army came to Washington, Louis Howe drove out to their encampment with the President's wife, and then fell asleep in the car while Mrs. Roosevelt circulated among the veterans asking if the coffee was good. From that day on the bonus was dead.

Hoover was never again discussed as a candidate for the office he had once held. But for twenty years there was never an election of any kind in which Democratic orators did not invoke his name, making it synonymous with Depression and disaster. At Republican conventions every four years the delegates gave him rote applause and then ignored him. He fought on with his books and speeches which pointed out that, for all that the Democrats did, the general prosperity levels of before the crash were not reached again until well into the 1950's.

For his efforts the most conservative elements of the Republican Party, who had once hated and feared him, made him into something of an idol. But by then it was safe for them to praise him, for they knew the possibility was past that he might try again for the Presidency.

Mellon died, Mills died, Louis Howe, Dawes, Al Smith. In 1944, when Lou Henry Hoover died, Eleanor Roosevelt sent him a kind note. A year later, when Eleanor Roosevelt's husband died, he wrote to her. Invited to attend the funeral, he did not appear.

With Harry Truman President, Hoover visited the White House for the first time since leaving it on March 4, 1933. Truman telephoned him at his hotel and, addressing him as "Mr. President," said he would come over to see him. Hoover replied that it would be improper for the President of the United States to call upon anybody. Truman laughed and said he'd guessed that Mr. Hoover would say that. And that he had therefore already dispatched a car to pick him up and bring him to the White House.

At Truman's request Hoover went to Europe to feed and clothe the hungry, even as he had a quarter of a century before. Truman also put him to work reorganizing the structure of the government as once, before the crash, he had wanted to do. He loved Harry Truman for permitting him to work and to contribute. He told his friends Truman added ten years to his life. When Truman left the White House he told the reporters the two of them had an "Ex-Presidents' Club" with Hoover as its leader and himself as its secretary.

As the years passed Hoover mellowed. Always active on behalf of children—his principal charity was the Boys' Club—he published a book of his letters to and from little boys and girls. At dinner parties he unbent, told stories, made quiet little jokes. That he could be charming came as a revelation to people who knew him only by reputation. "That just can't be Herbert Hoover," a senator's wife exclaimed to Arthur Krock after meeting him at Krock's home.

When the New Deal ran its course and disappeared into history, books appeared by former New Dealers admitting, openly or by implication, that the main lines of their best programs had been laid out by President Hoover in 1931 and 1932. Hoover cited the books as proof that only political obstructionism had blocked him from pulling the country through, that had he been given the cooperation Congress gave Roosevelt he would have succeeded on all fronts. He believed to his dying moment that the Depression had been beaten in the summer of 1932 and that only the specter of an oncoming Roosevelt Presidency had reversed the trend.

What it came down to, in essence, he said, was that he wanted restraint and local people dealing with local problems; and that the New Deal wanted wild spending and a giant centralized government taking complete charge of everything. But by then the whole thing was academic. To a prosperous postwar America, balanced budgets and tight constraints on spending belonged to history and not to current events. Hoover the dynamic engineer and Great Humanitarian, Hoover the planner and innovator and liberal, was simply Hoover the President with the breadlines.

A generation grew up knowing nothing of his great pre-1929 past, and thinking of him as reactionary and cold, a man with no sympathy for the unfortunate, a failure. Very old, something of the aura of dead days clung to him. Once, for a time, he had commanded the support and admiration of the world. In the end a chosen few said of him that the world had dealt as cruelly with him as with any man who ever lived. But only a very few. That he believed America had lost something very precious after 1933, that he believed the beautiful jug was broken into a thousand pieces, did not concern the Americans.

Herbert Hoover in his personal life was instinctively kind. And in a practical way. On a fishing trip shortly after leaving the Presidency he was told of a needy family living nearby. He went to their shack, had the children committed to hospitals for medical assistance, made telephone calls to raise food and clothing money. When he and his former Secretary of the Interior, Ray Lyman Wilbur, arrived at the scene of an auto accident, the former President of the United States immediately leaped forward to pull the victims gently from the wreckage, lay them down by the side of the road, cover and tend them.

Earlier, as President, he hired a teacher to minister to the needs of the children living in the tiny hollows and creek hamlets near his fishing camp along the Rapidan. Year after year he paid her salary. It is doubtful if the children or their parents realized how completely it was his own self-created project. For he always wanted to work that way—without the recipient of his generosity knowing who the benefactor was. Scores of times in his long life, friends died. He always assigned someone to check, quietly, the state in which the widow and children would find themselves. If he discovered financial problems, he arranged jobs or gifts. But he always screened his actions so that the people would never know who was helping them. He said a feeling of gratitude towards him would injure or at least change his relationship with them.

When his participation could not be concealed—as when, during the Presidency, he supplemented the government salaries of certain aides, he did it in matter-of-fact fashion that discouraged emotional display by the people being aided. Even on the bitter day of March 4, 1933, his last day in the White House, he wrote a note and put it in the desk which would be Franklin Roosevelt's, asking Roosevelt to keep a certain man on in the government—the man would have difficulty securing employment if Roosevelt let him go. Roosevelt complied with the request.

Men who rise to great position almost inevitably leave behind broken relationships. It was not the case with Hoover. The friends he made, he kept. Men he had worked with since college days remained his friends until death. His aides from Belgian Relief, Commerce, the White House, stayed with him. To Lewis Strauss they were like a club grouped around The Chief. Once a Hoover man, they said, always a Hoover man. A telephone call from him would send them flying across the nation or the world. In exchange his home and his heart were open to them.

Of Hoover's intellectual depth and grasp there can be no doubt. Bernard Baruch said the man soaked up facts like a sponge. Henry Lewis Stimson, Hoover's Secretary of State and Roosevelt's Secretary of War, said Hoover was capable of more intense and prolonged intellectual effort than any man he had ever met. (And Stimson served every President from Theodore Roosevelt to Harry Truman.)

Given all this, it was to his friends a hurt almost too painful to bear that Hoover was the most hated President in history. Hoover was blunt; he was impatient of meaningless niceties; he was no showman and no politician; he would not stoop or pander; he was uncompromising. But how had it possibly come about that the overwhelming majority of Americans detested him personally? How, his friends asked themselves, could it have happened that, as Gilbert Seldes pointed out, a certain type of bitter laughter heard in any room in 1932 meant that someone had told a brutal anti-Hoover joke?

Hoover had bestrode the earth in seven-league boots before 1929. He had never failed at anything. It was impossible to look at him on Notification Day, August 11, 1928, and not feel that his election and Presidency would bring forth the brightest period of our history. Hoover was the finest flower of our system. It was bewildering, phenomenally so, to look at him on March 4, 1933, and see him as the discredited leader whose name would be poison in the mouths of millions for decades to come.

What happened?

There was something in Hoover himself that caused it. That

something was his fate and his country's fate. Perhaps he was, as Franklin Roosevelt thought, not what he seemed. Or that in any other time he would have served eight glorious years and gone out of office covered with laurels.

There are those who feel Hoover can be characterized by the words "dogmatic," "unflexible," "unintelligent." His inadequacies, they say, were far deeper than a mere lack of spirit and of fire; it was that he misunderstood the situation, not that he was a poor performer. To those who see him this way, he will always be the unimaginative President whose methods and beliefs, put to the test, failed.

There are those who see him as having been crucified because he was too pure—and that this pureness, this idealism, was the something that brought him low. America's democracy brought him to high position; and America's democracy brought him down because democracy gives every man a vote. And every man is not selfless, not faultless, as Hoover thought the Americans were.

Hoover had seen Europe, seen Asia, the Arab countries, Latin America. It was his career, after 1914, to help those who suffered in foreign lands. No one ever did more than he for more people. He was at home in a dozen countries—had maintained residences in them—but his heart stayed at home. He remained throughout an American patriot.

Why, then, did he not bring an end to the suffering of the American people during the Depression as he had alleviated the hunger of the Europeans during and after the War? Why did he not rise out of himself, throw aside the Quaker gray cloak and lead a revolution in American ways?

These questions resolve themselves into two issues.

First, could he look like he was curing the Depression? The answer is that he could not. On visits to West Branch in his maturity he used to look at a school friend who became an auctioneer and murmur, "If only I had a voice like that." Hoover shrank from display. Some said it was because he was intrinsically cold. Others, that he was too respectful of his American listeners and of himself to sink to stage dramatics and rhetoric. Deep in Hoover's feeling for Americans was his thought that they were better than the Europeans. On a local level, personal charity could be endured because it was a matter of human kindness between individuals and families. But it could not be made a national, institutionalized way of life, because it was impersonal, degrading and in the end futile.

The other question is whether in fact he had cured the Depression, as he thought he had. In later years he used to say that in retrospect he could have done better. But that is true of everything we all do. Hoover was infuriatingly stubborn in the eyes of his subordinates. He would not bend his principles. "One, with God, is a majority," the Quakers said. But where is God? Hoover thought God stood for traditional America. His enemies shouted that he did not understand the Americans because of his long years abroad; he replied that he had shown the way to cure the Depression, but that new elements, new ways, pushed aside that traditional America which was fighting its way out, and substituted degrading, meaner measures.

There are many "ifs" with Hoover. Could he but have raised his voice. Might he not have unbalanced the budget and gone for deficit spending—as every one of his successors did? His supporters answer that flamboyance is not achievement; and that unbalanced budgets lead to welfare states and welfare catastrophes and postponed disasters.

He remains an enigma. William Allen White said it would take decades for history to render judgment on him. Decades have come and gone, but the judgment is still hanging in the balance.

Hoover died in 1964, aged ninety. In his last moments he lapsed into speaking in the Quaker fashion, calling the doctors and nurses "thee" and "thou" as he had addressed the people around him when he was a boy in the little town on the prairies of the middle frontier. He was buried on a slight rise there, where, he said, they had taught him sufficiency, pride and individualism—in West Branch, in Iowa.

BIBLIOGRAPHY

Abels, Jules, *In the Time of Silent Cal.* New York, G. P. Putnam's Sons, 1969.

Allen, Frederick Lewis, *Since Yesterday: The Nineteen Thirties in America.* New York, Harper & Brothers, 1939.

Angley, Edward, ed., *Oh, Yeah?* New York, The Viking Press, 1931.

Anonymous (Robert Sharon Allen), *Washington Merry-Go-Round.* New York, Horace Liveright, 1931.

———, *More Merry-Go-Round.* New York, Horace Liveright, 1932.

Anonymous (Clinton Wallace Gilbert), *The Mirrors of Washington.* New York, G. P. Putnam's Sons, 1921.

Anonymous (Ray Thomas Tucker), *Mirrors of 1932.* New York, Brewer, Warren and Putnam, 1931.

Bird, Caroline, *The Invisible Scar.* New York, David McKay Company, 1966.

Clapper, Olive Ewing, *Washington Tapestry.* New York, McGraw-Hill, 1946.

Clapper, Raymond, *Watching the World* (edited by Olive Ewing Clapper). New York, McGraw-Hill, 1944.

Corey, Herbert, *The Truth About Hoover.* Boston, Mass., Houghton Mifflin, 1932.

Darling, Jay Norwood, *As Ding Saw Hoover.* Ames, Iowa, Iowa State College Press, 1954.

Eisenhower, Dwight D., *At Ease: Stories I Tell to Friends.* New York, Doubleday & Company, 1967.

Emerson, Edwin, *Hoover and His Times.* Garden City, N.Y., Garden City Publishing Company, 1932.

Farley, James A., *Behind the Ballots.* New York, Harcourt, Brace and Company, 1938.

Fáy, Bernard, *Roosevelt and His America.* Boston, Mass., Little, Brown and Company, 1933.

Fields, Alonzo, *My Twenty-one Years in the White House.* New York, Coward-McCann, 1961.

Flynn, Edward J., *You're the Boss.* New York, The Viking Press, 1947.

Fowler, Gene, *Beau James: The Life and Times of Jimmy Walker.* New York, The Viking Press, 1949.

Galbraith, John Kenneth, *The Great Crash: 1929.* Boston, Mass., Houghton Mifflin, 1955.

Graves, Lloyd M., *The Great Depression and Beyond.* New York, Press of J. D. McGuire, 1932.

Hallgren, Mauritz, *Seeds of Revolt*. New York, Alfred A. Knopf, 1933.

Handlin, Oscar, *Al Smith and His America*. Boston, Mass., Little, Brown and Company, 1958.

Hickok, Lorena, *Reluctant First Lady*. New York, Dodd, Mead and Company, 1962.

Hill, Edwin C., *The American Scene*. New York, Witmark Education Publications, 1933.

Hoover, Herbert Clark, *Campaign Speeches of 1932*. New York, Doubleday, 1933.

———, *Memoirs*, Vol. I, *Years of Adventure: 1874–1920*; Vol. II, *The Cabinet and the Presidency: 1920–1933*; Vol. III, *The Great Depression: 1929–1941*. New York, The Macmillan Company, 1951–52.

Hoover, Irwin Hood, *Forty-two Years in the White House*. Boston, Mass., Houghton Mifflin, 1934.

Hunt, Frazier, *The Untold Story of Douglas MacArthur*. New York, The Devin-Adair Co., 1954.

Johnson, Claudius O., *Borah of Idaho*. New York and Toronto, Longmans Green and Company, 1936.

Johnson, Walter, *William Allen White's America*. New York, Henry Holt and Co., 1947.

Jones, Jesse, *Fifty Billion Dollars: Thirteen Years with the RFC*. New York, The Macmillan Company, 1951.

Josephson, Matthew, *Infidel in the Temple*. New York, Alfred A. Knopf, 1967.

Joslin, Theodore, *Hoover Off the Record*. New York, Doubleday & Company, 1934.

Krock, Arthur, *Memoirs: Sixty Years on the Firing Line*. New York, Funk and Wagnalls, 1968.

Lathem, Edward Connery, *Meet Calvin Coolidge: The Man Behind the Myth*. Brattleboro, Vt., Stephen Greene Press, 1960.

Liggett, Walter W., *The Rise of Herbert Hoover*. New York, The H. K. Fly Company, 1932.

Lippmann, Walter, *Interpretations 1931–1932*, selected and edited by Allan Nevins. New York, The Macmillan Company, 1932.

Lohbeck, Don, *Patrick J. Hurley*. Chicago, Ill., Henry Regnery Company, 1956.

Lowry, Edward G., *Washington Close-Ups*. Boston, Mass., Houghton Mifflin, 1921.

Lyons, Eugene, *Herbert Hoover*. New York, Doubleday & Company, 1964.

MacArthur, Douglas, *Reminiscences*. New York, McGraw-Hill, 1964.

Markey, Morris, *This Country of Yours*. Boston, Mass., Little, Brown and Company, 1932.

Mason, Alpheus Thomas, *Harlan Fiske Stone*. New York, The Viking Press, 1956.

McGee, Dorothy Horton, *Herbert Hoover: Engineer, Humanitarian, Statesman*. New York, Dodd, Mead and Company, 1959.

Meltzer, Milton, *Brother, Can You Spare a Dime? The Great Depression, 1929–1933*. New York, Alfred A. Knopf, 1969.

Mencken, Henry L., *Making a President: A Footnote to the Saga of Democracy*. New York, Alfred A. Knopf, 1932.

Michelson, Charles, *The Ghost Talks*. New York, G. P. Putnam's Sons, 1944.

Moley, Raymond, *After Seven Years*. New York, Harper and Brothers, 1939.

———, *Twenty-seven Masters of Politics*. New York, Funk and Wagnalls, 1949.

Morley, Christopher, *Fifth Avenue Bus*. New York, Doubleday, Doran, 1933.

Myers, William Starr, and Walter H. Newton, *The Hoover Administration: A Documented Narrative*. New York, Charles Scribner's Sons, 1936.

O'Connor, Harver, *Mellon's Millions*. New York, Henry Day Company, 1933.

Parks, Lillian Rogers, in collaboration with Frances Spatz Leighton, *My Thirty Years Backstairs at the White House*. New York, Fleet Press Corporation, 1961.

Peel, Roy V., and Thomas C. Donnelly, *The 1932 Campaign*. Farrar & Rinehart, 1935.

Perkins, Frances, *The Roosevelt I Knew*. New York, The Viking Press, 1946.

Ringel, Fred J., ed., *America As Americans See It*. New York, Harcourt, Brace and Company, 1932.

Robinson, Elsie, *I Wanted Out*. New York, Farrar & Rinehart, 1934.

Roosevelt, James, and Sidney Shakett, *Affectionately, F. D. R.* New York, Harcourt, Brace and Company, 1959.

Russell, Francis, *The Shadow of Blooming Grove: Warren G. Harding in His Times*. New York, McGraw-Hill, 1968.

Schlesinger, Arthur M., Jr., *The Age of Roosevelt: The Crisis of the Old Order*. Boston, Mass., Hougton Mifflin, 1957.

Seldes, Gilbert V., *The Years of the Locust: America, 1929–1933*. Boston, Mass., Little, Brown and Company, 1933.

Shannon, David A., ed., *The Great Depression*. Englewood Cliffs, N.J., Prentice-Hall, 1960.

Smith, Ira R. T., with Joe Alex Morris, *Dear Mr. President . . . . The Story of Fifty Years in the White House Mail Room*. New York, Julian Messner, 1949.

Snyder, Louis L., and Richard B. Morris, eds., *A Treasury of the World's Great Reporting*. New York, Simon and Schuster, 1949.

Sobel, Robert, *Panic on Wall Street*. New York, The Macmillan Company, 1968.

Starling, Edmund W., and Thomas Sugrue, *Starling of the White House*. New York, Simon and Schuster, 1946.

Steinberg, Alfred, *Mrs. R.: The Life of Eleanor Roosevelt*. New York, G. P. Putnam's Sons, 1958.

Stiles, Lela, *The Man Behind Roosevelt: The Story of Louis McHenry Howe*. Cleveland, Ohio, World Publishing Company, 1954.

Stimson, Henry Lewis, with McGeorge Bundy, *On Active Service in Peace and War*. New York, Harper & Brothers, 1948.

Stoddard, Henry, *It Costs to Be President*. New York, Harper & Brothers, 1938.

Stokes, Thomas, *Chips Off My Shoulder*. Princeton, N.J., Princeton University Press, 1940.

Stratton, Maud, *Herbert Hoover's Home Town: The Story of West Branch*. West Branch, Iowa, Maud Stratton, 1948.

Thirteen Correspondents of *The New York Times*, *We Saw It Happen*. New York, Simon and Schuster, 1939.

Timmons, Bascom N., *Portrait of an American: Charles G. Dawes*. New York, Henry Holt and Company, 1953.

Train, Arthur, *The Strange Attacks on Herbert Hoover*. New York, John Day Company, 1932.

Tugwell, Rexford Guy, *The Brains Trust*. New York, The Viking Press, 1968.

Warner, Emily Smith, *The Happy Warrior: A Biography of My Father*. New York, Doubleday, 1956.

Warren, Harris Gaylord, *Herbert Hoover and the Great Depression*. New York, Oxford University Press, 1959.

Waters, Walter W., as told to William C. White, *BEF: The Whole Story of the Bonus Army*. New York, John Day Company, 1933.

Watson, James, *As I Knew Them*. Indianapolis, Ind., The Bobbs-Merrill Company, 1936.

Weaver, John D., *Another Such Victory*. New York, The Viking Press, 1948.

Wecter, Dixon, *The Age of the Great Depression, 1929–1941*. New York, The Macmillan Company, 1948.

White, William Allen, *A Puritan in Babylon: The Story of Calvin Coolidge*. New York, The Macmillan Company, 1938.

Wilbur, Ray Lyman, *Memoirs*. Stanford, Calif., Stanford University Press, 1960.

Wilson, Carol Green, *Herbert Hoover: A Challenge for Today*. New York, M. Evans and Company, 1968.

Wilson, Edmund, *The American Earthquake*. New York, Doubleday, 1958.

Woolfe, S. J., *Drawn From Life*. New York, Whittlesey House, 1932.

MAGAZINES

Quotations from various magazines are cited in the Notes. In addition, two recently published books, *Time Capsule 1929* (New York, Time-Life Books, 1967) and *Time Capsule 1932* (New York, Time-Life Books, 1968), were useful. Both are composed of extracts from *Time* for the years indicated.

NEWSPAPERS

A comprehensive reading of every issue of any newspaper for a given period—in this case, the year 1932—will give a feeling for the way in which people lived and thought during the time in question. Although it was necessary to consult other, more detailed, newspaper stories, such as those found in *The New York Times*, the paper I selected for my every-issue reading was the New York *Daily News*.

Newspapers, unlike books and to a certain extent magazines, largely exist on minutiae. Most of the minutiae I studied in the New York *Daily News* for January 1, 1932, to December 31, 1932, I immediately forgot. Some of it stays with me. The endless references in all kinds of stories to "the days of our prosperity" or "in former times" or "during the Golden Decade" or "in happier periods" tell something of the hopelessness that existed and grew in America during the days of that year.

That the annual White House egg-rolling contest for children drew the smallest crowd in history tells something about Washington in the spring of Herbert Hoover's last full year in office.

The chances people took for money strike at one today. Store employees faced down armed robbers to protect cash registers, and cabbies died rather than give up two dollars in change. The robbers, caught, usually proved to be desperate men or women with no police records. "I couldn't stand it for the children to be hungry"; "My husband hasn't worked for two years and I had to do something."

It is possible, thirty-five years later, to sense the desperation of New York's merchants through their advertisements. Month after month their prices dropped so that it was possible to furnish a dining room with a solid mahogany table, chairs, sideboard, with a chandelier and silver and china, for less than two hundred dollars. A traveler could go to Europe, steamer passage, hotel and rail reservations paid, and stay a month there, for less than three hundred dollars. Meals in good restaurants cost a dollar and a half. Live-in maids worked for meals and a dollar a week; sleep-out maids got five dollars a week and lunches.

The immense popular interest in the comeback of an ancient (by boxing standards) Jack Dempsey was reflected in the sports pages of the *Daily News*. Close to bankruptcy, Dempsey campaigned through scores of minor opponents, boxing four-round "exhibitions" and never venturing upon a real bout. In his final "exhibition" he was savagely mauled by the clownish Kingfish Levinsky, who, during the golden age of sports, when Dempsey was young and America prosperous, would have been a laughable opponent. Toward the end of the fourth round, Levinsky stepped back and gestured at the weary Dempsey to come and fight. Francis Wallace, writing in the *News*, said it was the saddest moment in American boxing history. In the end the crowd, which, I believe, had wanted to be assured that Dempsey was the Dempsey of old, booed and hissed him. He had taught them, unwillingly, that he could not come back. They believed by extension that they could not come back either.

As the Great Depression entered into its climax, the films and the popular fiction of the magazines grew swankier and swankier. (In time of prosperity the heroine wears gingham; in a depression she wears ermine.) The fiction of *The Saturday Evening Post*, for example, always lavishly illustrated, never showed anyone in anything but batwing collar and tailcoat. Only Packards and Pierce-Arrows transported the characters in the story. But in the newspapers the real world showed. I remember one example of the type of piece the *News* ran on the page it devoted each day to a fictional short story. In the story, the former first violinist in an exclusive restaurant loses his job. Failing to find work, he goes to a remote quarter of the city and plays his violin in the street in the hope that people will throw him a few pennies or a nickel from their windows. (When I read the story I suddenly remembered having done just that as a very young child—wrapping up four pennies in paper and dropping them out of the window for two men whose music floated up to my parents' apartment.) In the *News* story the musician, ashamed of his new profession, tells his wife he has obtained work as a respected violinist. One day, visiting a friend, she glances out of the window and sees her husband playing his violin in the street. He is doing something just one step above begging. She draws back in horror. The next morning she gives him a hat. It is not proper, she says, for a first violinist to go to work informally dressed, bareheaded. With his new hat he goes to the streets.

Read three and a half decades after it was written, on paper grown yellow and crumbly, in a publication whose other pages report falling markets, foreclosures, evictions, unemployment, the story was tremendously moving. I had never heard of the author and so know nothing of his other work—if there is any. But I believe the story presented as fiction was fact. It spoke of the Great Depression as much as statistics do. More feelingly, perhaps.

It was this kind of minutiae that I remember from three months spent in the Newspaper Division of the New York Public Library. Herbert Hoover, the man and the President, was largely submerged in the masses of detail about America in the Depression. Franklin Roosevelt the Governor and Presidential candidate, and, finally, President-Elect, emerged more clearly. He was always smiling. Anyone who reads the papers for the year 1932 will understand a good deal about the way we elect our Presidents.

MANUSCRIPT COLLECTIONS

In the Library of Congress Manuscript Division I found valuable information and viewpoints in the Papers of Charles Sumner Hamlin, Felix Frankfurter, Breckinridge Long, William Gibbs McAdoo, Josephus Daniels, Raymond Moley, James Couzens, Emily Post, Edward T. Clark, George Van Horne Moseley, Ogden Livingston Mills, and others.

THE PAPERS OF HERBERT HOOVER

These Papers are housed in the Presidential Library at West Branch, Iowa. I am indebted to Dr. Franz Lassner, former head of the Library, and to archivists Dwight Miller and Martha Smith for the help they gave me during my weeks in West Branch.

It remains to be said, however, that these Papers are far from complete. One day, hopefully, all the material concerning President Hoover will be deposited in the Presidential Library which bears his name.

SOURCE NOTES

(The numbers in the left-hand columns refer to pages in this book.)

CHAPTER ONE

3. "Want to yell": Michelson wrote in the *New York World*, August 11, 1928.

4. Six microphones: Details of the day were lavishly described in all newspapers.

4. "No damned salutes": quoted in the *New York World*, August 12, 1928.

5. Hoover against Smith: Stokes, p. 234.

6. "I'll not kiss any babies": Arch Shaw, a longtime friend, quotes Hoover in Lyons, p. 190.

6. "An almost supernatural figure": Michelson, p. 27.

6. "If any difficult situation should arise": Hughes is quoted by Peel and Connelly, p. 4.

7. "I have endeavored to present to you": Elizabethton, Tenn., Oct. 6, 1928.

7. All through the evening he chalked in the figures: Stokes, p. 246.

7. Al Smith sat in the 69th Regiment Armory: Warner, p. 227.

7. She ran to a telephone: ibid., p. 226.

7. People were infected by the attitude of their host: Stokes, p. 246.

7. "He should have conceded three hours ago": quoted by Olive Ewing Clapper, p. 9f.

8. Went for a long tramp through the hills: Carol Green Wilson, p. 175.

CHAPTER TWO

10. "It always rains on moving day": That these were the words with which Coolidge greeted his last day in office was "authoritatively learned" by the *New York Herald Tribune*, said its March 5, 1928 edition.

13. Never heard him tell a funny story: Watson, p. 279.

14. Visitors' Gallery hurriedly cleared: Newspapers noted that among those ushered out was the visiting British politician Winston S. Churchill.

14. Others grinned: Edwin Lefèvre in *The Saturday Evening Post*, Jan. 4, 1930.

16. Most dangerous thing in the world: Hoover made the remark to Washington's Gridiron Club on Dec. 14, 1929.

CHAPTER THREE

18–20. The descriptions of early-day West Branch are largely from Stratton. Incidents in the life of the young Hoover are from his memoirs, Vol. I.

20. Solemn song at her father's funeral: Stratton, p. 13.

21. Stone too large: Stratton, p. 70.

22. *David Copperfield* as the most important book: Christian Gauss in *The Saturday Evening Post*, Nov. 5, 1932.

24. Lasted half a century: ibid.

26. "Ho for Kansas": Stratton, p. 65.

27. Known as "Boy" Hoover: Corey, p. 111.

CHAPTER FOUR

(Much of the material in this chapter is derived from Vol. I of Hoover's memoirs.)

31. Studying the buttons on his vest: Ding, p. 16.

32. "Highest-paid man of his age in the world!": quoted by Wilson, p. 52.

33. Jordan's letter is quoted in Wilson, p. 71.

35. Page's letter to President Wilson is quoted in McGhee, p. 109.

36. "Let the fortune go to hell": quoted in Lyons, p. 81.

39. "Weary titan . . . exhausted prize fighter": quoted in McGhee, p. 182f.

40. Like a limp flag: Ding, p. 22.

42. Harding had never heard of Mellon: Abel, p. 214.

42. No Hoover, no Mellon: Russell, p. 433.

43. Schools sometimes had polo teams: A friend of the writer who was a teacher in Jamaica High School, Long Island, in 1929, also remembered that students often took five years to get through school. No opprobrium was attached to their slowness.

CHAPTER FIVE

45. Hoover's dislike of Harding's Cabinet meetings: Ex-President Hoover mentioned his distaste several times to Dr. Franz Lassner, former head of the Presidential Library at West Branch.

45. "Playmates": Hoover uses the term for Harding's associates several times in his memoirs.

45. Harding's use of first names: Irving Hood Hoover, p. 238.

46. Held up proceedings when a cigarette went out: Lowry, p. 156.

46. Coolidge that way also: Woolf, pp. 44 and 309.

46. Enjoyed seeing them run: *Mirrors of Washington*, p. 73.

47. Never allow wives into stores: Starling, p. 210.

47. Coolidge's sleeping habits: *Mirrors of Washington*, p. 71, and Stokes, p. 140.

47. Coolidge's concern over his nickel: Starling, p. 213.

48. "Now we will have to get to work": quoted by Stokes, p. 81.

48. Coolidge's cousin was H. Parker Willis, former editor of the New York Journal of Commerce. The conversation of the cousins was detailed in White, *The Puritan in Babylon*, p. 390f.

49. Coolidge and the rabbit: Randolph, p. 79.

49. "Power and the glory of the Presidency went with him.": The sentence is one of the very few self-revelatory ones in Coolidge's autobiography.

49. Rob Roy's dreams and Coolidge's interpretations of them are discussed by Everett Sanders in the June 17, 1933, *Saturday Evening Post*.

50, 51. Hoover's meetings with Coolidge: Hoover, *Memoirs*, Vol. II, p. 190f.

50. Roosevelt's 1920 opinion of Hoover was contained in a letter sent to their mutual friend, Hugh Gibson, American Minister to Poland, on January 2, 1920. Gibson sent the letter to Hoover; it is in the Hoover Papers.

50. Coolidge's remark is quoted by Watson, p. 248.

50. "We'll see about that lateh": quoted in the *Mirrors of Washington*, p. 56.

51. "Wonder boy . . . smart boy, . . . miracle worker": quoted in the *Mirrors of Washington*, pp. 58 and 61; Lathem, p. 353; Stokes, p. 138; and *Time*, October 24, 1932.

51. Mellon's comment on Hoover is quoted in Watson, p. 256.

CHAPTER SIX

55. Impressions of the Depression were gained in various interviews conducted by the author.

55. A million people: Edmund Wilson, p. 204.

56. Miss Ferguson wrote on the change in parties in *The Saturday Evening Post*, November 12, 1932.

56. Eighty percent of the mail . . . 60 percent of the newspaper space . . . along the Pennsy tracks: Henry Morton Robinson, p. 102.

56. Markey saw a rancher: Markey, p. 168.

56. The empty skyscrapers: Davis wrote in the *New Republic*, June 1, 1932.
57. "Inevitable collapse . . . alarmist, . . . unwarranted": quoted in Hoover, *Memoirs*, Vol. III, pp. 9, 11.
57. "It will purge the rottenness": ibid., p. 30.
58. "Leave it alone": quoted in Hoover, *Memoirs*, Vol. III, p. 30.
58. "But President Hoover": William Allen White in *The Saturday Evening Post*, March 4, 1933.
58. The conversation about skyscrapers is reported by Woolf on p. 308.
59. "I am convinced we have passed the worst": The President's statement was made on May 1, 1930.
59. Clark's letters to Coolidge are in the Library of Congress.
60. Sackett's conversation with the President: Joslin, p. 88f.
60. Von Hindenburg's letter is printed in Joslin, p. 99f.
61. "It is a cruel world": quoted by Joslin, p. 91.
61. "Perhaps the most daring statement": ibid., p. 91.
62. "It seemed to me": Hoover, *Memoirs*, Vol. III, p. 82.
62. "No sooner is one leak plugged up . . . There is no end to it.": quoted by Joslin, p. 5.
63. Invariably appeared solemn and sad": Peel and Donnelly, p. 51.
63. More depressed than ever before in his life: Hoover, *Memoirs*, Vol. III, p. 86.
63. No cry of leadership: Seldes, p. 251.
64. "Fears of a moratorium": Herbert Bayard Swope of the *New York World* to Ogden Mills, December 31, 1931.
65. Adamic wrote of his experience for *Harper's Magazine*, May, 1931.
65. The plight of the miners: Markey, p. 28f.
66. " 'Why in God's name . . . ?' ": quoted in *Time*, July 18, 1932.
66. He should appear at relief stations: White is quoted by Walter Johnson on p. 425.
66. "This is not a showman's job.": quoted by Joslin, p. 3.
66. Refused to hold such a low opinion: Seldes, p. 255.
67. Olive Clapper mentions the situation of the reporter who coined the 1928 slogan on p. 10 of her book.
67. The telegram to Weber and Fields: *Time*, April 4, 1932.
67. He told Raymond Clapper: Olive Clapper, p. 3f.
67. "Oh God, I've got to fire six men.": Raymond Clapper, p. 13.
67. She herself feared robbery, riots, bloodshed: ibid., p. 14.

67. "What this country needs is a great poem": quoted by Morley, p. 37.

68. His silence: Mark Sullivan remarks in the March 11, 1933, *Saturday Evening Post* that the President could be entirely silent even when on a weekend devoted to relaxation at the camp along the Rapidan.

68. One sentence from him in her life: Parks, p. 32.

68. The servants hiding in the closets are described in Parks, pp. 43 and 220, and Irving Hood Hoover, p. 104.

68. The last President to dress for dinner every night: Fields, p. 29.

68. "HELP US! HELP US!": The letter is in the Hoover Papers.

CHAPTER SEVEN

69. The Cox visit and Father Cox's statement are detailed in *More Merry-Go-Round*, p. 14f.

70. Mellon paid: Seldes, p. 177.

70. "The Nation cannot afford extravagance": quoted in Lowry, p. 154.

71. "He doesn't smoke lightly": ibid., p. 156.

71. "I have often thought that": Stokes, p. 79.

72. "Ol' Andy Mellon": quoted in Starling, p. 207.

72. "Whose extraordinary rise": O'Connor, p. 227.

72. A throne of prestige more powerful than the White House: *Washington Merry-Go-Round*, p. 164.

72. The magnificent art gallery is now the National Gallery of Art, Washington. After Mellon's death his two children generously supported the gallery. His daughter, dying in 1969, was called the country's richest woman.

73. A lonely and tragic figure: Stokes, p. 79.

73. "Only ten servants in the house": quoted in *More Merry-Go-Round*, p. 134.

73. "Poor old Andy.": Norris is quoted by O'Connor, p. 327f.

CHAPTER EIGHT

76. No one on the outside knew he was there: Joslin, p. 165.

76. "Did I tell 'em?": quoted by Joslin, p. 166.

77. "I have other things to do": ibid., p. 194.

77. "He took no notice": Joslin, p. 215.

78. The Leon Errol incident is described in Timmons, p. 292f, and in other books.

78. In Dawes' eyes: Timmons, p. 305.

78. Afraid to be seen coming to the RFC offices: Jones, p. 232.
79. "The hostess who used to give luncheon parties": Miss Randolph wrote in the New York *Daily News* for Feb. 17, 1932.
79. A New Mexico doctor advertised: *Time*, August 8, 1932.
80. Backbone of the pawnbroker business: New York *Daily News*, June 2, 1932.
80. "Why are they doing that?": Thirty-five years later the voice of an acquaintance of the writer still trembled when she recalled the incident.
80. "We will either feed these people": Borah is quoted by Seldes, p. 99.
80. "As long as I sit at this desk they won't get by.": quoted by Anne O'Hare McCormick in *The New York Times*, Nov. 6, 1932.
81. A blond young man: Miss Robinson wrote in the New York *Daily News* for January 28, 1932.
81. "I haven't had a steady job in more than two years.": New York *Daily News*, February 15, 1932.
82. The meeting with Rudy Vallee is described in the April 4, 1932 issue of *Time*.

CHAPTER NINE

85. "Awful arrogant fellow": quoted by Perkins, p. 11.
85. Walker's views on the young Roosevelt are described in Fowler, p. 262.
86. Women would help Mrs. Lane while the men smoked together: *Mirrors of Washington*, p. 10.
86. The conversation between Roosevelt and Senator Lodge's daughter is described in Fay, p. 225f.
86. A copy of the letter from Hoover to Roosevelt is in the Hoover Papers.
87. "You know it is impossible": quoted by Perkins, p. 41.
87. Smith cornered Mrs. Roosevelt: ibid., p. 41f.
88. Flynn describes his call to Roosevelt on p. 71.
88. Details on Howe are from Stiles, Farley and *Twenty-Seven Masters of Politics*.
89. Roosevelt was incapable of understanding a problem unless he saw it with his own eyes: Perkins, p. 97f.
90. "Eddie, my reason for asking you to stay overnight": quoted by Flynn, p. 82.

91. "Can't you ever get anything through that thick Dutch head?": Howe is quoted by Stiles, p. 220f.

91. "These are all debts that I must clear up.": quoted by Flynn, p. 85f.

92. The exchange between Frankfurter and Mrs. Moscowitz is in the Frankfurter Papers.

92. Expert forgers operated under Louis Howe: *Twenty-Seven Masters of Politics*, p. 134.

93. "Say they need no other issue": Jay Franklin in *Liberty Magazine*, April 23, 1932.

93. "Why not call both of them?": Seldes, on p. 254, says he was told that Mellon "shook with mirth" when the joke reached his ears.

Chapter Ten

96. "The cylinder-head is cracked": quoted by Edmund Wilson, p. 232.

96. The most elaborate table of any President: Irving Hood Hoover, p. 50f, Parks, p. 223.

96. Details on serving procedures are from Irving Hood Hoover, p. 50f, Parks, p. 225f, Fields, p. 30.

96. Servants lived in fear of her glare: Irving Hood Hoover, p. 104.

97. Methods by which she gave orders are described by Irving Hood Hoover, p. 187, Parks, p. 80.

97. "Never a good morning": Irving Hood Hoover, p. 184.

97. Christmas gift details: Parks, p. 228, Irving Hood Hoover, p. 136.

98. This was the President's method of dieting: Morley, p. 51. Mrs. Parks, on p. 221 of her book, remarks that the President averaged nine to ten minutes on dinner and sometimes finished in eight minutes.

98. "Come on, you lazy man!": quoted by Joslin, p. 198.

98. "His awful habit": Mrs. Hoover is quoted by Ding, p. 20.

98. Dined alone with Mrs. Hoover but once each year: Ava Long, the former White House housekeeper, in the September, 1933, issue of *Ladies' Home Journal*.

98. Never any jokes: Stimson, p. 196f.

98. He thought of curtailing the lavish entertaining: Wilbur, p. 541.

100. Hoover dug into his own pocket: *Memoirs*, Vol. III, p. 120.

101. A hell on earth: Joslin, p. 219.

101. "He worked those about him until they could hardly drag one foot after the other.": Joslin, p. 170.

101. Never missed a single day through illness: Wilbur, p. 545.

101. The pleading wife is described by Joslin, p. 181f.

102. "My men are dropping around me": quoted by Joslin, p. 182.

102. Fumbled with the tackle: . . . caught the hooks: Starling, p. 283f.

102. Stare uncomprehendingly: Starling, p. 283.

103. Keynes is quoted in the August 6, 1932 *Saturday Evening Post* by Edwin Lefèvre.

CHAPTER ELEVEN

104. The Governors' Conference was extensively reported in all newspapers.

105. Eleanor Roosevelt thought she knew why: Tugwell, p. 108. He adds that she was "so enraged she could hardly be decent through the dinner."

105. "Throughout the length and breadth of the city": *Time*, June 20, 1932.

106. "Horrid" sound: Mencken, p. 45f.

106. "Ten million American workers": the *New Republic*, June 29, 1932.

106. "Lonely eccentric": *Time*, June 20, 1932.

106. Smile on his face and chewing gum: Mencken, p. 46.

107. "It was not wholly unexpected": quoted by Joslin, p. 245.

CHAPTER TWELVE

108. The situation in the garbage dumps and at the private incinerator is described in Edmund Wilson, p. 457f.

108. Insull's life was exhaustively discussed in the newspapers at the time of his fall.

110. Exactly ninety-eight cents in his pocket: *Time*, Aug. 8, 1932.

110. Dawes was uneasy and nervous: Stokes, p. 330.

110. First time he slept soundly: Jones, p. 74.

111. Jones describes the Loop scene on p. 72f.

111. The meeting is described by Jones, p. 74f.

111. "Make as good a trade as you can": quoted by Jones, p. 319.

112. "Impossible man": quoted Mason, p. 285.

112. "Feeble and wishy-washy": Mencken, p. 174.

113. "You are not representing the people of Bronx County": quoted by Flynn, p. 94.

114. The conversation with Howe is detailed in Stiles, p. 181.
114. Flynn had told him it was like a funeral march: Flynn, p. 100.
114. "I can go back to the hotel": quoted in Stokes, p. 315.
114. "Repeat 'Happy Days Are Here Again.' "; quoted in Stiles, p. 183.
115. The encounter with Long is described in Flynn, p. 95.
116. The Flynn-Howe conversation: Stiles, p. 185.
116. "This is the end for Louis . . . Of course he'll last": quoted by Stiles, p. 185f.
116. Raced up and down back stairs: Stiles, p. 188f.
116. "Is that your price?": quoted by Stiles, p. 186. In order to make room in the Senate for Byrd, Glass was offered the Secretary-ship of the Treasury. When he refused it, Swanson was given the post of Secretary of the Navy.
117. Hearst's switch is described by Arthur Krock in his chapter in *We Saw It Happen.*
117. The meeting between Smith and McAdoo and the later Smith-Baruch conversation are described by Frank R. Kent in *The Baltimore Sun*, Nov. 18, 1932.
117. Details of Smith's call to Garner's hotel: ibid.
118. "It's in the bag": quoted by Stiles, p. 187.
118. Nothing showed in his face: Stiles, p. 187.
118. Cermak filled the hall to its rafters: Stiles, p. 187. Cermak did not live to reap any benefit from his support of Roosevelt. A would-be assassin, shooting at President-Elect Roosevelt early in 1933, fatally wounded the Chicago mayor.
119. Sly smile uncovered McAdoo's teeth: Stokes, p. 322f.
119. His fellow players would agree: Irving Hood Hoover, p. 40.
121. Sulking: Daniel wrote in the next day's *New York Times.*
121. Everybody would be kept happy: Stiles, p. 192, Moley, *Twenty-Seven Masters of Politics*, p. 138.
122. "I shall vote for him": Mencken, p. 177.

CHAPTER THIRTEEN

129. Waters gives his background in his book, as he does the early details of the Bonus March.
134. Deputy Chief said to the Chief of Staff: Moseley manuscript.
134. "Dynamic . . . an inspiration": Eisenhower, p. 213.
135. The Army should move: Moseley manuscript.
135. He gave the plan to Secretary Hurley: Moseley manuscript.

135. A copy of the letter to Croly, written some time before the Bonus March, is in the Moseley Papers.

136. "Possible seeds of Revolution.": The letter, from Oliver Capen of Bedford, N.Y., and a copy of Strother's reply, are in the Hoover Papers.

136. "Our job": The Secret Service man is quoted by Waters, p. 59.

136. Waters-Glassford meeting: Waters, p. 62f.

138. "The first Communist republic": The story was an Associated Press dispatch printed in many papers.

139. "Hollow cheeks off breadlines": Dos Passos wrote in the *New Republic*, June 29, 1932.

139. "Here's a plant that can turn out everything": quoted by Dos Passos in the *New Republic*, June 29, 1932.

140. Plot to hang MacArthur: MacArthur, p. 97.

140. Secretly transferred tanks: Moseley manuscript.

142. "This is a swell country": Angelo is quoted by Waters, p. 121.

142. "I feel sick to the stomach.": Petrovna wrote in the New York *Daily News*, June 12, 1932.

145. "Did you get your orders from Wall Street?": quoted in the New York *Daily News*, June 14, 1932.

145. The young girl is described by Weaver, p. 129f.

146. "This marks a new era": Johnson is quoted in *More Merry-Go-Round*, p. 46.

147. She saw a menace she had never seen before: Elsie Robinson, p. 272.

147. "Tell them to sing 'America' ": quoted by Waters, p. 152.

CHAPTER FOURTEEN

(A very great part of the material in this chapter was gleaned from contemporary newspaper reports, including the account of Lee Mc-Cardel of the *Baltimore Evening Sun*, which received Honorable Mention for the 1933 Pulitzer Prize and is reprinted in Snyder and Morris. The incidents described were mostly itemized in newspapers then, with the exception of those mentioned below.)

153. The meeting with Hurley and MacArthur is described in Waters, p. 192.

158. Hurley disregarded the President's orders that the Bonus Army should be rounded up: This is made very clear by Donald Lisio in the *Wisconsin Magazine of History*, Autumn, 1967.

158. MacArthur believed the Bonus Army was collecting guns and desperadoes: A 1939 letter to former President Hoover from

James Savage of New York relates that a newspaper reporter informed MacArthur that there were guns and men who would use them, and that MacArthur took the reporter at his word. The letter is in the Hoover Papers. Army Intelligence also reportedly told MacArthur there were firearms.

158. The beginning of a Communist rebellion: Moseley in his Papers says there is no doubt the Bonus Army intended to seize government buildings as a signal to "Communistic" allies that the moment had come to spring to arms.

158. Hurley decided to pen nobody up: Lisio. Lisio indicates that it is his feeling that the proper course for the President was to request the resignations of the Secretary of War and Chief of Staff in the wake of their rout of the Bonus Army.

In later years, ex-President Hoover, in moments of irritation, was known to say privately that MacArthur had monstrously exceeded his orders and his military authority. Towards the end of both men's lives they lived as neighbors in the Waldorf Towers of the Waldorf-Astoria Hotel in New York. Their relations were amicable, but not overly close.

159. "We are acting on the order of the President": quoted by Hunt, p. 143.

159. Eisenhower-MacArthur conversation: Eisenhower, p. 216.

160. Watson-Hoover talks: Watson, p. 276f.

162. Moseley-Hurley talks: Moseley Papers.

162. Moseley-MacArthur talks: ibid.

162. The two additional Hurley calls: ibid.

163. "Too busy": Eisenhower, p. 217.

163. Tensely waited for the first shots: Stokes, p. 303f.

164. Absolutely essential that the men stand where they were: the *New Republic*, August 10, 1932.

164. Patton went down: Josephson, p. 99f.

165. Light could be seen from the Lincoln Study: *More Merry-Go-Round*, p. 51.

165. "That pitiful sight": Easby-Smith's letter is in the Hoover Papers.

165. Something about the fire struck at Eisenhower's heart: Eisenhower, p. 216.

165. Eisenhower wondered if indeed all this were so: Eisenhower, p. 216.

166. Distinguished Service Cross flapping from his shirt: Waters, p. 121.

CHAPTER FIFTEEN

169. Details of the Tugwell-Roosevelt conversations are from Tugwell, p. 357f.

170. "Sidewalks-of-New-York eyes": quoted by Fowler, p. 262.

171. Preferred cronies to those he called career-seekers: quoted by Fowler, p. 262.

171. Details on Walker as mayor are from Fowler.

172. "How would it be if I gave the little mayor hell?": Roosevelt is quoted in *Twenty-Seven Masters of Politics*, p. 209.

173. "Jim, you're through": quoted by Fowler, p. 325.

173. "So you'd rather be right than President!": quoted in *Twenty-Seven Masters of Politics*, p. 211. Moley does not indicate the name of the individual who flung the match. It could only have been Louis Howe.

173. "I'd like to be home": quoted by Fowler, p. 343.

174. "Heart appeared to be in the right place": *Time*, Sept. 26, 1932.

174. It seemed to him that it was like Europe just after the War: quoted by Anne O'Hare McCormick in *The New York Times*, Nov. 6, 1932.

174. "Perhaps this fellow can help us out.": ibid.

174. Looked like Mongolian peasants: Hitchcock, p. 32.

175. "We are going to change.": Breckinridge Long wrote a memorandum on his experiences in the campaign; it is in the Long Papers.

175. Long saw a cowboy . . . apples, with culls out: Long Papers.

175. "Is Hoover going to drive me out of here?": quoted by Seldes, p. 192.

176. "Why, I don't expect to do a thing, my dears": quoted by Stiles, p. 203.

176. "Sometimes worse than that": quoted by Stiles, p. 220.

176. " 'Are All the Hot Dogs Dead?' ": quoted by Stiles, p. 201.

177. "When a miracle man fails": Senator Johnson's defection from the Republican ranks was not an unpleasant experience for him. He told the reporters that he had not enjoyed a fight as much since the campaign of 1912, when he was Theodore Roosevelt's vice-presidential candidate on the Bull Moose ticket.

178. "There is a widespread conviction": *Liberty Magazine*, April 30, 1932.

178. The Wise-Frankfurter exchanges are in the Frankfurter Papers.
178. "The way most people feel": Rogers expressed his opinion in his column for April 27, 1932.

Chapter Sixteen

179. There must be some mistake: Long Papers.
179. "It looks pretty dark": quoted by Joslin, p. 301.
179. "We have got to fight to the limit": quoted by Joslin, p. 301.
180. The horse was one of nature's mistakes: *Memoirs*, Vol. I, p. 18.
181. He shocked Stimson: Schlesinger, p. 431.
181. The Gauss article appeared in *The Saturday Evening Post*, Nov. 5, 1932.
182. Irwin's article appeared in *Liberty Magazine*, April 21, 1932.
182. "It cannot be worse": quoted by Joslin, p. 299.
183. "If only they would leave me alone": quoted by Joslin, p. 300.
183. Castle wrote of his experiences in Chicago to Presidential Secretary Lawrence Richey, adding that The Chief should not be bothered with the matter, for it would only disturb him. The letter is in the Hoover Papers.
183. The Roqau-Newton exchange is in the Hoover Papers.
184. The President permitted himself to think Coolidge had seen it all coming: Dr. Franz Lassner told the writer that ex-President Hoover once bitterly remarked that "Coolidge stuck me with the Depression."
184. William Allen White thought: *The Puritan in Babylon*, p. 433.
184. Coolidge's talk with the barber: ibid., p. 435.
184. "It's too much of an effort": quoted in Lathem. The remark was made to Coolidge's Amherst classmate, Charles Andrews.
185. Mrs. Gann called it off: *More Merry-Go-Round*, p. 31.
185. Curtis' trip was detailed in all newspapers.
186. The letters between Richey and Theodore Roosevelt, Jr. are in the Hoover Papers.

Chapter Seventeen

187. Exactly as in Lincoln's time: Joslin, p. 61.
187. "No thought of making any stumping trip": Mills to Arthur Woods, September 24, 1932. The letter is in the Mills Papers.
187. "Talk right out": quoted by Joslin, p. 303.
188. "It is unnecessary to tell me": quoted by Joslin, p. 303.
188. He wanted to finish the job: quoted by Anne O'Hare McCormick in *The New York Times*, November 6, 1932.

189. "Nobody could approach his desk": Clark's letter to Coolidge is in the Clark Papers.
190. Awakened at three in the morning: Joslin, p. 305f.
190. "Jumpy": ibid., p. 306.
190. "Panic-stricken": Starling, p. 299.
191. "To hell with Hoover": quoted in *Time*, September 5, 1932.
191. Two terrified Iowa Republican leaders: Joslin, p. 304.
191. "It is not the crushing blow I had feared": quoted by Joslin, p. 304.
191. Joslin's view was that not more than half a dozen states were safe for him: Joslin, p. 313.
192. "You know things are not nice": quoted by Joslin, p. 306.
192. Joslin looked at them: Joslin, pp. 306 and 312.
192. Anne O'Hare McCormick wondered also: *The New York Times*, November 6, 1932.
193. "Heckle-proof": *Time*, October 17, 1932.
193. Stokes thought to himself: Stokes, p. 288.
194. The President's personal telepone calls: Joslin, p. 317f.
195. "It represents, as in Aristotle's definition": the *New Republic*, October 19, 1932.
196. Talk about West Branch: Joslin, p. 307.
196. Reveal himself to be what Joslin thought him to be: Joslin, 312.
197. Always simply "Franklin": Hitchcock, p. 41.
197. A reporter standing perhaps six or eight feet away: Farley, p. 177.

CHAPTER EIGHTEEN

199. "I've been traveling with Presidents since Roosevelt": the unnamed Secret Service man is quoted in *Time*, November 7, 1932.
199. Someone flung a large light bulb: Joslin, p. 321.
200. Armored cars patroled the route: Starling, p. 299.
200. A Calvary for the President: Stokes, p. 304.
200. Bewildered and stricken: Starling, p. 299.
200. Hands were shaking: Stokes, p. 305.
200. Found himself suddenly covered with perspiration: Starling, p. 300.
200. The Chief was not right: Joslin, p. 324.
201. At least he would not lie sprawling on the floor, ibid., p. 324.
201. "Why don't they make him quit?": quoted by Starling, p. 300.
201. "I know little about what the government is doing": Coolidge's

letter is in the Clark Papers, as are the following letters between the two men.

202. He had never talked to an audience which laughed: Lathem, p. 210.

202. Mrs. Coolidge listened over a radio: ibid., p. 209f.

202. "Burned out": quoted in Lathem, p. 215. The remark was made to Coolidge's Amherst classmate, Charles Andrews.

202. "I feel I no longer fit in": quoted by Henry L. Stoddard in the *New York Sun*, January 6, 1933.

203. "This fight has not been lost": quoted by Anne O'Hare McCormick in *The New York Times*, November 6, 1932.

204. His law partner sitting with his face in his hands: The law partner, Ralph Hemenway, wrote of the incident in *Good Housekeeping* for April, 1935.

204. "I tell you, lady": quoted by Anne O'Hare McCormick in *The New York Times*, November 6, 1932.

CHAPTER NINETEEN

206. "Where are you going?": Markey, p. 202.

207. "The invariable retort": quoted by Samuel Blythe in *The Saturday Evening Post* for October 15, 1932.

207. "Weariness shows in his slumping torso": William Allen White wrote in *The Saturday Evening Post* for March 4, 1933.

208. Tomatoes and eggs flung at the train: Carol Green Wilson, p. 231.

208. "My friends of Nevada County": The planned speech, typed by a machine with extra large print to facilitate its reading, is in the Hoover Papers. The actual speech, taken down by a stenographer, is also there.

208. Violated the traditions: His doing so was commented upon by every reporter.

209. "Will you say at this time": A stenographic report on the press conference is in the Hoover Papers.

209. "This afternoon I greet you": Both prepared speech and actual words are in the Hoover Papers.

210. The Joslin and Newton telegram is in the Hoover Papers, as are those indicating the developing election situation.

211. He called Joslin in Washington: Joslin, p. 324.

211. Shook hands with one man three times: Edward T. Folliard in the *Washington Herald*, November 17, 1932.

211. Mrs. Wilbur's thoughts: Charles Sumner Hamlin was told by

Mrs. F. A. Delano, who had talked with Mrs. Wilbur. Hamlin noted the matter in his diary, November 20, 1932.

211. "All right, that's that": quoted by Joslin, p. 325.

211. Details on the scene at the Biltmore are from a variety of papers.

212. Losers always spurt in the beginning: Stiles, p. 216.

212. Mrs. Roosevelt's thoughts on life in the White House: quoted by Perkins, p. 69.

213. "I put this sherry away in Albany twenty years ago.": quoted by Stiles, p. 216.

213. Robert Gros wrote of his feelings to Allan Hoover, the President's son, the next day. He asked for a chance to shake the President's hand. His letter is in the Hoover Papers.

213. The balcony scene was described in all newspapers.

214. The President-Elect's talk with his son: Roosevelt, p. 231.

CHAPTER TWENTY

215. The stenographic report of the news conference, and the telegrams are in the Hoover Papers.

216. Young wrote in the *Star* of the following day, November 10, 1932.

216. "It will work out some way": quoted by William Allen White in *The Saturday Evening Post*, March 4, 1933.

217. "Curiously enough": ibid.

218. Most difficult to know or understand: Howard is quoted by Schlesinger, p. 243.

218. Moseley thought bitterly of the contrasting scene: Moseley Papers.

219. She pitied him from the bottom of her heart: Randolph, p. 168.

219. The conversation with Roosevelt was recorded by a stenographer listening on an extension; a copy of the report is in the Hoover Papers.

219. Roosevelt's hair had gotten mussed: Irving Hood Hoover, p. 221.

220. To Hoover he was "Mills": Moley, *After Seven Years*, p. 77.

220. He looked at the Great Seal: ibid., p. 73.

220. He thought to himself that Roosevelt was amiable, pleasant: A memorandum dictated by President Hoover and now in the Hoover Papers adds he was "very badly informed and of comparatively little vision."

220. An ignorant young man in need of education: Hoover so de-

scribed Roosevelt to Secretary of State Stimson; the description is quoted by Schlesinger, p. 444.

222. A man idling along: Edmund Wilson, p. 441.

222. The two most dangerous men in the country: Tugwell, p. 434.

222. "I am still Franklin": The letter is in the Daniels Papers.

223. Details of the fishing trip are from several newspapers.

CHAPTER TWENTY-ONE

225. Details on the Hoover-Couzens negotiations are found in Hoover, *Memoirs*, Vol. III, p. 206f.

226. A copy of the letter is in the Hoover Papers.

226. "Cheeky documents": quoted by Schlesinger, p. 477.

226. "Madman": Stimson's diary entry is quoted by Schlesinger, p. 177.

227. "We are on the verge": A copy of the letter is in the Hoover Papers.

227. Robinson and Glass told him nothing could be done: Hoover, *Memoirs*, Vol. III, p. 213.

228. The Rand revelations about the luncheon with Tugwell: Hoover, *Memoirs*, Vol. III, p. 214f.

228. "When you have been in Washington as long as I": James Roosevelt told the story many times, and at least once during a television interview. Also quoted in Steinberg, p. 188.

228. Roman holiday . . . Roosevelt learned from Hitler: Hoover, *Memoirs*, Vol. III, pp. 214 and 215.

228. "There is nothing more we can do": quoted by Joslin, p. 366.

229. A Secret Service man came into Hoover's office: This incident and many of the immediately following were obtained by reading newspapers of the day following the Roosevelt Inauguration.

230. "What interesting steel structures": James Roosevelt has described the trip in the car several times and indicated these were the approximate words the President-Elect used. Newspaper sources for the following day, the day after the Inauguration, say that although Roosevelt talked to Hoover somewhat, Hoover did not reply at all.

230. Krock and Owen wrote in the next day's *New York Times*, March 5, 1933.

230. The Roosevelt letter to Gibson, written on January 2, 1920, was sent to Hoover by Gibson and is in the Hoover Papers.

231. Details of the swearing-in are from various newspapers and from the author's observation of a newsreel of the event.

231. Mrs. Roosevelt's comments on the day: *The New York Times*, March 5, 1933. The gloom and solemnity can be sensed by watching the Inauguration newsreel; and it is striking how little applause there was at any point. The handclapping was perfunctory even when President Roosevelt uttered his famous words about nothing to fear but fear itself.

232. "If I fail I shall be the last one.": quoted by Peel and Donnelly, p. 312.

INDEX